The World Will Never See the Like:

THE GETTYSBURG REUNION OF 1913

John L. Hopkins

Savas Beatie
California

First edition, first printing

ISBN-13: 978-1-61121-684-4 (hardcover)
ISBN-13: 978-1-61121-685-1 (ebook)

Library of Congress Cataloging-in-Publication Data
Names: Hopkins, John L., 1957- author.
Title: The world will never see the like : the Gettysburg reunion of 1913 / by John L. Hopkins.
Other titles: Gettysburg reunion of 1913
Description: El Dorado Hills, CA : Savas Beatie LLC, [2023] | Includes bibliographical references and index. | Summary: "This is the story of the largest reunion of Union and Confederate veterans ever held: its genesis and planning, the obstacles overcome on the way to making it a reality, its place in the larger narrative of sectional reunion and reconciliation, and the individual stories of the veterans who attended"-- Provided by publisher.
Identifiers: LCCN 2023025662 | ISBN 9781611216844 (hardcover) | ISBN 9781611216851 (ebook)
Subjects: LCSH: Gettysburg Reunion, 1913. | Gettysburg, Battle of, Gettysburg, Pa., 1863.
Classification: LCC E475.57 .H67 2023 | DDC 973.7/349--dc23/eng/20230606
LC record available at https://lccn.loc.gov/2023025662

Printed and bound in the United Kingdom

SB
Savas Beatie
989 Governor Drive, Suite 102
El Dorado Hills, CA 95762
916-941-6896 / sales@savasbeatie.com / www.savasbeatie.com

All of our titles are available at special discount rates for bulk purchases in the United States. Contact us for information.

For Apple, Anna, Callie, and Sarah

TABLE OF CONTENTS

LIST OF ILLUSTRATIONS

ABBREVIATIONS

ACHS	Adams County Historical Society
CU	Cornell University
GAR	Grand Army of the Republic
GBMA	Gettysburg Battlefield Memorial Association
GNMP	Gettysburg National Military Park
LOC	Library of Congress
LV	Library of Virginia
NARA	National Archives and Records Administration
NYHS	New York Historical Society
PSA	Pennsylvania State Archives
RIHS	Rhode Island Historical Society
UCV	United Confederate Veterans
UNCCH	University of North Carolina-Chapel Hill
USC	University of South Carolina
UDC	United Daughters of the Confederacy
USAMHI	U.S. Army Military History Institute
VHS	Virginia Historical Society
WSL	Washington State Library

Preface

Europeean civilization, explained the correspondent of London's *Daily Telegraph*, "with its centuries of strife and bloodshed has not yet furnished a spectacle comparable to that witnessed today on the historic battlefield of Gettysburg." He wrote those words in a dispatch published not in 1863 in the midst of the bloodiest battle of the Civil War, but in 1913 during a reunion of more than 53,000 Union and Confederate veterans held to mark its fiftieth anniversary.

From June 29 to July 5, the old soldiers filled a 280-acre encampment between the Emmitsburg Road and Seminary Ridge in the largest Blue-Gray reunion ever held. It was front-page news across the country, covered by more than 150 reporters and photographers. Colonel James Martinus Schoonmaker, a Union veteran and Medal of Honor winner who helped organize the reunion, called it "a celebration unparalleled in the history of the world."

Those who attended were convinced that its impact would reverberate through the years. "It will go down in history as an event fraught with more power for good than any event since the signing of the Declaration of Independence," declared Alfred B. Beers, commander-in-chief of the Grand Army of the Republic, the largest fraternal organization of Union veterans. "All that the great Reunion of the Blue and the Gray means to the American people is yet to be realized," wrote a daughter who accompanied her veteran father to the event. "It will be realized more and more with the flight of years—it will be talked about and written about as long as the American people boast of the dauntless courage of Gettysburg." Yet today, the 1913 Gettysburg reunion is all but forgotten.

I first stumbled upon this extraordinary event in Carol Reardon's superb *Pickett's Charge in History and Memory*. The dozen pages she devoted to it whetted my appetite, so I went in search of a book-length treatment, confident that J. Thompson Brown, a Confederate veteran who attended, had been correct in his assertion that the "history of this grand and final Reunion of the Blue and Gray . . . will surely be written." I quickly discovered that the commission created by the State of Pennsylvania to plan the reunion had produced a handsomely bound final report of some 280 pages, heavy on official documents and transcripts of dignitaries' speeches, and distributed 25,000 copies around the country, one of which landed in the library of the liberal arts college in Ohio where I worked. So far, so good. Two books had been written by participants: *From Maine to Gettysburg, 1863–1913*, by Elsie Dorothea Tibbetts, who accompanied her 15th Maine veteran father to the reunion, and *Handgrips: The Story of the Great Gettysburg Reunion*, by New Hampshire veteran Walter H. Blake, both published within a year of the event, and both offering a mixture of first-hand observations and recycled anecdotes from the newspaper coverage. John William Corrington, a professor of literature at Loyola University in New Orleans—who named two of his children Robert Edward Lee and Thomas Jonathan Jackson—published a short story titled "Reunion. Gettysburg: 1913" in the *Southwest Review* in the early 1960s, while in 2009 Carl Eeman's novel *Encampment* posited an alternative history in which thousands of black veterans participated in the reunion. In 2013, to mark the centennial of the event, James Rada produced *No North, No South: The Grand Reunion at the 50th Anniversary of the Battle of Gettysburg*, a 96-page overview heavily illustrated with more than 100 photos.

And that was about it. The full story of the great reunion—its genesis and planning, the obstacles overcome on the way to making it a reality, its place in the larger narrative of sectional reunion and reconciliation, to say nothing of the often poignant, occasionally comical, at times unbelievable individual stories of the veterans who attended—had never been told. So, I resolved to do it.[1]

Acknowledgments

Any acknowledgment of the many sources of help I received during the lengthy process of researching this book must begin with the scores of nameless newspaper reporters (bylines were not in common use in the early part of the last century

[1] In 2019, just as I was putting the finishing touches on this manuscript, Thomas R. Flagel's *War, Memory, and the 1913 Gettysburg Reunion* was published by the Kent State University Press. Flagel's primary focus is on what motivated men to attend the reunion and he highlights four veterans—two Union, two Confederate—to support his contention that those motivations were more complex than the narrative of national reconciliation that dominated contemporary news coverage.

who covered the great reunion, and the people at organizations like Proquest, Newspapers.com, and Newspaperarchives.com who have made a vast trove of old newspapers readily available online. The staff at the Pennsylvania State Archives in Harrisburg, which houses the records of the commission that planned and organized the reunion, as well as those at the Gettysburg National Military Park Library and Research Center and the Adams County Historical Society were unfailingly helpful and kind. Michael Sherbon of the Pennsylvania Archives deserves special thanks for his assistance in obtaining many of the images contained herein. Jana Meyer at the Filson Historical Society in Louisville, Kentucky, Shawn Connery of the Seymour Library in Auburn, New York, and Richard Mansley at the Newtown Historic Association in Newtown, Pennsylvania, provided invaluable information about three veterans who figure prominently in this tale, while Michael Mills at the Hudson Museum in Hudson, Michigan, produced a photo of a Union and Confederate veteran who had met during the war, were reunited in Gettysburg in 1913, and then traveled back to Michigan to continue their personal reunion. Mary Morris at the Clarke County Historical Association in Berryville, Virginia, supplied the letter from a Virginia veteran with which this book closes.

This book began as a nights-and-weekends project, wedged into whatever gaps I could find between my day job and my family. Over the course of almost 40 years in public relations, I have written well over a million words on behalf of various employers and clients, not one of which had a shelf life of more than a couple of weeks. This book is the most complex writing project I have ever undertaken, and by far the one of which I am most proud. I am enormously grateful to Theodore P. Savas for giving me this opportunity and to everyone on the team at Savas Beatie for their guidance and support through the publication process.

I have been richly and undeservedly blessed in this life, above all by the love of my wife, Apple, and our three wonderful daughters: Anna, Callie, and Sarah. This book is dedicated to them.

Chapter 1

The Greatest Event Gettysburg Has Ever Seen

On an early spring day in 1908, a well-dressed, silver-haired man with an empty right sleeve made his way into the Union League on South Broad Street in Philadelphia. Henry Shippen Huidekoper had recently been named to the commission charged with designing a monument to commemorate the 34,000 Pennsylvania troops who fought at Gettysburg. But today he had come to call upon Gov. Edwin S. Stuart on another matter.

"He stated that he had given much thought to the fact that in July 1913 it would be fifty years since the Battle of Gettysburg," Stuart later recalled, "and he wished to impress upon me the importance of incorporating in my next message to the Legislature in January 1909 a recommendation that the event be properly celebrated under the auspices of the State of Pennsylvania."[1]

In July 1913, it would also be 50 years since a 24-year-old Lieutenant Colonel Huidekoper suddenly found himself in command of the 150th Pennsylvania during the first day's fight at Gettysburg, after Col. Langhorne Wister had to assume brigade command. For three quarters of hour, Huidekoper and his men withstood the onslaught of Brig. Gen. Junius Daniel's North Carolinians and Col. J. M. Brockenbrough's Virginians on McPherson's Ridge. Already wounded in the leg, Huidekoper was struck by a second bullet that shattered his right arm. After applying a makeshift tourniquet to stanch the bleeding, he continued to rally the

---

1 Letter, Edwin S. Stuart to Lewis E. Beitler, Oct. 10, 1913, Fiftieth Anniversary of the Battle of Gettysburg Commission: Correspondence, Record Group 25.24, Box 2, Pennsylvania State Archives (PSA). Hereafter cited as "Commission Correspondence."

150th as the fighting grew more desperate, but soon became faint from loss of blood and was forced to leave the line and make his way through the streets of Gettysburg to a field hospital that had been set up in St. Francis Xavier Roman Catholic Church on West High Street. There his arm was amputated, and there he remained when the Union lines west and north of town finally collapsed and the Confederates poured in.[2]

Huidekoper would rejoin his regiment in December but found that the loss of his arm hampered his ability to serve and resigned his commission in March 1864. He went on to live a long and full post-war life—as commander of the Pennsylvania National Guard, postmaster of Philadelphia, and vice president and general manager of the Metropolitan Telephone and Telegraph Company—but his wartime service remained a defining moment, as it was for so many of his comrades. He was elected president of the 150th Pennsylvania Regiment Veterans Association and commander of the Pennsylvania Commandery of the Military Order of the Loyal Legion of the United States and attended reunions faithfully. In 1905, he was awarded the Medal of Honor for his actions at Gettysburg.[3]

*   *   *

Through the four years of the Civil War, more than 2 million men served in the Union Army and Navy, a bit more than half the Northern military age male population, while the Confederacy put some 750,000 men under arms, three out of four military-aged men in the South. When the war ended, they returned home not just to starkly different conditions, but to different receptions as well. True, the boys in blue were hailed as the saviors of the Union and were cheered to the echo as they marched in the Grand Review in Washington, D.C., on May 23 and 24, 1865. But as they mustered out regiment by regiment in the weeks and months that followed and made their way home, their travels often marked by the consumption of copious amounts of liquor, incidents of petty theft, and fistfights with the locals in the communities through which they passed, the Northern press began to voice concerns about this horde of semi-savages now let loose upon the civilian population. "By midsummer," historian Brian Matthew Jordan writes, "gasping editors declared that the nation was fatally afflicted by an 'epidemic' of veteran misdeeds." The defeated Confederates, on the other hand, returned home to a far less ambivalent reception, in no small measure because the people and land to which they returned had been so thoroughly devastated. The war had destroyed "two-thirds of the assessed value of Southern wealth, two-fifths of the

2 David G. Martin, *Gettysburg July 1* (Cambridge, MA, 1995), 245, 378, 456.

3 H. S. Huidekoper obituary, *The Harvard Graduates' Magazine* (March 1919), 27:325-327.

South's livestock, and one-quarter of her white men between the ages of 20 and 40. More than half the farm machinery was ruined, and the damages to railroads and industries were incalculable . . . Southern wealth decreased by 60 percent." And while there were no parades, receptions, or speeches in the town square as there had been when they went off to war, those who returned were welcomed home as something akin to tragic heroes, men who had fought long, hard, and well, despite all hardships and against long odds.[4]

The initial contrast in Northern and Southern attitudes toward their returning veterans would carry over in many ways through the post-war decades. "In the South," writes James Marten in *Sing Not War*, "veterans would always be those proud, ragged, honorable men who limped home with their heads held high. If they succeeded in their postwar lives, they would do so despite the hardships they survived. If they failed, who could blame them?" But in the North, "marginalized veterans were often seen as agents of their own decline, almost purposefully swimming against the stream of progress, economic growth, and opportunity. They may have served bravely in the war, but as the country moved deeper into peacetime, they were expected to get over their experiences and move on."[5]

For the first decade or so after the war, most veterans focused on trying to pick up the threads of their pre-war lives. For tens of thousands, that meant learning to navigate life with a missing arm or leg, a wound that refused to heal, or memories of the carnage of combat that could not be laid to rest. In the South, it also encompassed the rebuilding of a shattered infrastructure and economy and resisting and subverting Reconstruction by every possible means in order to maintain effective white control of millions of newly emancipated African Americans. But as the years passed, veterans on both sides became increasingly concerned with preserving the history of what they had done, and the memory of those who had died. The former Confederates, who had more to explain and justify in defeat, were first into the literary arena. "The most that is left to us is the history of our struggle," Jubal A. Early wrote to Robert E. Lee in November 1868, "and I think that ought to be accurately written. We lost nearly everything but honor, and that should be religiously guarded." Early himself had already published the first book-length work by a significant commander on either side, *A Memoir of the Last Year of the War for Independence, in the Confederate States of America*, in late 1866, and exercised significant influence over what viewpoints were printed in the *Southern*

---

4 Brian Matthew Jordan, *Marching Home: Union Veterans and Their Unending Civil War* (New York, 2014), 48; James M. McPherson, *Ordeal by Fire: The Civil War and Reconstruction* (New York, 1982), 476.

5 James Marten, *Sing Not War: The Lives of Union and Confederate Veterans in Gilded Age America* (Chapel Hill, NC, 2011), 20.

Historical Society Papers. In the decades that followed, dozens of other major figures would follow suit, including James Longstreet, William T. Sherman, and Ulysses S. Grant, whose publisher rang up advance sales of 300,000 copies of the Union commander's memoirs, completed just days before he died. Campaign studies and regimental histories appeared by the score, and thousands of enlisted men and officers offered their personal recollections and fought out controversies about the details of engagements large and small in the pages of publications like *Confederate Veteran* and *The National Tribune.* In the 1880s and 1890s, memorials to the dead moved gradually outward from cemeteries to town squares and the downtowns of major cities, growing larger and more elaborate as they did so. Cleveland's magnificent Soldiers and Sailors Monument, dedicated on July 4, 1894, soars 125 feet above Public Square and cost $280,000 to construct. The formal dedication of the Robert E. Lee monument, the first and largest of the memorials on Richmond's Monument Avenue, drew more than 100,000 people in May 1890.[6]

The last decades of the nineteenth century were the heyday of fraternal organizations in America, and Civil War veterans were not immune to their allure. They formed regimental, brigade, and corps associations, as well as specialized groups for Signal Corps veterans and former prisoners of war, many of which held annual reunions. Towering above them all in both membership and political clout was the Grand Army of the Republic (GAR), the largest organization of Union veterans, with almost 7,000 local posts across the country, including every state of the old Confederacy. The influence of the United Confederate Veterans (UCV), founded two decades later, was more narrowly confined to the South. While the GAR's membership probably never included much more than a third of surviving Union veterans at any given time, that still added up to more than 425,000 men at its zenith in 1890. If that number is suggestive of the political power wielded by veterans in the post-war decades, it is only one of many such data points. Five of the seven U.S. presidents who held office between 1869 and 1901 were Union combat veterans: Ulysses S. Grant, Rutherford B. Hayes, James A. Garfield, Benjamin Harrison, and William McKinley. A sixth, Chester A. Arthur, served as quartermaster general for the state of New York. Due in no small measure to their political influence, by 1893, "pensions for Union veterans accounted for 43 percent of federal expenditures" and 19,518 of those veterans were living in federal or state soldiers' homes. Historian William B. Heseltine has calculated that south of the Mason-Dixon line "[the] 585 top military and civil leaders

---

6 Jubal A. Early to Robert E. Lee, Nov. 20, 1868, quoted in Gary W. Gallagher, "Jubal A. Early, the Lost Cause, and Civil War History," in Gary W. Gallagher & Alan T. Nolan, eds., *The Myth of the Lost Cause and Civil War History* (Bloomington, IN, 2000), 39; Gaines M. Foster, *Ghosts of the Confederacy: Defeat, the Lost Cause, and the Emergence of the New South* (New York, 1987), 101.

of the Confederacy furnished to the postwar South 418 holders of elective and appointive offices," from governor's mansions and state legislatures to both houses of Congress, an outcome he attributes "in part to their own abilities and thanks in no small measure to the imbecility of their conquerors." And while Confederate veterans had access neither to federal pensions nor federal soldiers' homes, in that same year of 1893, just over 27,000 Confederate veterans were receiving state pensions or living in state soldiers' homes, at a total cost of $1,126,736. This was less than one percent of the total spent in the North on 876,068 Union veterans, but it was nonetheless a significant amount in a region still recovering from the economic and demographic impact of the war.[7]

With regimental and national associations, reunions and monument dedications, soldiers' homes, and periodicals written by and for themselves, Civil War veterans in the 1880s and 1890s created a place they could call their own in a rapidly changing nation. "Quite literally 'marching to the beat of a different drummer,' veterans marked time on a calendar now solemnized by enlistment dates . . . discharge dates, and the anniversaries of wounds, imprisonment, and battles—both great and small," notes Brian Matthew Jordan. "Certain sacrifices could not be shared; certain nightmares could not be explained," James Marten adds. "And those experiences had cemented relationships among soldiers stronger than any other connection."[8]

As the new century began, the world outside the one the veterans had formed for themselves was changing in ways that must have seemed little short of magical to men who, in their teens, had followed mounted officers into battle, torn paper cartridges open with their teeth, and marveled at the sight of the world's first ironclad warships. In 1903, the Wright brothers electrified the world with the first powered flight. Five years later, Henry Ford's first Model T rolled off the assembly line. Fresh from victory in the Spanish-American War, where the sons of Union and Confederate veterans had fought side by side, the United States was assuming a larger role on the world stage, and in December 1907, President Theodore Roosevelt dispatched the 16 battleships of the "Great White Fleet" on a globe-circling, muscle-flexing cruise to drive home the point. Henry Huidekoper and his fellow veterans were also keenly aware that their ranks were thinning. GAR membership

---

7 Stuart McConnell, *Glorious Contentment: The Grand Army of the Republic, 1865-1900* (Chapel Hill, NC, 1992), 153; William B. Heseltine, *Confederate Leaders in the New South* (Baton Rouge, LA, 1950), 95; Marten, *Sing Not War*, 17. Wallace C. Davies provides a fine overview of the growth and impact of the GAR and UCV in their heyday in *Patriotism on Parade: The Story of Veterans' and Hereditary Organizations in America, 1783-1900* (Cambridge, MA, 1955). For further insight into the GAR, see Mary R. Dearing, *Veterans in Politics: The Story of the G.A.R.* (Baton Rouge, 1952).

8 Jordan, *Marching Home*, 74; Marten, *Sing Not War*, 258.

had fallen by almost a third from its peak in 1890. "The wartime conditions, remembered as of yesterday," observed the *Philadelphia Public Ledger* in 1903, "seem infinitely remote, as though they must have belonged to some elementary period of civilization with which we no longer have anything in common."[9]

The semi-centennial of those three bloody days in July would be an opportunity to remind their fellow citizens, perhaps for the last time, that the unity and prosperity the nation enjoyed in the twentieth century had its roots in the hallowed ground of a hundred Civil War battlefields, of which none loomed larger than Gettysburg.

*   *   *

Five months after Huidekoper first broached the idea to the governor, Col. John P. Nicholson, a veteran of the 28th Pennsylvania and chairman of the Gettysburg National Park Commission, invited 30 prominent Gettysburg citizens to a meeting at the Eagle Hotel and urged them to take the lead in organizing a suitable commemoration of the fiftieth anniversary of the battle. At a subsequent town meeting on September 25, a committee of seven, chaired by the Reverend J. A. Singmaster, president of the Gettysburg Theological Seminary, was appointed to take up the matter with Governor Stuart.

There were many reasons to celebrate the battle's anniversary, Singmaster told the citizens gathered in the courthouse that night, but "the commercial reason, the benefit it would be to the community, was not one of the motives that should urge the commemoration." Moreover, "it should not be celebrated as a matter of mere local pride, for the event belonged to the nation and not the community." Judge Samuel McCurdy Swope concurred, declaring that the "patriotism of the suggestion of a celebration ought not to be questioned because it comes from the town."[10] "[It] promises to be the greatest event Gettysburg has ever seen or ever will see," said the *Gettysburg Star and Sentinel*. "Not only will the citizens of Gettysburg be interested, but all who participated, as well as many influential men throughout the country."[11]

If Singmaster's forswearing of "the commercial reason" seemed a tad defensive, there was good cause. When the Army of Northern Virginia began its retreat

---

9 *Philadelphia Public Ledger*, July 3, 1903, quoted in Jim Weeks, *Gettysburg: Memory, Market, and an American Shrine* (Princeton, NJ, 2003), 58. For GAR membership over time, see *Proceedings of the 53rd Annual Encampment of the Dept. of Ohio G.A.R.* (Columbus, OH, 1919), 66. For UCV membership, see Caroline E. Janney, *Remembering the Civil War: Reunion and the Limits of Reconciliation* (Chapel Hill, 2013), 180.

10 "50th Battle Anniversary," *Gettysburg Compiler*, Sept. 16, 1908.

11 "Fiftieth Anniversary," *Gettysburg Star and Sentinel*, Sept. 16, 1908.

southward on July 4, 1863, with the Army of the Potomac following cautiously in its wake, Gettysburg's 2,500 citizens emerged from their cellars to find a shattered landscape: crops trampled, orchards destroyed, fences tumbled down or burned, barns and stores stripped of provisions, livestock and poultry gone, and thousands of dead horses and mules, swollen to twice their size and rotting in the heat. Then there were the men: more than 7,000 Union and Confederate dead, some hastily buried in shallow graves, others still lying where they had fallen, and more than 20,000 wounded. "This town, and the vicinity within a space of country surrounding it of eight or ten miles, is literally one vast and over-crowded hospital," reported the *Philadelphia Public Ledger*. Gettysburg, one local observed, was "one vast, hideous charnel house."[12]

Surveying the devastation, many townspeople wondered, not unreasonably, how and by whom they would be made whole for their losses. But in their haste to answer that question, the impression they made on Union officers and enlisted men was not favorable. "They are a miserly crew," wrote Lt. Robert S. Robertson of the 93rd New York, "and have no souls or conscience where a penny is concerned. Some took the pumps out of their wells, and others charged the soldiers for the privilege of drawing water. I paid a dollar and a half for a small loaf of bread which could be bought in New York for 8 cents."

"After satisfying themselves that there was really no further danger to be apprehended from the Rebels," recalled a Connecticut private, "the fugitives of the people of Gettysburg came sneaking back and expressed their gratitude for the saving of their homes from destruction by charging wounded officers five dollars each for carrying them back two miles to the officers hospital, and five cents a glass for cool water for the parched and fevered lips of wounded soldiers. Others hurried to headquarters, before the dead had all been buried, whimpering and whining even to tears about the timber cut for breastworks, or the fence rails used to cook their defenders' meals, and wanting to know how they were to get their pay for them; as well as for the trampled wheat where there had been such agonizing struggle in defense of our common country during those bloody hours."

Lorenzo Crounse, a reporter for the *New York Times*, was equally scathing in his assessment. "[I]nstead of lending a helping hand to our wounded, and opening their houses to our famished officers and soldiers, they have only manifested indecent haste to present their bills to the military authorities for payment of losses inflicted by both armies," Crounse wrote in an article that appeared on July 9. "Their charges, too, were exorbitant—hotels, $2.50 per day; milk, 10 and 15 cents

---

12 Gregory A. Coco, *A Strange and Blighted Land: Gettysburg: The Aftermath of a Battle* (El Dorado Hills, CA, 2017), 40, 169. Coco provides an extraordinarily detailed and brutally vivid portrait of the battle's impact on the landscape and people of Gettysburg and Adams County.

per quart; bread, $1 and even $1.50 per loaf; twenty cents for a bandage for a wounded soldier! And these are only a few specimens of the sordid meanness and unpatriotic spirit manifested by these people, from whose doors our noble army had driven a hated enemy."[13]

Crounse was just one of the horde of reporters, photographers, and artists who descended on the town to document the aftermath of the longest, bloodiest battle ever fought on American soil, and again four months later for the dedication of the new national cemetery. John B. Bachelder, who arrived three days after the battle, was another. In *Gettysburg: Memory, Market, and an American Shrine*, historian Jim Weeks writes, "Bachelder believed Gettysburg represented the climactic struggle he had been anticipating since attaching himself to the Army of the Potomac the previous year. Unlike other photographers and bohemians who recorded Gettysburg and then departed, Bachelder spent the remaining three decades of his life promoting Gettysburg as the focal point of his trade in images. In the process, he shaped public perceptions of Gettysburg as both a shrine and a tourist site."[14]

Bachelder's panoramic "isometrical map" of the battlefield, published the year after the battle, was an immediate hit and ultimately sold thousands of copies. He followed up in 1873 with a popular guidebook, *Gettysburg: What to See and How to See It*, which was informed by his post-war interviews and correspondence with hundreds of Union and Confederate officers. And it was Bachelder who popularized "the copse of trees" near the center of the Union line where the Confederates briefly broke through during Pickett's Charge as "the High Water Mark of the Rebellion," a phrase that he coined.

The residents of Gettysburg "knew their town had made history," Weeks notes, "and that history as displayed on an epical landscape could be packaged and sold. An open letter 'to the people of Adams County' by the *Adams Sentinel*'s editor in 1865 saw the battle as 'one of the chief events in recorded history,' and an opportunity that 'the providence of God has put within the power of the people of this county.'"[15]

By the mid-1880s, Gettysburg boasted six hotels, two rail lines that brought a steady stream of visitors, and a growing cottage industry of battlefield guides, relic and souvenir vendors, and refreshment stands to serve them. Union veterans arrived regularly for reunions or to dedicate state and regimental monuments and

---

13 Ibid., 251-252; Lorenzo Crounse quoted in Allen C. Guelzo, *Gettysburg: The Last Invasion* (New York, 2013), 471. For more on contemporary criticism of the behavior of Gettysburg's citizens in the aftermath of the battle, see Margaret S. Creighton, *The Colors of Courage: Gettysburg's Forgotten History* (New York, 2005), 157-162.

14 Weeks, *Gettysburg*, 23.

15 Ibid., 27.

were welcomed by "a band resplendent in navy uniforms fringed by gold braids, brass-spiked Prussian helmets, and white belts."[16]

In the early 1890s, local photographer and entrepreneur William Tipton helped secure approval for an electric trolley line through the battlefield and opened Tipton Park on 13 acres near the southern end of its route at Devil's Den, complete with a refreshment stand, a dancing pavilion, and a photographic gallery. The Harrisburg and Gettysburg Railroad built a branch line that bisected the field of Pickett's Charge on its way to the Round Tops, where Round Top Park offered similar attractions to crowds of day-trippers from Baltimore and Philadelphia, some of whom never set foot on the battlefield itself.

The economic benefits of battlefield tourism, however, were a mixed blessing. As Weeks observes, "Although the local papers boosted tourism, they often regretted its stultifying effect on industry. 'It has prevented the location of factories here and has retarded the growth of the few we have,' the *Gettysburg Star and Sentinel* lamented in 1900." Three years later, the same paper complained, "Boys are brought up peddling in the streets who ought to be in school or in shops learning a useful trade; men who ought to be at work spend whole days waiting around in carriages and annoying visitors."[17] And the note struck by Crounse would reverberate over the years. In its coverage of the twenty-fifth anniversary of the battle in 1888, the *Times* declared that "[n]owhere else in the wide world is the art of squeezing so thoroughly understood and so harshly practiced as at Gettysburg."[18]

*   *   *

Governor Stuart did not disappoint Henry Huidekoper or the citizens of Gettysburg.

On January 5, 1909, in his biennial message to the General Assembly, he urged the creation of a commission "with authority to invite the cooperation of the other States" to plan a fitting observation of the fiftieth anniversary of the battle. He reminded the legislators that "the Commanding General of the Union forces was a distinguished Pennsylvanian, and on that memorable field thousands of Pennsylvania's sons won imperishable fame. Of Pennsylvania commands, there were engaged, or present on the field, sixty-nine regiments of infantry, ten regiments

16 Ibid., 68.

17 Ibid., 73-74.

18 Ibid., 73.

of cavalry and seven batteries of artillery. Many of the men of these commands are still living, and many will be living on the fiftieth anniversary of the battle."[19]

One could be forgiven for suspecting that when the assembled legislators heard the words "still living" they silently added "and voting."

In May, both houses of the legislature approved an act authorizing the governor to create the Fiftieth Anniversary of the Battle of Gettysburg Commission (hereafter cited as the Pennsylvania Commission) and appropriating $5,000 for its preliminary expenses. Governor Stuart appointed nine men, all Union veterans and GAR members, including a past commander-in-chief, Brevet Brig. Gen. Louis Wagner, who was elected its chairman.

Wagner was born in Giessen, Germany in 1838, and came to America at age 11 with his parents, settling in Philadelphia. After serving as an apprentice to a lithographer, he started his own printing business in 1859. When the Civil War came, he helped raise a company of infantry and joined the 88th Pennsylvania as first lieutenant of Company D. Promoted to captain, he was wounded in the leg and captured at the Second Battle of Bull Run in August 1862. After being paroled, he returned to his regiment and was promoted to major. He was wounded a second time at Chancellorsville, this time seriously enough to be deemed unfit for further field service. Now a lieutenant colonel, Wagner asked to be given command of Camp William Penn, in Chelton Hills, Pennsylvania, where he was responsible for training thousands of African American volunteers for service in the United States Colored Troops (USCT). He was promoted to brigadier general just before the war ended.

After the war, Wagner returned to Philadelphia, where he served as the city's first director of the Department of Public Works, and later as president of the Board of City Trusts. A temperance man and devout Presbyterian, he was active in Union veteran organizations almost from the moment the war ended, ultimately becoming "one of Pennsylvania's most prominent Grand Army men" and national commander-in-chief of the GAR in 1880.[20]

He was not a man to suffer fools gladly. According to the *Washington Post*, Wagner, who walked with a cane due to the wound he received at Bull Run, "has adopted a novel method of avoiding questions as to the cause of his lameness. When introduced to a stranger he hands the latter a card, which reads: 'No sir; it is not either rheumatism or the gout; neither was I thrown out of a carriage or kicked

---

19 *Report of the Pennsylvania Commission for the Fiftieth Anniversary of the Battle of Gettysburg*, revised edition (Harrisburg, PA, April 1915), 3.

20 Louis Wagner obituary, *Proceedings of the 48th Annual Encampment of the Dept. of Pennsylvania, G.A.R.* (Harrisburg, PA, 1914), 32-33.

by a horse. At 5:33 p.m. on Saturday, August 30, 1862, at the second battle of Bull Run, I foolishly got in the way of a rebel bullet and lost 3 inches of the shinbone of my right leg. That is what is the matter.'"[21]

*　　*　　*

One of the Pennsylvania Commission's first acts was to write to the governors of every U.S. state, commonwealth, and territory, inviting them "to share in this important anniversary and to help make it an event worthy of its historical significance and an occasion creditable and impressive to our great and reunited Nation." Ultimately, all would appoint representatives to work with the commission, including Union veterans Joshua L. Chamberlain from Maine, Elisha Hunt Rhodes from Rhode Island, and Daniel E. Sickles of New York, and Confederates Evander M. Law of Florida and S. A. Cunningham, editor of *Confederate Veteran* magazine, representing Tennessee.

In February 1910, the members of the commission met in Washington with President William Howard Taft, Vice President James S. Sherman, and members of Pennsylvania's congressional delegation, seeking to engage the interest of the federal government in the reunion project. In June, that effort bore fruit as the House and Senate passed a concurrent resolution authorizing the appointment of a committee consisting of three senators and three representatives to confer with the Pennsylvania Commission and report back their recommendations "as to the proper action to be taken by Congress to enable the United States fittingly to join in the celebration of the Fiftieth Anniversary of the Battle of Gettysburg."

The congressional committee was composed of four Republicans and two Democrats. It included Rep. Daniel F. Lafean, whose district encompassed Gettysburg, Sen. George T. Oliver of Pennsylvania, and two others with Pennsylvania roots: Sen. Weldon B. Heyburn of Idaho, born to Quaker parents near Philadelphia, and Rep. James A. Tawney of Minnesota, who was born and raised in Mount Pleasant, not far from Gettysburg. Five were too young to have served in the Civil War. One, Rep. John Lamb of Virginia, was a Confederate veteran.[22]

With the organizational structure for planning the great event taking shape, it was time to bring all the players together and begin work in earnest. The commission invited the members of the congressional committee and the state representatives appointed thus far—about two dozen, including those from Virginia, North Carolina, and South Carolina—to join them for a general conference on October 13 and 14 in Gettysburg.

---

21 "Interviews with Capital's Visitors," *Washington Post*, Jan. 13, 1912.

22 *Pennsylvania Commission Report*, 5-6.

They arrived by train from Harrisburg in mid-afternoon and were taken in carriages over the ground of the first day's fight west and north of town. That evening after dinner, the local organizing committee and the Citizens Band escorted them from the Eagle Hotel to a public meeting at the courthouse, where it soon became apparent that the passage of almost 50 years had not entirely reconciled the former combatants on every point.

The Reverend J. Richards Boyle, a member of the commission and veteran of the 111th Pennsylvania, began well by voicing his support for the erection of statues of Lee and his commanders on the battlefield, which "received vigorous applause from the audience." He then declared that Union victory in the war had brought about a great good—an oblique reference to the abolition of slavery—preserved the integrity of the nation, and "prevented the Mexicanization of the United States."

Representative Lamb of the congressional committee, who had commanded a company of the 3rd Virginia Cavalry in the war, rose next. First elected to the House in 1896 and now in his seventh term, he was known as "an earnest and forcible" speaker whose "fidelity to the 'Lost Cause' and her leaders has made him many friends outside of his own neighborhood and constituency," according to the 1907 edition of *Men of Mark in Virginia*. "He believes that the South was right in 1861, and that with five thousand more men at Gettysburg she would have established her independence."[23]

Lamb now "reviewed with great feeling the southern defeat at Gettysburg . . . [and declared] that of the men who charged with Pickett not one out of thirty owned a slave nor had their ancestors done so before them. He claimed slavery had little to do with the war and said the state's rights contention was uppermost." Lamb also took a shot at Lt. Gen. James Longstreet, almost seven years in his grave but still capable of stirring the ire of Southerners who could forgive neither his post-war embrace of the Republican party nor, even worse, the criticisms he had leveled against the sainted Lee. Lamb said a young boy had recently declared that Longstreet must have been drunk on the third day at Gettysburg. "Yes," he roared, "but there are more ways of becoming intoxicated than by drinking liquor. People become drunk with envy, with hatred and with enthusiasm."

John E. Gilman, commander-in-chief of the GAR, was next to speak and "in a more or less sarcastic way referred to a number of the former speaker's statements, especially to his depreciation of slavery as a cause of the war." Lamb leapt to his feet

---

23 "Friction at Commissioners' Mass Meeting, *Gettysburg Times*, Oct. 14, 1910; Lyon Gardiner Tyler, *Men of Mark in Virginia*, 5 vols. (Washington, D.C., 1907), 3:202.

to respond, but Wagner, who was chairing the meeting, refused to recognize him and told him to sit back down.

Augustus E. Willson, Republican governor of the predominately Democratic state of Kentucky and the first non-veteran to speak, attempted to calm the increasingly troubled waters. "If I did not know I was away from my state," he began, "if I did not know what I was here for, if I did not know I was in Gettysburg, I would believe you were all from Kentucky. We all look alike. We are all Americans. That is why the Civil War lasted so long. If there had been a foreign army opposing an American army the war would have been over in a hurry. But so far as this Mexican business is concerned, we don't know anything about it. That is a different breed from ours." Willson closed by pointing with pride to the fact that there were fewer immigrants in Kentucky than in any other eastern state. "His address," the *Gettysburg Times* noted, "was received throughout with great enthusiasm."

The evening's final remarks came from Senator Heyburn of the joint congressional committee, whose irritation with the back-and-forth among the previous speakers was evident. "If we are to come here in 1913 to fight again the battle of Gettysburg," Heyburn said, "and to point out when one army was victorious and the other defeated we would better stay away. Let's have done with these discussions about north and south. We are brothers and brothers, if they have a quarrel, do not on every anniversary fight it all over again. They forget about it. Let us gather here three years hence to commemorate the victory of a great national principle. If we come with any other spirit the celebration will be a failure and we would better not have it."[24]

By the following morning, passions had cooled. The weather was clear and beautiful, and the group toured the scene of the second and third days' fight before returning to the hotel and formally convening the first general conference of the commission and its state representatives at 10:45 a.m. Senator Oliver of Pennsylvania asked Wagner if the commission had prepared any tentative plans for the anniversary celebration, and was told it had not, as one purpose of the conference was to gather advice on that score. A roll of the states was called for suggestions and proceeded as far as Illinois, with each representative pledging his state's support but offering no concrete ideas for how the event should be structured.

---

24 "Friction at Commissioners' Mass Meeting, *Gettysburg Times*, Oct. 14, 1910. For more on the efforts of Jubal Early and others to blacken Longstreet's postwar reputation, and his own sporadic and sometimes counterproductive attempts to fight back, see William Garrett Piston, *Lee's Tarnished Lieutenant: James Longstreet and His Place in Southern History* (Athens, GA, 1987) and Jeffrey D. Wert, *General James Longstreet: The Confederacy's Most Controversial Soldier* (New York, 1993).

At this point a motion was made to suspend the roll call and "a prolonged and desultory discussion took place."[25]

"Gen. George H. Roberts of Idaho, declared he had no plans to suggest and had no thought of one, but expected that a tentative plan would be presented and thrashed out," the *Gettysburg Compiler* reported. J. B. Greenhut, a veteran of the 12th and 82nd Illinois Infantry and now a wealthy department store owner in New York City, said he supposed that the commission would have "some ideas in a crystallized form that could be approved or disapproved," while John R. King of Maryland "drew attention to the uselessness of talking and no plans to discuss." Senator Oliver thought the commission "had started at the wrong end and should formulate a plan for discussion."[26]

Dan Sickles, the last surviving corps commander on either side at Gettysburg, was asked to weigh in and said he thought it entirely proper for the commission to hear the views of the conference before preparing a plan, but that "whatever else might be determined upon, a permanent Peace Monument of some kind should, if possible, be dedicated on the field at the time of the Jubilee celebration."[27]

The meeting closed just before 1:00 p.m. with a flurry of motions: to hold the anniversary commemoration on July 1-4, 1913, "with the final day being devoted to the subject of National and International Peace"; to request that the conference members formulate tentative plans for the celebration and submit them in writing, within 30 days, to the commission; to request that each state furnish transportation for its surviving veterans to and from the event; and to confer on the commission and the congressional committee "full power to make all arrangements for the proper observance of the Fiftieth Anniversary of the Battle of Gettysburg."[28]

Over the course of the next several weeks, the commission received suggestions regarding the program for the anniversary celebration from several state delegates. King, the Maryland representative, suggested that the army place 50 pieces of artillery on the field, to fire a salute each day, and that the reunion culminate on the night of July 4 "with a great display of Fire Works and a great chorus to sing 'The Star Spangled Banner' and 'Auld Lang Syne.'" Samuel M. Bushman, Jr., an attorney and the delegate from New Mexico who had been born and raised in Gettysburg, declared, "I believe the celebration should be such that it will bring to Gettysburg more people who have the anti-military spirit, than those who

---

25 Fiftieth Anniversary of the Battle of Gettysburg Commission Minutes, 13, Record Group 25.27, Box 1, PSA. Hereafter cited as Commission Minutes.

26 "The Great Anniversary," *Gettysburg Compiler*, Oct. 19, 1910.

27 Commission Minutes, 13.

28 Ibid., 13.

believe in the virtues of war. I agree most heartily with the suggestion of Genl. Sickles, that it is now time that there be dedicated upon the Gettysburg Field a great and grand monument to Peace; and that should be the concern of the National Government."[29]

Sickles himself wrote, "I would like to see the veterans of both sides— confederate and union soldiers surviving—meet at Gettysburg on this occasion. . . . If we could have both sides at Gettysburg, in goodly numbers, it would make the occasion historical—a national love feast. . . . By the way, should we not ask Congress for an appropriation?—at least for the Peace monument, of which I have before spoken?—and perhaps something added for expenses, music, printing, and a volume of all our proceedings, speeches, etc., a copy of which should be in every public library in the United States, including schools."[30]

Martin G. Brumbaugh, the superintendent of schools in Philadelphia who was serving as delegate from Puerto Rico (and would later be elected governor of Pennsylvania) submitted a professionally printed brochure in which he outlined a detailed proposal for the four days of the celebration, each of which was to have a specific theme and focus. On July 1, the veterans themselves would gather "to commemorate the close of all Sectional strife and the beginning of an era of Fraternity and Brotherhood on the part of all who participated in the memorable battle of fifty years ago." July 2 would be military day and feature a grand parade of "at least 10,000" active-duty servicemen and 5,000 state militia, reviewed by the president and the secretaries of war and the navy. The states would hold their individual exercises on July 3, and on July 4 the celebration would reach its climax with the dedication of the peace memorial by the president, before an audience that would include—in addition to the veterans, of course, who seemed to be shrinking into the background of this scenario—both houses of Congress, the justices of the Supreme Court, the governors of every state and territory, and "a male chorus of 5,000 voices massed and uniformed as a living flag and singing national patriotic songs."[31]

The minutes of the commission do not note how this ambitious proposal was received, but at their next meeting, on December 20, the members voted to appoint a four-man executive committee and charged it with preparing a plan and program for the consideration of the commission and its state representatives. The tentative

29 Letter, John R. King to Louis Wagner, Oct. 31, 1910; Letter, Samuel M. Bushman, Jr. to Louis Wagner, Nov. 10, 1910, Commission Correspondence, RG 25.24, Box 2.

30 Letter, Daniel E. Sickles to Louis Wagner, Nov. 23, 1910, Commission Correspondence, RG 25.24, Box 2.

31 Letter, Martin G. Brumbaugh to Louis Wagner, Nov. 5, 1910, Commission Correspondence, RG 25.24, Box 2.

program sketched out by Wagner in a letter to newly elected Pennsylvania Gov. John K. Tener a few weeks later followed generally the lines of Brumbaugh's four-day proposal, albeit without some of the more eye-popping specifics concerning the size of the parade and the number of singers in the chorus. But Wagner was quite clear that the commission expected the celebration would culminate in "the laying of the cornerstone of a permanent Peace Memorial, to be authorized and erected by the Government of the United States."

"We shall request the General Government to furnish the camp equipage that may be found necessary," Wagner wrote, "and the several States to provide transportation for the veteran soldiers residing within their jurisdiction. We shall ask the Gettysburg National Park Commission to locate the various camps, and shall invoke the aid of Pennsylvania to defray the transportation expenses of her own surviving soldiers, and the actual cost incurred in providing the chorus and the officially invited officers of the State and General Government."[32]

When the executive committee, composed of Wagner, R. Dale Benson, J. Richards Boyle, and Lewis T. Brown, who was elected chair, held its first meeting in Philadelphia on December 30, it authorized Wagner "to confer with the officers of the Railway Companies centering at Gettysburg regarding the matter of improved transportation to that place; and also to communicate with the Citizens' Committee of Gettysburg, suggesting a conference between that Committee and the Commission on the subject of transportation and other matters of public accommodation."[33]

Brown died in March 1911 and was not replaced on the executive committee; Wagner succeeded him as chair. By the time the next meeting of the full commission convened in July, the Pennsylvania legislature had authorized further expenditures up to a total of $250,00 for the semi-centennial celebration, which, assuming the federal government set up and ran the camp itself, would be more than sufficient to cover the costs of programming, transportation for the state's veterans, and accommodations for VIPs. There had been little other activity, however, and the minutes begin to suggest some concern on that score. On a motion from Benson, "it was ordered that at its next meeting the Commission should invite authorized representatives of the various railroads and railways centering in Gettysburg,

32 Letter, Louis Wagner to John K. Tener, Feb. 17, 1911, Commission Correspondence, RG 25.24, Box 2. Tener was born in County Tyrone, Ireland, and pitched for two seasons with the National League's Chicago White Stockings (later the Cubs) before going on to a successful career in business. He was elected president of the National League in December 1913 and juggled those duties with his final year as governor.

33 Commission Minutes, 16.

and the Gettysburg Citizens' Committee, to meet with it, to confer respecting transportation, entertainment, and kindred matters."[34]

Three more months went by, and in October, Boyle moved that the members of the Gettysburg National Park Commission be invited to meet and confer with the commission. A further motion from Benson authorized the executive committee to employ a field secretary and a press agent "to aid in extending and publishing the work of the Commission."[35]

As 1911 drew to a close, the meetings with the citizens' committee, the park commission, and the railroad representatives, first called for a year earlier, still had not been scheduled. Lieutenant Colonel Lewis E. Beitler of the National Guard of Pennsylvania had been appointed field secretary for the Pennsylvania Commission and he, in turn, was dickering with William A. Connor of the Associated Press, who had expressed interest in taking on the press agent job for a salary of $100 per month. The commissioners wanted to spend no more than $50, and he was ultimately hired at that salary for a period of 10 months, to commence January 1, 1912. Beitler was also endeavoring to arrange a joint session with the members of the congressional committee, who had not met with the commission in more than a year.

Meanwhile, the idea of confining the celebration to four days, to say nothing of the desultory pace at which preparations seemed to be proceeding, was beginning to cause some uneasiness among the citizens of Gettysburg. The front page of the December 27 edition of the *Compiler* sounded the alarm:

> With hundreds of thousands of veterans as proposed guests, it follows that many of these guests will bring a wife, a daughter, a son, a granddaughter or grandson, and the guests and their immediate relatives will be a tremendous throng such as Gettysburg has never seen since the great battle. . . .
>
> Limited to survivors of the battle and as many more of the general public gives a grand total of 100,000 which is more than likely to be swollen to two, three, four or many times that number . . .
>
> The two railroads entering the town are single track roads and these two roads with their well known ability to handle crowds can not carry more than 20,000 a day, take care and return the cars and provide for a freight traffic such as this big a throng will require. . . .

34 Ibid., 20.

35 Ibid., 22.

Next, if every one of the 1,000 residences in Gettysburg were thrown open to the visitors, if every public place was prepared for their lodging, this town would be crowded to its utmost capacity with 15,000 people . . .

Again, the water system of Gettysburg that has successfully taken care of encampments forming a community of four times the population of the town might be able to provide for 50,000 or more but not for hundreds of thousands for a four days' celebration. . . .

[T]he physical impossibility of a four days' celebration demands an anniversary of such length as the circumstances require, two weeks, three weeks, or as long as the Gettysburg campaign covered, two months.[36]

A number of local residents also weighed in. J. Frank Hartman of the Gettysburg Department Store declared that "preparations to provide provisions for an enormous four days' crowd would be such a plunge that it would be doubtful whether any of our business men would be willing to take the risks. To stock up to meet the emergency and run the chance of a fizzle of a four days' show was not an inviting prospect."

"I would say it is impossible to carry out the program as tentatively outlined," said J. A. Cox, local agent for the Reading Railroad. "There are almost insurmountable difficulties in transporting such a large number to and from Gettysburg. . . . I think four to six weeks would be required to hold the celebration as planned."

Robert C. Miller was secretary of the Gettysburg Board of Trade and proprietor of the Jennie Wade House, a popular Gettysburg tourist attraction. He also was editor of the Republican weekly, *The Star and Sentinel*, but he crossed party and competitive lines to share his concerns with the readers of the *Compiler*, the Democratic weekly. "It is a very grave question in my mind whether these veterans should be taken care of in tents. Hot tents, close quarters near the ground, with risk of storms might produce a condition disastrous to the health of men of their age."

William Beales, the town's postmaster, voiced the unspoken concern on many minds that "a four days' celebration would be such a crowded, unsatisfactory thing that the town would be more hurt than helped, [and] that the visitors would leave with impressions that might keep them from ever returning."[37]

*   *   *

36 "50th Anniversary Plans," *Gettysburg Compiler*, Dec. 27, 1911.

37 "Four Day Anniversary of the 50th Anniversary Is a Physical Impossibility," *Gettysburg Compiler*, Jan. 3, 1912.

On January 11, 1912, more than a year after the executive committee had authorized Wagner to reach out to the town, J. A. Singmaster of the citizens' committee finally met with the members of the Pennsylvania Commission, along with Senator Oliver, chairman of the joint congressional committee, John Nicholson of the Gettysburg National Park Commission, and the commanders of the GAR and UCV, in Washington. He read a lengthy communication from the committee, which outlined its concerns about the available water supply, transportation, accommodations, sanitation, medical facilities, and public safety. Based on the town's past experience with reunions, he estimated the probable number of visitors, veteran and non-veteran, at "not less than seventy-five thousand" and broached the idea of extending the celebration for a full month, "which was actually the period of the Gettysburg campaign in 1863." Several large tents could be erected at different points around the battlefield, which "great orators, singers and bands might visit in turn" during the course of the month.

"We pledge our hearty cooperation to make the celebration a success," Singmaster declared, "but we feel that the great project must in no sense depend for execution on our feeble efforts. Its accomplishment rests on the wisdom and the available resources of the Commission. We have no fears of its success, provided the seriousness and magnitude of the celebration be properly apprehended."[38]

Wagner made no formal acknowledgment of Singmaster's statement, which covers five full pages in the meeting minutes, but did report on the commission's work to date, including the broad outline of the four-day celebration, the appointment of state representatives, and Pennsylvania's appropriation of $250,000. He then asked the members of the joint congressional committee to help secure passage of legislation directing the U.S. Army to lay out, equip, supply, and operate the camps that would house the veterans during the celebration and authorizing the federal government to take the lead in securing a design for, and funding the construction of, "a permanent Peace Memorial [that] shall take the form of an imposing gateway, or entrance to the Gettysburg National Military Park . . . signifying National Unity and Peace" and topped with a heroic statue of Abraham Lincoln reading the Gettysburg Address. "It is our judgment," Wagner declared, "that such a work as this would fittingly express the spirit and meaning of the proposed observance of the Fiftieth Anniversary of the Battle of Gettysburg; that its cost would not exceed an expenditure such as Congress would willingly authorize—say, a maximum of $500,000; and that standing as a Benedictus above this great bivouac of our patriot dead it would be, for all time, an eloquent object lesson in American unity, valor and good-will. We regard the erection of this

38 Commission Minutes, 33-34.

memorial as by far the most important part of the proposed celebration of this anniversary, and we hope . . . that such measures will be taken through you by the National Legislature as will guarantee the laying of the cornerstone of the structure by the President of the United States, at high noon, on July 4, 1913."[39]

Had the veterans taken a closer look at the composition of the Congress in 1912, they might have been less confident in their assertion that it "would willingly authorize" $500,000 for the design and construction of a peace memorial. Twenty years earlier, when their political power and influence in the life of the nation was approaching its zenith, 178 Union and Confederate veterans were serving in Congress: fully half the Senate and four out of every 10 members of the House. By 1912, there were just 23: one senator out of 10 and three congressmen out of 100. A half-million dollars for yet another monument on a field already crowded with them was not going to be an easy lift.[40]

In April, the members of the joint congressional committee shepherded through the House and Senate a concurrent resolution directing the secretary of war to prepare a detailed report on the logistics of operating a camp for 40,000 aging veterans—a seat-of-the-pants estimate, but the only one offered by the commission—from drinking water and sanitation needs to tents, field kitchens, and medical facilities. [41] "This resolution of Congress was in line with the suggestions of the Citizens' Committee as conveyed by Dr. J. A. Singmaster to the Pennsylvania Commission [in January] and ignored by them," the *Gettysburg Compiler* noted with satisfaction, and echoed "what the Compiler has been advocating for many months."[42]

The report that was presented to Congress on May 10 estimated the total cost of running the camp at just over $358,000, a figure later pared to $300,000.[43]

That same week, the three-man executive committee of the Pennsylvania Commission finally met with representatives of the two railroads serving Gettysburg—the Western Maryland and the Philadelphia and Reading—who estimated that their combined maximum daily capacity was 18,500 passengers. They also stressed that in order to achieve that maximum "it would be necessary to have the expected traffic gathered at main points in the respective states, and

39 Ibid., 27-28.

40 These numbers were compiled by reviewing the Wikipedia biographies of every member of the 52nd and 62nd Congresses.

41 The largest reunion of Union and Confederate veterans to date, at the dedication of the Chickamauga and Chattanooga National Park in September 1895, had drawn about 25,000.

42 "50th Anniversary Plans," *Gettysburg Compiler*, Apr. 10, 1912.

43 *Pennsylvania Commission Report*, 12.

forwarded thence by special trains and on special schedules to the final transfer points on the Reading and Western Maryland Roads. Otherwise . . . there would be danger of congestion and failure."[44]

Meanwhile, tensions were growing between Wagner and the town of Gettysburg. "Our work of arranging the Fiftieth Celebration of the Battle of Gettysburg is hindered," he wrote to Singmaster, "and the people interested with me [are] annoyed by the general circulation of one of your papers which seems to have reached the conclusion that it is its business to see that this Celebration does not take place. Would it not be well for you to call a meeting of your Committee to consider this subject and to determine that so far as the people of Gettysburg are concerned they will cooperate with our Commission, instead of endeavoring to spread abroad the impression that your city is not large enough to take care of the Celebration?"[45]

"The cry that the town cannot handle the crowds has reached New York," noted the *Gettysburg Times*, "and had such an effect, according to General Wagner, that the matter of withdrawing the state appropriation to send veterans here was seriously considered. Other states may view the matter in the same light if the agitation is continued."[46]

"The policy of the head of the Commission of doing nothing along the many practical details of the event," the *Compiler* shot back, "would have made the celebration a monumental failure, if the Congressional Committee had not realized the wisdom of the suggestions of our people and had them studied, with the result that the success of the celebration is assured by the transfer of all authority over the details to the Secretary of War."[47]

As the criticism in the Gettysburg press mounted, Wagner—in a dynamic that will be familiar to any public relations person—became increasingly frustrated with W. A. Connor, the commission's press agent. He complained repeatedly to the other executive committee members about Connor's performance and declared that "his services to date were unsatisfactory."[48]

Whatever headaches the editors of the *Compiler* and the citizens' committee were causing Wagner must have paled to insignificance with the arrival of two letters from Senator Oliver of the joint congressional committee. The first informed him that the committee had drawn up a tentative bill, based on the report of the

---

44 Commission Minutes, 57.

45 Ibid., 58.

46 "Might Hurt the 50th Anniversary," *Gettysburg Times*, May 8, 1912.

47 "Grand Army of Republic," *Gettysburg Compiler*, Jun. 12, 1912.

48 Commission Minutes, 53, 83.

secretary of war concerning the cost of the camp, and "was willing to recommend an appropriation of $150,000 by the National Government, provided a similar amount be contributed by the State of Pennsylvania out of the $250,000 pledged by her Legislature for this Celebration." The second declared, "If this is done I will prepare the necessary bill and introduce it just as soon as I hear from you, but, if immediate action is not taken, I want to say plainly that neither I nor the Congressional Committee will be responsible for the failure of this scheme." The commission also was advised to defer the question of the Peace Memorial until the next session of Congress.[49]

The letters arrived just ahead of the second general conference of the commission and its state representatives, which had been scheduled for May 27–29, 1912, in Washington, to enable the state delegates to lobby their respective congressional delegations in support of the reunion appropriation. Only now, instead of seeking support for $300,000 to fully fund the costs of the camp plus another $500,000 for the peace memorial, the goal had been reduced by 80 percent.

"I am feeling very sore and disappointed over the action of the Congressional Committee," wrote Dale Benson of the executive committee. "I feel like a bird with its wings clipped."[50] "[T]he indisposition of that Committee seriously to consider the proposition of the Commission for the erection of a substantial and worthy Peace Memorial, by the General Government . . . has likewise disappointed me," admitted fellow executive committee member J. Richards Boyle. "In my opinion this proposed Memorial is by far the most important feature of the celebration which the Commission has suggested."[51]

A few weeks later, Boyle resigned from the Pennsylvania Commission.

*   *   *

When the *Compiler*'s editors got wind of Boyle's resignation, they laid it squarely at the feet of their nemesis: "General Louis Wagner, as Chairman of the Commission, has been autocratic and often unpleasant in insisting upon having his way. The Commission, composed of men advanced in years naturally have no desire to antagonize him and let him have his way. This has led straight to a do-nothing policy with a necessary day of reckoning ahead. The present condition of affairs must be some unpreparedness which can not help but reflect upon the

49 Letter, George T. Oliver to Louis Wagner, May 17, 1912, Commission Correspondence, RG 25.24, Box 2.

50 Letter, R. Dale Benson to Lewis Beitler, June 1, 1912, Commission Correspondence, RG 25.24, Box 2.

51 Letter, J. Richards Boyle to John K. Tener, June 26, 1912, Commission Correspondence, RG 25.24, Box 2.

Commission and it is not surprising that this should result in a resignation. The surprise is that all the Commissioners do not resign and allow their Chairman to face the reckoning for which in a great measure he is responsible."[52]

To fill Boyle's place on the commission, Governor Tener appointed James Martinus Schoonmaker, a Union cavalry veteran, Medal of Honor winner, successful businessman and railroad executive, and one of Pittsburgh's wealthiest men. In notifying Wagner, the governor admitted that the appointment violated "the sentiment which has heretofore controlled such selections, in appointing only those who participated in the engagement. However, this sentiment should not control, in my opinion, when we can command the service of a man of Col. Schoonmaker's ability."[53]

Congress finally passed the $150,000 appropriation in late August. It explicitly gave the war department full responsibility for the establishment and operation of the reunion camp, leaving the Pennsylvania Commission in charge of "the order of exercises during the celebration" and, by default, anything having to do with the accommodation of non-veteran visitors and the transportation of tens of thousands of people to and from Gettysburg. With the appropriation passed, the joint congressional committee considered its work complete. "The concurrent resolution . . . specifically defined [our] duties to be the recommendation of such legislation as might be necessary to enable the United States Government to participate in the celebration of the Fiftieth Anniversary of the Battle of Gettysburg," Senator Oliver wrote to Wagner. "No further duty was imposed on the commission [sic] and I therefore cannot construe the resolution any other way than to regard its mission as terminated."[54]

Summer turned to fall and at last, with some prodding from Governor Tener, the commission met on October 1 for the first time since the second general conference in May. Benson, the only remaining member of the executive committee besides Wagner, again raised the critical question of rail transportation, and the urgent necessity of "the early appointment of an experienced and expert railroad man of recognized ability and standing in his profession to be the Master of Transportation, with supreme authority in all matters pertaining thereto." His motion that such a position be created, and the executive committee be authorized and directed to appoint someone to fill it, passed unanimously.[55]

52 "Anniversary Official Resigns," *Gettysburg Compiler*, Aug. 21, 1912.

53 Letter, John K. Tener to Louis Wagner, Sept. 7, 1912, quoted in Commission Minutes, 88.

54 Letter, George T. Oliver to Louis Wagner, Jan. 23, 1913, Commission Correspondence, RG 25.24, Box 2.

55 Commission Minutes, 89.

The motion met the same fate as many that had preceded it. Wagner took no action, and when the commission next met, on December 13 in Gettysburg with Governor Tener in attendance, the position remained unfilled.

The commissioners were losing patience. Following Schoonmaker's presentation of a detailed report on his meetings with the senior management of the Reading and Western Maryland railroads, including maps and blueprints of the work they had undertaken, at the cost of several hundred thousand dollars, to expand the capacity of their Gettysburg facilities, the commissioners unanimously referred "the entire subject of increased railroad accommodations at Gettysburg, the appointment of a Master of Transportation, the securing of reduced Gettysburg rates for the Veterans, etc." to him "as a Sub-Committee on Transportation, with full power to act." It also authorized Schoonmaker to add to his subcommittee whatever additional members he deemed best, whether they were part of the Pennsylvania Commission or not.[56]

In turn, Schoonmaker suggested the establishment of a half-dozen additional subcommittees, on entertainment, invitations, and other critical topics, whose composition also would not be restricted to members of the Pennsylvania Commission. Wagner objected vehemently, but other commissioners supported the idea, as did Governor Tener, who spoke at length of the importance of the reunion and how "the eyes of the entire country were upon Pennsylvania." He framed the issue as delicately as he could, saying that Wagner should not be allowed, "however willing and able, to burden himself with the vast amount of work, every day growing larger and larger, nor should the present Commissioners seek likewise to do it all themselves."[57]

Wagner, who alone seemed serenely unconcerned that the opening of the reunion was barely six months away, was unmoved. Such an approach would be a mistake, he insisted, and in any case a decision to completely alter the plans and organization of the commission should not be undertaken lightly; it should be deferred until the next meeting in January. Governor Tener asked for and received Wagner's assurance that the question would be settled at the January meeting, and on that less than satisfactory note, the commission adjourned. Its third general conference was scheduled for January 23, 1913.

On December 21, Dale Benson resigned. The executive committee of the Pennsylvania Commission was now officially a one-man band.

*   *   *

56 Ibid., 101.

57 Ibid., 104.

When the commissioners met with Governor Tener on January 23, just prior to the opening of the third general conference in Philadelphia, several things quickly became apparent. First, the army officers detailed to plan and lay out the great camp on 280 acres of battlefield land leased from local farmers by the war department had that work well in hand, and Schoonmaker was working closely and effectively with the railroads on the transportation question. So far, so good. On the other hand, the $250,000 appropriated by the Pennsylvania legislature was not going to be sufficient to cover the state's share of the camp expense, plus the cost of transportation for all Pennsylvania veterans to and from the reunion, plus the cost of accommodating and entertaining hundreds of dignitaries and special guests. This was to say nothing of providing any of the support the citizens of Gettysburg were begging for in terms of additional police, hospital, and sanitation resources, as well as thousands of cots to provide temporary accommodations in public buildings and private homes for the expected throng of non-veteran visitors.

Perhaps most alarming, Wagner revealed that he had not yet invited President-elect Woodrow Wilson or any of the other dignitaries the commission was counting on to attend, and that none of the details of the program for the four days of the reunion had been finalized. He suggested to the other commissioners that "the opinions of the Representatives in attendance upon the General Conference might first be obtained thereon."

In executive session, Governor Tener reopened the question of establishing subcommittees, which had been tabled at the last meeting. Wagner remained adamantly opposed and Schoonmaker was just as firmly in favor, stressing that they were the only way to accomplish "the vast amount of work that now confronts the Commission, and that will daily grow larger." Tener reminded Wagner of the two resignations he had already received, warned that others were pending, and stated bluntly that the subcommittees must be formed "if success and not failure is to result." At last, the old general gave way.[58]

The public sessions of the third general conference were no less contentious. On behalf of the citizens' committee, J. A. Singmaster continued to press for assistance for the town. As usual, this was met with derision from Wagner who, according to the *Gettysburg Times*, "declared that we are neither patriotic nor progressive enough to sacrifice a little to make the celebration a success." "When Dr. Singmaster said there were a number of buildings in town like the Court House, school houses, etc. that could be converted into sleeping quarters if 5,000 cots would be provided

58 Ibid., 111, 118.

for the purpose," the *Star and Sentinel* added, "he was interrupted by Gen. Wagner shouting 'Get the money and put the buildings in shape.'"[59]

Editor Robert Miller of the *Star and Sentinel* had had enough, and in the January 29 edition he let Wagner have both barrels:

> General Wagner's remarks may be taken to indicate a disposition to unload the responsibility for possible failure on Gettysburg and he may as well be told now that the town does not propose to be the official scapegoat to relieve him.
>
> If it is General Wagner's desire to provoke an exchange of opinion he may understand that Gettysburg considers a man of his pugnacious and irritable temperament a positive calamity in a position in which he can control the preparations for a great celebration like this and in which he can insult at will the other parties interested who are compelled to appear before him. . . .
>
> Whatever is the reason, General Wagner has shown a spirit of positive animus toward the town that was manifest before any opposition to him or any of his plans had developed here. He has taken advantage of every opportunity in public speaking to display that sentiment. His domineering attitude has caused several of the more active members of the Commission to resign, and it has impaired the efficiency of the efforts of the others. His conduct in this matter considered, as well as his feelings of hostility and bias toward this community, leads to the conviction that the successful issue of the work with which the Commission is charged, depends upon the immediate resignation of its Chairman.[60]

Governor Tener had come to the same conclusion. Days after the conference ended, he asked for Wagner's resignation. The general, obstreperous to the last, told his fellow commissioners that he would "retire" from the commission on March 1. He asked that, upon his retirement, the commission's scrapbook be presented to him and, with what must have been a mixture of incredulity and relief, the commissioners readily agreed.[61]

When the news broke, an unnamed member of the commission told the *Gettysburg Times*:

> General Wagner's methods as an executive were displeasing almost from the start, and at times threatened to impair the commission's usefulness. A man of indomitable courage and marked will-power, and evidently feeling that in his capacity as president his wishes

---

59 "Slap for Gettysburg," *Gettysburg Times*, Jan. 25, 1913; "50th Anniversary Plans," Gettysburg Compiler, Jan. 29, 1913.

60 "Gettysburg vs. Gen. Wagner," *Gettysburg Star and Sentinel*, Jan. 29, 1913.

61 Commission Minutes, 121.

were entitled to more consideration than those of other members, he frequently assumed an arbitrary attitude. Of kindly heart, the general is given to abruptness of expression. Not infrequently members of the commission feel humiliated by the general's autocratic air during conferences of the commission.[62]

"With the passing of General Wagner from the Commission," declared the *Compiler*, "it is believed that the situation is cleared for quick, and as thorough work as can be done in the next four months."[63]

There was plenty of work to do.

62 "Wagner Out But Did Not Resign," *Gettysburg Times*, Mar. 1, 1913.

63 "Wagner Out," *Gettysburg Compiler*, Mar. 5, 1913.

Chapter 2

To Be Present Should Be Our Ardent Desire

A s Governor Tener and the Pennsylvania Commission struggled with planning and logistics for the great reunion, scores of states were making ready to send their veterans to Gettysburg, and in the case of most northern states, appropriating at least some funds to provide for their transportation. Massachusetts allocated $32,000, Maine $18,000, and New Jersey $20,000. As one moved farther west, the costs became more daunting, and the appropriations smaller. Montana approved just $2,000 to send 20 veterans—10 Union, 10 Confederate—to the reunion.[1]

Washington State appropriated $15,000, but only after overcoming opposition from an unlikely source. A group of Union veterans wrote to the governor to object to what they saw as misplaced priorities. "Our Soldiers' Home in this State is already inadequate to shelter and care for those entitled to admission, many of whom are now on the waiting list and in need of proper care; and our Soldiers' Relief Fund, provided by law and raised by taxation, has been drawn against to the limit and the need for additional funds is increasing, therefore we do not feel like spending money for railroad fare and hotel bills while the above conditions exist, nor in asking any unnecessary further taxation at this time." Their view did not prevail, and the state solicited competing offers from several rail lines who hoped to provide the special train to transport her veterans. In a letter to the state auditor, an official of the Chicago, Milwaukee and Puget Sound Railway appealed

1 *Pennsylvania Commission Report*, 36-37.

to cold political calculus: "It has been intimated that the state of Oregon would approach Washington with the intention of getting you to join with them. I hardly think, however, that Governor Lister or yourself would care to lose the identity of Washington in such an arrangement. The only return you are getting for the money expended in the transportation and expenses of the veterans is the publicity it will give to the State of Washington and I think this can be better brought about by using a railroad that is identified with the State and traverses the State from the West to the East." The governor and auditor were unmoved, and the Great Northern Railway, headquartered in Minnesota, ultimately won the contract.[2]

Unfortunately, Washington's appropriation fell $5,000 short of the amount necessary to transport the 152 Yanks and 15 Rebels who wished to attend. State officials hoped a statewide fund-raising campaign could make up the difference and couched their appeal in terms no less hard-headed than those of the Chicago, Milwaukee and Puget Sound Railway. "Eliminating the sentiment of the matter, which is a vital issue, the idea of $5,000 being raised by subscription to insure the attendance of all eligibles, would be a good advertisement for the state," Fred Llewellyn, adjutant of the Washington National Guard, told the *Seattle Times*. "The special train will be decorated with banners advertising the state and boosting literature will be provided for distribution throughout the East. The veterans will be the best boosters in the world, and if the people of Washington do their part toward sending them back there to their old battlefield, it would be an excellent investment from a selfish point of view, if not advisable, and so highly commendable, from any other."[3]

As it turned out, the statewide appeal was unnecessary. Horace C. Henry of Seattle, a veteran of the 14th Vermont who had fought at Gettysburg and built a successful post-war career as a banker, real estate developer, and partner in a railroad construction company, announced that he would guarantee the $5,000 needed, in anticipation of the next session of the state legislature passing an additional appropriation.[4]

Some states, including New York, Rhode Island, Vermont, and Indiana, established their own commissions to coordinate the work of soliciting, vetting, and fulfilling the veterans' transportation requests. "The clerks employed were kept busy," noted the report of the New York commission, "many corrections having

2 Undated letter to Gov. Lister, signed by 17 Union veterans; Letter, J. G. Thomson to C. W. Clausen, May 10, 1913, Manuscript Collection, Washington State Library, Tumwater, WA.

3 "Adjutant-General Asks Citizens to Assist Old Soldiers," *Seattle Times*, June 8, 1913.

4 "H. C. Henry Comes to Relief of Veterans," *Seattle Times*, June 13, 1913.

to be made in the applications, by reason of errors committed by the applicants, requiring the re-mailing of documents and letters of information."[5]

South of the Mason-Dixon line, it was a different story. "I cannot believe it even possible that the State Governments can afford to make appropriations to transport their Veterans to the battlefield at Gettysburg," Bennett H. Young of the UCV wrote to the Pennsylvania Commission. He was correct. Despite the best efforts of Lt. Col. Lewis Beitler, the Pennsylvania Commission's field secretary, who crisscrossed the South calling upon governors and state legislators and meeting with the editors of major newspapers to urge support for the reunion, Alabama, Florida, Georgia, Louisiana, Mississippi, Tennessee, and Texas made no appropriation at all. Virginia's legislature passed an enabling act authorizing county supervisors to appropriate funds to transport local veterans to the reunion but allocated no state money for the purpose. South Carolina was the only exception among the states of the old Confederacy; its legislature appropriated $1,000.[6]

If the fiftieth anniversary celebration was to be the "love feast" that Dan Sickles hoped for, it was imperative that Confederate veterans be persuaded to attend alongside their former foes in numbers larger than at any previous Blue–Gray reunion. But in the absence of state funding, Bennett Young declared, "To secure such attendance the desire to go must be quickened so that the individuals will be willing to pay their own expenses." Moreover, the Southerners would need to be absolutely certain that the event would in no way be a celebration of their defeat. And even though Blue-Gray reunions had become more common than they had been 20 years earlier, that was still going to be a pretty tall order.[7]

One of the earliest such events had taken place in the summer of 1881, when the GAR post in Carlisle, Pennsylvania, organized an excursion for 600 Union veterans to Luray, Virginia, in the Shenandoah Valley, where they were entertained by nearly 2,000 Confederate veterans. Other reunions had brought together a few hundred members of individual units that had fought one another, like the 5th Virginia and 28th New York, who exchanged visits at Niagara Falls in 1883 and Staunton, Virginia, the following year. In 1887, some 400 veterans of the Philadelphia Brigade gathered with 300 survivors of Pickett's Division in Gettysburg where Sallie Pickett, Maj. Gen. George Pickett's widow, hosted a reception and signed autographs for veterans of both sides. The following year,

---

5 *Fiftieth Anniversary of the Battle of Gettysburg 1913: Report of the New York State Commission* (Albany, NY, 1916), 17.

6 Letter, Bennett H. Young to Louis Wagner, May 25, 1912, Commission Correspondence, RG 25.24, Box 2; *Pennsylvania Commission Report*, 36-39.

7 Young to Wagner.

however, when 20,000 Union veterans and their families came to Gettysburg to mark the 25th anniversary of the battle, most old Rebels stayed away, unwilling to take part in what they suspected would feel too explicitly like a glorification of Union victory.[8] "A number of prominent confederates, including Lieutenant-General Gordon, General Hooker of Mississippi, and others were present," recalled Sickles, "but not many of the rank and file."[9]

One old soldier stated the case plainly. "I do not see how any man who came back in April of 1865 to smoking ruins and desolated fields, who fought for existence through six bitter years of reconstruction and remembers the wormwood of those days can celebrate side by side with the victors in our defeat in the most important battle of the war," he told the *Richmond Times-Dispatch*. "I, for one, cannot go to Gettysburg where the Grand Army will celebrate with festival the battle which broke the backbone of the Confederacy," declared another, "while we recall it only with tears of deep sorrow."[10]

Brigadier General Evander M. Law, who had led a brigade in Hood's Division at Gettysburg and assumed temporary command of the division when Hood was wounded on July 2, encountered that sentiment head on when he attempted to persuade the Florida legislature to support the reunion. As he wrote bitterly to field secretary Beitler, "I have made every possible effort to get even a small appropriation from the state without success, solely on account of the presence in our state senate of two men who unfortunately happened to be at the battle of Gettysburg, and who opposed every movement in that direction, appealing to senatorial courtesy to sustain them and blocking every effort I made. Thank God, we have few such narrow-minded cranks in the state. We have numbers of G.A.R. Posts as well as U.C.V. Camps and the utmost fraternity and good will exists among them everywhere throughout the state. . . . I feel deeply mortified at the failure of the legislature to second my efforts in a great and patriotic cause."[11]

It was going to take a concerted effort, spearheaded by UCV commander C. Irvine Walker, to turn out a respectable number of ex-Confederates despite parsimonious state legislators and the veterans' own concerns about the tenor and message of the reunion. "As such attendance is absolutely necessary to accomplish the high, noble, patriotic objects for which your Commission was constituted,"

8 Janney, *Remembering the Civil War*, 160-161, 175-178; William Buckley, *Buckley's History of the Great Reunion of the North and the South* (Staunton, VA, 1923), 11, 93.

9 Letter, Daniel E. Sickles to Louis Wagner, Nov. 23, 1910, Commission Correspondence, RG 25.24, Box 2.

10 Both quoted in Janney, *Remembering the Civil War*, 267.

11 Letter, Evander M. Law to Lewis Beitler, May 15, 1913, Commission Correspondence, RG 25.24, Box 5, PSA.

Walker wrote to the Pennsylvania Commission, "you would be most certainly authorized to incur the expense necessary to stimulate the same." He proposed the establishment of a "quasi Southern Publicity Bureau," assured them that its expense would be "inconsiderable, compared with the great good obtained," and nominated himself for the job. "Excuse me for saying it, but owing to peculiar and exceptional circumstances, there is no living Ex-Confederate better able or better situated than I am, to lead in this work and elicit the support and assistance necessary to accomplish this part of your grand work." Law warmly endorsed the idea. "Walker is a tireless worker and is widely known in Confederate circles throughout the south and if his plan should be adopted, no one would be better fitted to do the work." The commission ultimately agreed, employing Walker at a salary of $100 per month.[12]

Walker, a native of Charleston, South Carolina, had commanded the 10th South Carolina and was seriously wounded leading his men at Ezra Church in July 1864. After the war, he and his father had reopened their antebellum stationery and printing business, which eventually merged with the publishing house Evans and Cogswell. Walker was one of the organizers of the Carolina Rifle Club, ostensibly a social club, but actually a quasi-military organization that Walker called "the most powerful means by which the white men were enabled to quell the negro and his carpetbag masters, and regain the political control of the State." Walker presented the group with the 10th South Carolina's battle flag, behind which they marched proudly in the months leading up to the "redeemer" election of former Lt. Gen. Wade Hampton as governor in 1876. Walker boasted that "the Carolina Rifle Club had the honor of being the first military body of white men which paraded in the streets of the city [of Charleston] or the State, bearing arms and the first to march under the Confederate Banner, since the struggles of the War had ceased." He began to take an active interest in the UCV after attending their 1894 reunion and was elected commander in chief in 1911.[13]

Walker now wrote to the men of the UCV that they "have been offered by the State of Pennsylvania and the Union Veterans the hand of peace and amity, with such cordiality, fairness, and consideration, that they should know it, and he thinks should accept and grasp it. . . . Your Commander feels that the time has come, when, by invitation of our one-time foes, we can unite with them in

---

12 Letter, C. Irvine Walker to Louis Wagner, September 12, 1912, Commission Correspondence, RG 25.24, Box 2; Letter, Evander M. Law to Louis Wagner, October 8, 1912, Commission Correspondence, RG 25.24, Box 5.

13 William Lee White and Charles Denny Runion, eds., *Great Things Are Expected of Us* (Knoxville, TN, 2009) xix-xx; C. Irvine Walker, quoted in John M. Coski, *The Confederate Battle Flag: America's Most Embattled Emblem* (Cambridge, MA, 2005), 49.

celebrating that permanent peace, which we pray may forever bless this our great and glorious country. . . . Let us bury deep and forever, all bitterness, but never fail to perpetuate the glorious history of that record of high duty superbly done by you in your young manhood."[14]

"To be present on such an occasion, should be our proudest ambition, our ardent desire and our most determined purpose," said J. Thompson Brown of the UCV's R. E. Lee Camp #1 in Richmond. "The world has not and will never see the like. The conquered, but proud and immortal heroes, the honored guests of our invincible conquering host, celebrating the Peace Jubilee of a reunited and indissoluble country—American heroes all! . . . Let every Camp and every Veteran resolve now that in the written history of this grand and final Reunion of the Blue and Gray (which will surely be written), that its and his name shall be there for future generations to see, if he has to go as the sole and only representative of his Camp and County."[15]

Harvey M. Trimble, commander-in-chief of the GAR, echoed Walker's and Brown's sentiments. "Let us assemble there, and meet and greet each other hand to hand and heart to heart in the spirit of true friendship and brotherhood, born out of love for the Flag and devotion to our common Country. Thus will all the wounds of our former strife be healed, as they must sometime be, that this people, as a united and vital force, may effectively and mightily solve the problems of our Nation's destiny in world affairs and human progress."[16]

"I have always taken the ground that the bitterness that existed between the North and the South should be forgotten," Walker told the *Washington Post*, "but that the glories of that great struggle should be perpetuated. It was the most splendid example of American manhood the world has known."[17]

Editorialists in both North and South applauded the idea of the reunion, especially the willingness of Southern veterans to take part alongside their former foes. "Those who participate in this wonderful Reunion will present a sight that the world has never looked on before," declared the *Indianapolis News*. "There is no record of any Civil War that shows those who were at death grips

---

14 *Pennsylvania Commission Report*, 9-10.

15 Circular letter from J. Thompson Brown to First Brigade, Virginia Division, UCV, Jan. 15, 1913, Commission Correspondence, RG 25.24, Box 7, PSA.

16 Letter, Harvey M. Trimble to C. Irvine Walker, March 4, 1912, reproduced in *Pennsylvania Commission Report*, 15.

17 "Interviews with Capital's Visitors," *Washington Post*, Jan. 13, 1912.

meeting in common fellowship fifty years after, citizens of a country united as it never was before."[18]

According to the *Atlanta Constitution*, "Final evidence of the breadth and nobility characterizing the men of the sixties, and evidence no less conclusive of the disappearance of sectional bitterness, is offered in the attitude of the United Confederate Veterans toward the second call to Gettysburg."[19]

"The decision of the United Confederate Veterans . . . to accept the invitation extended through the Grand Army of the Republic to attend the celebration of the fiftieth anniversary of the battle of Gettysburg," declared the *Philadelphia Evening Telegraph*, "is what would be expected of the chivalrous men who upheld the cause of the South in the crucible era. Though the South was defeated in this supreme trial of valor, and saw its cause thenceforth decline until its collapse, a year and nine months later in the fall of Richmond, and Lee's surrender at Appomattox, there is nothing about the manner in which the Southern soldiers fought that does not redound to their glory. Both vanquished and victors gave sublime display of the heroism of the American race." [20]

Northern paeans to their "chivalrous" nature were all well and good, but the old Confederates felt honor required that they go to the reunion not only as Americans, but as Confederates. A circular letter to the Virginia Division of the UCV emphasized the importance of Southern veterans wearing their UCV uniforms at Gettysburg. "If a Veteran be too poor to get a gray blouse (all that is needed), that he may proudly stand by his colors (gray), as he rallied to his colors on this greatest battle-field on the top of Mother Earth, 50 years ago, let some Veteran endowed with worldly goods make such indigent Veteran a present of a gray blouse, or money to buy the same . . . that he may there proudly show his scars and empty sleeve or pants, as he marks the battle-lines with his crutch and fights his battles o'er with his erstwhile foe, but now an *honest* and *sincere* friend and host, and as true *blue* as the blue uniform he wears."

Of even greater symbolic importance was the Confederate battle flag. In the immediate post-war years, most Southerners had heeded the admonition in Father Abram J. Ryan's widely reprinted poem, "The Conquered Banner," to:

---

18 "The Gettysburg Reunion," *Indianapolis News*, Mar. 29, 1913, quoted in *Pennsylvania Commission Report*, 187-188.

19 "At Gettysburg," *Atlanta Constitution*, May 5, 1912.

20 "The Gettysburg Celebration," *Philadelphia Evening Telegraph*, May 10, 1912, quoted in *Pennsylvania Commission Report*, 186-187.

Furl that banner, softly, slowly,

Treat it gently—it is holy—

For it droops above the dead;

Touch it not, unfold it never,

Let it droop there, furled forever,

For its people's hopes are dead.[21]

By 1870, however, shot-torn battle flags had begun to reemerge at memorial ceremonies and monument dedications. According to those unfurling them, they did so simply to honor the battlefield valor of the Confederate dead. But just as during the war the battle flag had come to be seen as the de facto national flag of the Confederacy, by degrees it took on broader symbolism during the heyday of the Confederate memorial period in the 1880s and 1890s as the emblem of the nation that was no more, the "Lost Cause." At the 1890 dedication of the Robert E. Lee monument in Richmond, veterans marched behind their old battle flags, while scores of new flags waved from windows and porches along the parade route. With each passing year, more and more new Confederate flags—many produced by Northern businesses like Annin & Co. and the American Flag Manufacturing Co.— lined the streets and adorned public buildings in the host city of the annual UCV reunion. "We have wrapped it round our hearts!" the Reverend Randolph H. McKim told his fellow veterans at the 1904 reunion. "We have enshrined it in the sacred ark of our love; and we will honor and cherish it evermore—not now as a political symbol, but as the consecrated emblem of an heroic epoch; as a sacred memento of a day that is dead; as the embodiment of memories that will be tender and holy as long as life shall last." A day perhaps not entirely dead after all. "It is too dear to us to be furled," declared Clement A. Evans, chairman of the UCV's historical committee in 1906, "for it proclaims a Cause that was never lost."[22]

The public rehabilitation of the battle flag did not always sit well with members of the GAR, who suspected that most Southerners shared Evans's unreconstructed sentiment, if not his boldness in proclaiming it. An 1887 proposal by the war department to return more than 550 captured flags to the Southern states evoked howls of opposition and was ultimately withdrawn by President Grover Cleveland, who came in for some pointed commentary along the way about his own decision to hire a substitute during the war. The flags, wrote the members of one Iowa GAR

---

21 Circular letter, Jan. 15, 1913, Commission Correspondence, RG 25.30, Box 4; Ryan poem quoted in Coski, *The Confederate Battle Flag*, 45.

22 Coski, *The Confederate Battle Flag*, 64, 57.

post, "have no other meaning than a representation of treason." The display of Confederate banners during the Lee monument dedication drew a rebuke from GAR Commander-in-Chief John Palmer, who saw in it evidence that "there still lurks in the hearts of a few a desire, by the display of the flag, to fire the hearts of the young generation of the south to rebellion." While Congress ultimately voted to return the captured flags in 1905, for some Union veterans they would always remain treasonous symbols. Louis Wagner was solidly among that cohort, and if his attitude were to prevail in the councils of the Pennsylvania Commission, the effort to create a Blue-Gray reunion of historic proportions would surely fail. [23]

Andrew Cowan, a veteran of the 1st New York Independent Battery and Kentucky's representative to the commission, therefore set about the delicate task of attempting to shift the irascible chairman's view. "We Union men who have lived in the South, among the survivors of the Southern armies, no longer object to such exhibitions," he wrote to Wagner. "Their flag is only a memory, but it is dear to them, and I know the strength of this Southern sentiment. I am accounted a hard and fast Republican and a strong defender of the justice of the Union cause, for which I fought through more than four years with the Army of the Potomac, and prominently at Gettysburg, but I should not now object to survivors of Lee's Army appearing anywhere in uniform and carrying the Southern flag, provided the flag of our Country was also carried by them. Unless your Commission should be willing to accept conditions of that nature, I doubt if the Celebration can be made one of 'Peace and Good Will.'"[24]

The question of Rebel flags was not the only issue vexing the members of the commission. In reporting to the executive committee on his travels across the south, Lewis Beitler noted that he also had received a number of inquiries from Confederate veterans as to "whether negro members of the G.A.R. would participate at Gettysburg." The question was a natural one. Since its founding, the GAR had been open to all honorably discharged Union veterans "without distinction of party or creed, rank or color." Pennsylvania alone had at least 36 integrated posts, plus another 21 all-black posts. Maryland was home to 23 black posts, including six in Baltimore, which for almost 20 years had sponsored an annual excursion to Gettysburg in September to commemorate the issuing of the Emancipation Proclamation, an event that some years drew thousands of African

23 Ibid., 68, 67.

24 Letter, Andrew Cowan to Louis Wagner, June 28, 1911, Commission Correspondence, RG 25.24, Box 5.

Americans to town. The minutes note that these issues "were discussed and left for further consideration and later disposition."[25]

*　　*　　*

Flags or no flags, the transportation problem had to be solved if ex-Confederates were to attend in sufficient numbers to make the reunion a success. In Virginia, the R. E. Lee Camp's J. Thompson Brown launched a grassroots lobbying effort, writing to county supervisors and asking local chapters of the United Daughters of the Confederacy (UDC) for their help "in persuading the Board of Supervisors in their respective Counties, to act upon the authority given them [by the state legislature] to appropriate free railroad-fare to every Veteran in their respective Counties."[26]

The UDC, however, was more focused on what it could do directly. In a circular letter to its entire national membership, Mrs. Alexander B. White, the group's president general, wrote, "It was hoped that the legislatures of the Southern States would make appropriations to send their Veterans to Gettysburg, but practically none have done it, and alas, so many of our dear Veterans are too poor to meet the expenses of the trip themselves. . . . I hope every Chapter will make every effort to send their Veterans. These old men who made the signal glory of the South would appreciate this gracious kindness on your part and it gives you such a charming way of ministering to their pleasure, for many of them I fear, for the last time."[27]

Irvine Walker of the UCV followed up with a letter marked "confidential" to all UCV camp commanders, urging them "to quietly interest some of your citizens of means and influence to help the Daughters in this work. It may not do for you, as Commander to ask the subscriptions, but you can enlist the Sons [of Confederate Veterans] or other well wishers."[28]

A number of newspapers also got into the act, including the *Montgomery Advertiser*, which raised enough to send four residents of the Alabama Soldiers Home in Mountain Creek to the reunion, and the *Charlotte Observer*, whose editorial on the subject was headlined "Chip In, At Once!" The *Houston Post* found

25 Andre M. Fleche, "'Shoulder to Shoulder as Comrades Tried': Black and White Union Veterans and Civil War Memory," *Civil War History*, Vol. 51, No. 2 (June 2005), 181; James P. Weeks, "A Different View of Gettysburg: Play, Memory, and Race at the Civil War's Greatest Shrine," *Civil War History*, Vol. 50, No. 2 (June 2004), 179; Barbara Gannon, *The Won Cause: Black and White Comradeship in the Grand Army of the Republic* (Chapel Hill, 2011), 204, 206, 219-220; Commission Minutes, 40.

26 Circular letter, Jan. 15, 1913, Commission Correspondence, RG 25.30, Box 4.

27 Circular letter from Mrs. Alexander B. White to UDC chapters, April 29, 1913, quoted in Commission Minutes, 151.

28 Circular letter from C. Irvine Walker to UCV camp commanders, May 17, 1913, Commission Correspondence, RG 25.24, Box 23, PSA.

a way to leverage its altruism to sell a few more papers as well. During the six days that the editors solicited donations, they also ran a coupon that readers could use to nominate an old Rebel they wished to see provided for from the limited funds available. Each coupon could be used to cast a single vote, and the editors specified that it "must be clipped from a copy of The Houston Post and must be brought to the offices of the Post before 8 p.m. Thursday, June 26, 1913 to be counted." They also made clear that this effort was for Confederate veterans only. Any Yanks in Houston who wished to attend the reunion were on their own. The paper ran daily updates on the vote tallies, along with a list of donors that included the Houston Ice and Brewing Company and the American Brewing Association. Enough money was raised to send 19 veterans to Gettysburg, including nine who had fought in the battle.[29]

South Carolina, the only state whose legislature had made any appropriation, saw one of the most aggressive and successful efforts, led by *The State*, Columbia's morning paper. "South Carolina failed to do a proper part toward enabling the Confederate Veterans of this State who participated in the Battle of Gettysburg to reach the battlefield and take part in the most notable gathering the world has ever seen," the editors wrote. "The State asks its readers to supplement the appropriation of $1,000 made by the legislature with $1,000, and to do so within six days. . . . This is a matter for either prompt action or permanent neglect. The State Company subscribes one hundred dollars to the fund." Each day, the paper reported on the progress of the fundraising effort and published letters from those who had contributed. John W. Carlisle of the 13th South Carolina sent $20, and the son of another veteran gave $5. The citizens of Ridge Spring sent a check for $7.10, along with a detailed accounting of the 17 individuals who had chipped in, most in the amount of 25 or 50 cents apiece. P. W. Sullivan added a caustic postscript to the letter accompanying his contribution. "Where are the politicians who have professed such great love for our grand old soldiers?" he asked. "Some for years past would make us believe they would give all, even die for them. Now let them put up or hush up."[30]

The UDC played an active role in *The State*'s campaign and in similar fundraising efforts across the South. The members of B. W. Ball Chapter raised enough to defray the transportation expenses of five Confederate veterans from

29 "Fifty Dollars Raised for Gettysburg Fund," *Montgomery Advertiser*, June 22, 1913; "Chip In, At Once!" *Charlotte Observer*, June 25, 1913; "Veterans to be Sent to Gettysburg," *Houston Post*, June 21, 1913; "19 Veterans Will Arrange for Journey," *Houston Post*, June 27, 1913.

30 "Make Good South Carolina's Failure," *The State*, June 18, 1913; "Four More Days to Raise Fund," *The State*, June 20, 1913; "Gettysburg Fund Growing Slowly," *The State*, June 21, 1913; "Gettysburg Fund Has Accessions," *The State*, June 25, 1913.

Cross Hill by selling ice cream and staging plays. The Winnie Davis Chapter in Yorkville raised $38, the R. E. Lee Chapter in Anderson, $5. Across the state line in North Carolina, UDC chapters in Hertford and Hendersonville each raised enough to pay the expenses of three veterans, while those in Kinston and Littleton sent one apiece. But the 55 members of the Orren Randolph Smith Children's Chapter of the UDC, in Henderson outdid them all by raising $211.70.[31] "The camp could not have made the trip without the help of our friends . . . [and] the enthusiasm of the children of the Orren Randolph Smith Chapter, who went through the town and raised the required amount necessary for the twenty-two members who could go to attend," wrote J. T. B. Hoover, commander of the UCV's Henry L. Wyatt Camp and a veteran of the 3rd North Carolina Artillery.[32]

*   *   *

The question of whether the veterans would be permitted to wear their UCV uniforms and carry their old battle flags to the reunion encampment at Gettysburg was still unanswered as the third general conference opened at the Union League in Philadelphia on January 23, 1913. Chairman Wagner told the conference that over the past several weeks, the commission had received communications from a number of UCV camps "demanding that their members be permitted to wear their old uniforms." The man who had spent 15 months training thousands of freedmen to fight for the Union did not look kindly on such demands. Former Confederate Gen. Felix H. Robertson of Texas, however, declared that if Union veterans were permitted to wear their GAR uniforms, the same courtesy should be extended to those who wore the gray. Other veterans disagreed, including Elisha Rhodes of Rhode Island, who declared, "Let us go to the encampment as American citizens."[33] Charles Burrows, New Jersey's representative, offered a motion that it was the sense of the meeting that there should be no uniforms or flags except those of the United States. This brought Robertson to his feet.

Historian William C. Davis has called Robertson "almost without doubt the most reprehensible man in either army to wear the uniform of a general. Only by the narrowest of margins did he escape being tried by his own government for what later generations would call war crimes." In October 1864, Robertson's

31 "Money for Worthy Purpose," *Charleston News & Courier*, June 24, 1913; *Minutes of the 17th Annual Convention, United Daughters of the Confederacy, North Carolina Division* (New Bern, NC, 1913), 100.

32 J. T. B. Hoover, "The Reunion of the Blue and Gray Held at Gettysburg, Pa., July 1st to 5th, 1913," July 9, 1913, Typescript, Vertical Files 11-61-B: 50th Anniversary, Grand Reunion 1913: Participant Accounts, Gettysburg National Military Park Library (GNMP).

33 "Want to Wear Gray Uniforms," *Gettysburg Times*, Jan. 24, 1913.

cavalrymen, along with Confederate guerrillas led by the infamous Champ Ferguson, murdered scores of wounded black troopers from the 5th U.S. Colored Cavalry, as well as some of their white officers, in what came to be known as the Saltville Massacre. In February 1865, Confederate Secretary of War John C. Breckinridge ordered a court of inquiry, but through the chaotic final months of the Confederacy, Robertson declined to return to Virginia from Georgia to face the charges and the war ended before he could be brought to justice. "Eventually, he settled in Waco," Davis writes, "where he practiced law, supported the Ku Klux Klan, and relished in minor celebrity as an aging Confederate general."[34] Now, in an impassioned speech seasoned with profanity, which newspaper accounts of the conference omitted, he declared, "I want to bring there and show you and wave in your faces again the very Texas Brigade battle flag that we shook in your faces there July 3, 1863. If you were able to drive it back then, its faded colors can do you no harm now."[35]

Warming to his subject, Robertson continued:

There was never a greater mistake in the history of the world than the Civil War; but, on the other hand, you veterans of the Grand Army of the Republic have never made peace, and the credit for the feeling now existing between the people of the North and the South is due to your sons and not to any of you. We only quit fighting when we were forced to, speaking for myself, we would have been fighting yet if we had not seen that it was a hopeless task to defeat you.

We were forced into the Union, and now we ask that you take us as we are. Allow the old Confederates to go to Gettysburg in their tattered uniforms. Many of them do not know that the war is over, and if you decide that these gray uniforms must be left at home a large number of those who wear them will refuse to attend the great encampment.

I think I speak for every Southern soldier when I say that if you intend celebrating a victory, then do not permit us to join in it; but if it is peace you are commemorating, all we ask as a subdued people is that we come in whatever garb we may see fit.[36]

34 William C. Davis, "Felix Huston Robertson," in William C. Davis and Julie Hoffman, eds., *The Confederate General*, 6 vols. (Washington, D.C., 1991), 5:100-101.

35 "Tener Arbitrates Uniform Quibble," *Philadelphia Inquirer*, Jan. 25, 1913.

36 "Lively Meeting of Commission," *Gettysburg Times*, Jan. 25, 1913.

Wagner, diplomatic to the last, proceeded to add fuel to the fire when he ordered the secretary "to record his objection on the minutes of the conference to the sprinkling of 'damns' in the remarks of General Robertson."[37]

Just as it appeared that the conference might dissolve in acrimony, Governor Tener came to the rescue. "I want it well understood by the whole Confederate soldiery," he said, "that you are coming as guests of the State of which I have the honor to be the Chief Executive, and it will make no difference to him or the State whether the man from the South comes in civilian attire or wears the old gray uniform."[38] He closed by noting that "if General Robertson had any more adjectives and expletives on his chest, he might come up to Harrisburg and be free to swear like a trooper," at which the conference erupted in laughter, and Burrows withdrew his motion. Wagner must have been seething.[39]

*   *   *

The governor and James Schoonmaker, who would formally replace Wagner as chairman of the commission in March, now had barely five months to make up for two years of dithering. In short order, contracts were awarded for the camp's water system, lighting, and latrines. George F. Baer, a Union veteran and president of the Philadelphia and Reading Railroad, was appointed to the commission to help sort out the transportation issues. Governor Tener worked with the legislature to pass two additional appropriations: $165,000 to defray the expense of transporting all Pennsylvania veterans to the reunion, and $195,000 for all other costs not directly related to the establishment and operation of the camp itself. The latter included leasing a portion of the grounds and buildings at both the Pennsylvania College and the Lutheran Theological Seminary for the accommodation of the commission and its guests, as well as the additional police, sanitation, and hospital resources in town that the Gettysburg Citizens Committee had been begging for. Schoonmaker established committees on transportation, program, invitation and reception, military affairs, and press, while field secretary Beitler took steps to secure a tent and seating for at least 10,000 people, in which the main elements of the reunion program would be held. Beitler hired Thomas M. Jones, a veteran Harrisburg newspaper man, as the commission's new publicity agent and made arrangements with the war department and the president of the Pennsylvania Undertakers' Association "for the use of a certain portion of the National Cemetery at Gettysburg, should the necessity arise." There were contracts

37 "50th Anniversary Plans," *Gettysburg Compiler*, Jan. 29, 1913.

38 Ibid.

39 "Tener Arbitrates Uniform Quibble."

to be let for taxicabs from the Auto Livery Company of Washington, badges to identify the commission's guests and the press from Whitehead & Hoag, and 3,600 flags to decorate the graves in the national cemetery. Beitler was directed to hire two stenographers "and such other clerks as the increasing work required." The torrent of correspondence now crossing his desk encompassed everything from purchase orders for linens, towels, and 158 cuspidors to outfit the VIPs' rooms at the college, to a request from the widow of an 8th Ohio veteran who had hoped to attend the reunion that his body be interred in the national cemetery before the great event began.[40]

"When I feel that I can't move another peg," former GAR commander Ell Torrance wrote to Beitler, "I think of you at Gettysburg—up early and late, incessantly besieged by all kinds of people seeking information on all sorts of subjects and demanding concessions that would bankrupt a South American republic—and recalling your genial smile, patient forbearance, heroic behavior and Christian fortitude, I take new courage and trudge along a little farther."[41]

The Philadelphia and Reading and the Western Maryland railroads were expanding their yard facilities at Gettysburg, constructing additional tracks and sidings to accommodate up to 100 passenger coaches at a time. The commission decided that the great camp would be open from Sunday, June 28 until Sunday, July 6 to allow more time to transport veterans to and from the reunion. The UCV told its members that they were welcome "to wear their U.C.V. uniforms and carry their camp flags. Confederate battle flags which waved at Gettysburg in 1863 could be carried with great propriety."[42]

By the first week in April, 200 laborers were at work on the camp site: laying water mains from newly dug wells, raising hundreds of poles for electric lights, framing up scores of temporary structures from camp kitchens to field hospitals, pitching the first of 5,000 tents in which the veterans would sleep, and constructing the hundreds of long wooden tables and benches at which they would eat. For the army, the encampment was an opportunity to demonstrate that it had learned from the medical and hygiene disaster of the Spanish-American War mobilization, when deaths from typhoid fever and other diseases in the stateside assembly camps for U.S. volunteers had outnumbered combat deaths by more than four to one. The war department tapped Maj. James E. Normoyle of the quartermasters corps, fresh

---

40 Commission Minutes, 130-131; "Rousing Cheer Ends Meeting," *Gettysburg Times*, May 16, 1913.

41 Letter, Ell Torrance to Lewis Beitler, August 8, 1913, Commission Correspondence, RG 25.24, Box 23.

42 "Heroes in Gray Urged to Attend," *The State*, June 8, 1913.

from overseeing relief work for thousands of people forced from their homes by flooding around Dayton, Ohio, to take on the logistical, sanitary, and commissary challenges of running a temporary camp for tens of thousands of elderly men.

The question of exactly how many of the old soldiers would attend remained unanswered. A circular letter to the governors of every state a year earlier had yielded little data, and the working assumption—little more than a guess—was 40,000. In early April, a new letter, containing the fullest official information yet released concerning the details of the camp and the reunion, was sent to GAR posts, UCV camps, and newspapers nationwide. Among those details was the fact that every veteran who wished to be quartered in the great camp would be required to produce either his honorable discharge papers, pension certificate, or an affidavit from his post or camp commander before receiving credentials.[43] This set off an avalanche of correspondence between veterans and the Pennsylvania Commission, and with their respective state commissions to apply for transportation, from which some more concrete numbers began to emerge. Still, the picture was murky, and Schoonmaker and Governor Tener called for a fourth and final general conference of the commission in Gettysburg on May 15-16, at which each state representative would be required to provide an estimate of the number of their veterans planning to attend. "It is recognized that to give this information you must do some tall guessing," Irvine Walker wrote to all UCV camp commanders. "So guess from what you know of local feeling."[44]

A canvass of the state representatives at the conference on May 16 yielded a total estimate of 44,000 veterans planning to attend the reunion, "which total all agreed was higher by far than what would actually attend." Schoonmaker forwarded both the estimate and the caveat to the war department and asked each representative to provide updated numbers no later than June 1.[45]

The editors of the *Compiler* thought it "absurd to ask veterans to tell before June 1 whether they want to see and hear what the commission don't yet know is to be seen and heard." They continued:

> Again the veterans should have been entitled to the knowledge of what they were being asked to attend. If it is only going to be a joy ride and a handshake why not say so. If there are to be speakers why should not a full program have been furnished the veterans? Has

---

43 *Pennsylvania Commission Report*, 22-27.

44 Circular letter from C. Irvine Walker to UCV camps, undated, South Caroliniana Library, University of South Carolina (USC), Columbia, SC.

45 Commission Minutes, 150.

this part of a speaking program been forgotten? Speakers of a national fame should have been booked months ago and now known. . . .

A lot of hot air of the dedication of a peace memorial has been shot into space and why this memorial has not been worked overtime as an attraction to the veterans can not be guessed at, unless a realization has at last struck home that to dedicate any such memorial it will have to be built of blocks of moonshine laid in place from an aeroplane.[46]

W. A. Connor, whose services as publicist had so displeased Chairman Wagner, was also concerned. Back at his post as Philadelphia correspondent for the Associated Press, he wrote to Beitler:

Have you definite knowledge that the president and the chief justice of the Supreme Court will attend and speak? I know that General Wagner at the outset arranged that these high officials should be there, but I have never read that they were formally invited, or that they had stated their intention of participating. I observe that one of Gen. Wagner's plans for a railroad loop has been vetoed by President Baer of the Reading Company, and I am filled with the fear that maybe President Wilson will also declare himself out of it as he is likely to be very busy with important matters at the time of the celebration.

I am anxious to see the thing big enough to be a great news story, but I am free to say that it hasn't "sized up" so far.[47]

In fact, both the president and the chief justice had politely declined the eleventh-hour invitations that had finally reached them, pleading prior engagements, as had former President William Howard Taft, Sallie Pickett, and Stonewall Jackson's widow, Anna.

At the June 1 reporting deadline, estimated attendance totaled 49,405. By June 15, less than two weeks from the scheduled opening of the great camp, it had risen again to 54,928. And on Friday, June 20, a lengthy telegram arrived in the commission's Harrisburg office from Secretary of War Lindley M. Garrison in Washington:

I am informed by Major Normoyle, the depot quartermaster in charge at Gettysburg, that you have advised him that the number expected at the Camp and the number required to be taken care of at the Camp, will be fifty thousand instead of forty thousand, and that he had been called upon by you to provide the extra hospitals, Red Cross stations, tentage and

---

46 "Celebration Hysteria," *Gettysburg Compiler*, May 28, 1913.

47 Letter, W. A. Connor to Lewis Beitler, June 9, 1913, Commission Correspondence, RG 25.24, Box 2.

supplies for the additional number. . . . If you have arranged that ten thousand in addition attend, you must provide the funds to take care of them. There are no funds available to me for this purpose, and I am positively prohibited by express Acts of Congress from incurring one dollar's worth of expenses over and above the amounts specifically appropriated for this particular purpose.[48]

Garrison ordered all supplies and work at Gettysburg beyond what was required for a camp of 40,000 halted immediately and notified the Associated Press of what was happening. When the wire service's story appeared in newspapers around the country, the Pennsylvania Commission was flooded with inquiries from veterans "all alarmed lest provision inadequate for their entertainment would be found at Gettysburg, should they attend in the numbers then proposed."[49]

A mad scramble ensued in Harrisburg. On Monday, June 23, an emergency appropriation was introduced in the state legislature, which was scheduled to adjourn on Thursday at noon, and the Pennsylvania Commission wired the war department "our firm belief in the unanimous passage of the appropriation by our General Assembly that week, and expressing the hope that the Department would therefore at once rescind its order of the 20th, and immediately resume forwarding supplies to and continue the work at Gettysburg necessary for the ten thousand additional Veterans." The response from Washington was a polite but firm refusal to do so "until State so appropriates."[50]

On Wednesday, June 25, as 83 Union veterans and five Confederates boarded a special train in Portland, Oregon to begin their four-day journey, a second crisis exploded. An Associated Press story out of Philadelphia headlined "No Torn Battle Flags to Fly at Gettysburg" appeared in newspapers across the South, from the *Atlanta Constitution* and *Richmond Times-Dispatch* to the *Charleston News & Courier*, *Montgomery Advertiser*, and *New Orleans Times-Picayune*:

> Word has gone out to veterans of both armies all over the country not to bring their tattered battle flags to Gettysburg next week for the celebration of the fiftieth anniversary of the battle, for they cannot be flown to the breeze in the encampment. Every precaution will be taken to prevent the stirring up of animosities and feeling on the part of the old soldiers, and this is one of the precautions considered necessary. The only flag which will be allowed in the encampment will be the Stars and Stripes.[51]

48 *Pennsylvania Commission Report*, 45.

49 Ibid., 47.

50 Ibid., 47.

51 "No Torn Battle Flags to Fly at Gettysburg," *Atlanta Constitution*, June 25, 1913.

The story cited no source for the announcement of the flag ban but given that its dateline was Wagner's hometown of Philadelphia, it's possible that the old warrior was playing one last card in the hope of having the final word on an issue that was important to him. A new round of anxious and indignant inquiries poured into the Pennsylvania Commission's headquarters, including one from S. A. Cunningham, who received the following reply: "Your telegram 25th asking about press reports concerning Confederate flags received. Such reports are utterly unauthorized. Pennsylvania, through Governor Tener, last January distinctly stated her position, and it is the same today as it was then."[52] By Thursday newspapers were reporting that the original story had been incorrect and that neither the Pennsylvania Commission nor the war department had barred Confederate flags from the camp. As an editorial in the *Charleston News & Courier* noted, however, "it is to be feared that some harm has been done. An error like this once started is hard to overtake and kill."[53]

Meanwhile, the Pennsylvania house and senate were deadlocked over the appropriation bill, as the deadline for adjournment approached and then passed. Not until 6:00 a.m. on Saturday, June 28 was the bill finally passed, just 36 hours before the first meal was scheduled to be served in the great camp. The news was telephoned to the war department, and it promptly reopened the spigot. By early Saturday afternoon, special express trains carrying thousands more tents, cots, blankets, and other supplies began arriving in Gettysburg, where crews worked through the night to be ready for the arrival of the first veterans on Sunday afternoon.[54]

This was good, because from Utah to Indiana and Vermont to Georgia, dozens of other trains were on the move, carrying thousands of veterans toward Gettysburg, and the largest Blue-Gray reunion the world would ever see.

52 "Gettysburg to See Confederate Flag," *The Tennessean*, June 27, 1913.

53 "Battle Flags at Gettysburg," *Charleston News & Courier*, June 26, 1913.

54 *Pennsylvania Commission Report*, 47-48.

Chapter 3

A Quart of Black Ants in a Pint Cup

The reunion camp covered 280 acres, from Confederate Avenue on the west to the Emmitsburg Road on the east, and from South Street to a point just north of the High Water Mark monument. More than 6,500 tents, each designed to hold 12 men but designated on this occasion to accommodate eight veterans each, were laid out along 47 miles of company streets illuminated by 500 electric lights. There were 173 field kitchens to feed the veterans, staffed by 2,170 cooks, kitchen helpers, and laborers, including 50 bakers who toiled around the clock in three shifts to produce more than 50,000 loaves of bread each day. Ninety 40-seat latrines had been dug, 35 pay telephones installed, and a temporary post office set up. Water lines crisscrossed the camp to feed 32 "bubbling ice water fountains" located at central points. At the southernmost edge of the camp, just west of the Codori house along the Emmitsburg Road, there was a 13,000-seat tent, where the main events of the four-day program, along with dozens of state and individual unit reunions, would take place.

Brigadier General Hunter Liggett and the 1,465 officers and men under his command were responsible for every aspect of the camp's operation. The army medical corps had set up two full field hospitals, three regimental hospitals, and 11 aid stations, anticipating that "the advanced age of the men the camp was to shelter, the season of the year, and the long journey many would take to reach the camp would result in an unusual morbidity, and probably a large mortality." One officer confided to a reporter from the *Washington Post*, "If I had a relative who was a civil war veteran, and who wanted to attend the reunion, I would do everything

Thousands of tents were laid out in neat company streets that crisscrossed the reunion camp's 280 acres. *Library of Congress*

in my power to keep him away from there."[1] A dozen mule-drawn ambulances and two motor ambulances were on hand, and on one of the new sidings in town sat a rail car filled with more than 100 coffins. One hundred fifty-five newspaper and wire service reporters and photographers had been accredited to cover the event and provided with accommodations within the army's headquarters camp, where their liaison was Lt. Simon Bolivar Buckner, son of the Confederate general of the same name. Four hundred sixty Boy Scouts from Pennsylvania, Maryland, and the District of Columbia were on hand to serve as messengers, guides, and assistants wherever needed. The roads crisscrossing the battlefield were patrolled by a squadron of the 15th U.S. Cavalry, including a young second lieutenant named George S. Patton, Jr., whose grandfather, Col. George Smith Patton of the 22nd Virginia, had been killed at the Third Battle of Winchester in 1864. This was not Patton's first visit to Gettysburg. In May 1909, a month before graduating from the U.S. Military Academy, he and his fellow cadets had participated in a two-day staff ride around the battlefield, during which he found himself thinking about other ancestors, like his great-uncle, Lt. Col. Waller T. Patton of the 7th Virginia,

1 *Pennsylvania Commission Report*, 39-42, 54; "Coffins for the Living," *Washington Post*, Jun. 25, 1913.

who was mortally wounded in Pickett's Charge. In a letter to his fiancée, Beatrice Banning Ayer, Patton wrote:

> There is to me strange fascination in looking at the scenes of the awful struggles which raged over this country. A fascination and a regret. I would like to have been there too.
>
> This evening after supper I walked down alone to the scene of the last and fiercest struggle on Cemetery hill. To get in a proper frame of mind I wandered through the cemetery and let the spirits of the dead thousands laid there in ordered rows sink deep into me. Then just as the sun sank behind South Mountains I walked down to the scene of Pickett's great charge and seated on a rock just where Olmstead [sic] and two of my great uncles died I watched the wonder of the day go out.
>
> The sunset painted a dull red the fields over which the terrible advance was made and I could almost see them coming growing fewer and fewer while around and behind me stood calmly the very cannon that had so punished them. There were some quail calling in the trees near by and it seemed strange that they could do it where man had known his greatest and last emotions. It was very wonderful and no one came to bother me. I drank it in until I was quite happy. A strange pleasure yet a very real one.
>
> I think it takes an evening like that to make one understand what men will do in battle. It was a wonderful yet a very foolish battle.[2]

*   *   *

Some veterans, perhaps concerned that the camp might be a bit too spartan for their tastes, had made their own arrangements. Several hundred found lodgings in boarding houses or private homes in town, where the going rate ranged from $1.50 to $3 a night. Hotels were a pricier option at $2.50 to $5 per night. The GAR post from Lowell, Massachusetts had secured the Rose farmhouse for its use, while the men of Carr's Brigade leased the Rogers house and six acres of surrounding land on the Emmitsburg Road. There they erected 100 tents of their own "where all comrades of the brigade, their friends, and our guests, can call to rest, smoke, swap war yarns of the old days, and make new acquaintances and friendships between Federals and Confederates that we trust will endure the few years we have yet to live." They invited two veterans from each of the 12 Confederate regiments in the brigades of Cadmus Wilcox, Edward Perry, and William Barksdale—men against

---

2 Letter, George S. Patton, Jr., to Beatrice Banning Ayer, May 11, 1909, in Martin Blumenson, ed., *The Patton Papers, 1885-1940* (Boston, 1972), 173.

whom they had fought fiercely along the Emmitsburg Road portion of the III Corps's advanced line on July 2—to join them.[3]

Charles McConnell, president of the Economical Drug Co. in Chicago and a veteran of the 24th Michigan, leased a plot of land just outside the camp boundaries and erected a large tent to serve as headquarters for his fellow Iron Brigade veterans. He also secured the services of Col. John A. Pattee and His Old Soldier Fiddlers, "fresh from their triumphant tour of the entire United States," to perform there every afternoon and evening. Pattee, also a veteran of the 24th Michigan (like many a post-war "colonel," his promotion was self-bestowed), had put together the popular vaudeville act, along with another Union veteran and two ex-Rebels, in 1910.[4]

A group of Pennsylvania veterans outdid them all. A year before the reunion, the surviving members of the "Old Bucktails"—the 1st Rifle Regiment, Pennsylvania Reserve Volunteer Corps—took an option on the entire Battlefield Hotel at Steinwehr Avenue and Baltimore Street, where they now converged from as far away as Texas, California, and Oregon. The old Bucktails considered themselves "probably the most comfortably quartered body in all the vast throng who were in attendance." They too invited a group of Confederates to join them, and the 10 Virginians "were assigned to a large parlor on the first floor of the hotel, and entered into the spirit of the occasion as readily as the most enthusiastic Bucktail." On the door to the parlor was a placard that read "The Devil's Den and the Ten Little Devils Inside." The Pennsylvanians also engaged "an old-time minstrel troupe" to provide daily entertainment at the hotel.[5]

After months of worrying and conflict with the reunion's organizers, the people of Gettysburg were as ready as they would ever be for the onslaught of visitors headed their way. In addition to offering accommodations in private homes, the town's churches were prepared to open their doors to those who could find no other place to lay their heads, charging 25 cents for a pillow, 35 cents for a pillow and cushioned pew, and 50 cents for the deluxe accommodations of pillow, pew, and blanket. The Eagle Hotel was prepared to serve 3,600 eggs a day, while another restaurant had laid in 2,500 pounds of ham. The state set up a temporary hospital to handle any medical emergencies among the non-veteran visitors, as well as half a dozen public comfort stations at key points. Governor

3 "Lowell's 'Boys' Arrive Early," *Boston Globe*, Jun. 29, 1913; "Survivors Wilcox Brigade, Attention," *Montgomery Advertiser*, Jun. 10, 1913.

4 "Veteran Gives Up Gettysburg Trip to Aid Sick Wife," *Detroit Free Press*, Jun. 30, 1913.

5 William H. Rauch, *Fiftieth Anniversary of the Battle of Gettysburg and Twenty-sixth Annual Reunion of the "Old Bucktails" or First Rifle Regiment, P.R.V.C.* (Philadelphia, 1913).

Tener ordered the entire state police force—191 officers and men—to Gettysburg for 10 days to provide security and traffic control in town and on the surrounding roads. A company from the Harrisburg Fire Department was on hand to augment the Gettysburg department.

Out on the Taneytown Road adjacent to the national cemetery, an enterprising group from Philadelphia leased 10 acres from Judge Samuel McCurdy Swope and erected a camp they dubbed "Meadeboro: The Tented Village" for those seeking more than a cushioned pew and a pillow. An advertising circular noted that it was situated "in the highest and best part of Gettysburg," adjacent to the trolley line and close by the cyclorama building. "It will be under close supervision, a detail of guards being provided, who will be on duty both night and day. . . . Meals of all kinds will be furnished in the Village, and quiet and rest will be assured to those who need repose after the fatigues incident to witnessing the various exercises each day."[6]

A reporter for the *Kansas City Star*, already in town to cover the reunion, was considerably less sanguine about the prospects for rest and repose:

> Did you ever try to cram a quart of black ants into a pint cup? Because if you ever did you can get a fair idea of what this town and the hills surrounding it will be like after 10 o'clock Monday morning. . . . Every scrap of room has been under charter in and near Gettysburg for months past. Every farmhouse has been prepared for the 'paying guest.' The cottages of the negroes in Gettysburg are in some cases under contract . . .

> It is possible that by persistently running trains into town—side tracking all returning empties to leave a clear track for the arrivals—that one hundred thousand people may be unloaded here.

> When that is done, the curtain will have been raised on a great, sordid, sweating melodrama of discomfort.[7]

*   *   *

In small towns and cities across the country, Saturday, June 28 was a day of departures.

In Detroit, 600 Union veterans got underway from the Michigan Central Depot as three of their comrades played "The Girl I Left Behind Me" on fife and drums from the rear platform of one of the cars. In Atlanta about a hundred

6 "Meadeboro: The Tented Village," undated pamphlet, Vertical Files 11-61: 50th Anniversary Grand Reunion: General Information, GNMP Library.

7 "But Pity the Poor Visitor," *Kansas City Star*, Jun. 29, 1913.

old Rebels were on the move, while in Indianapolis, 400 men, including 52 Confederates, accompanied by the governor, other state officials, and members of the Indiana National Guard hospital corps, steamed out of Union Station on two special trains. Indiana was one of several states that sent medical teams along with their delegations. Oregon and South Dakota required every veteran to provide a physician's certificate vouching for their fitness to undertake the journey.

It was a beautiful, cloudless morning in St. Albans, Vermont, as Frank Kenfield and his comrades boarded the special train that would carry them as far as New London, Connecticut, where they would take an overnight boat to Jersey City, New Jersey, there to entrain once again for the final leg of the journey to Gettysburg. Kenfield had enlisted as a second lieutenant in Company E of the 13th Vermont, a nine-month regiment, mustering in on October 1, 1862. Nine months and two days later, on July 3, 1863, he was in temporary command of his company as Pickett's and Pettigrew's men prepared to launch their desperate assault on the Union center. In the cannonade preceding the attack, he suffered a grievous shrapnel wound in the groin. Like so many of his comrades, the wound would continue to cause him pain for years after the war. In 1889, a surgeon's certificate filed with his application for a pension increase noted that Kenfield suffered from "an open ulcer, 3/8 inch across" on the left side of his penis. Nonetheless, six months after being mustered out of the 13th Vermont, he reenlisted for three years in the 17th Vermont as captain of Company C. He was wounded a second time, this time a gunshot wound in the left forearm at the Wilderness in May 1864, returned to duty at the end of June, and was captured a month later in the failed Union assault at Petersburg known as the battle of the Crater. He spent seven months as a prisoner of war. Today, however, he thought "all seemed joyous and happy. One would be led to think as he listened to their jokes and laughter, they were boys instead of men that had passed the allotted time of human life."[8]

The story was the same in Auburn, New York, where family members gathered to see off about 75 Union veterans from Cayuga County, who though "old and bent with age . . . declared that they would not miss the opportunity of visiting the old battlefield." "It's some different than when we went away fifty years ago," one of them told a reporter. "We went away from Auburn in cattle cars then and they weren't clean cattle cars either."[9] Each man wore a small bronze badge pinned to his coat. The upper part depicted two soldiers shaking hands and bore the inscription

8 Frank Kenfield, "Fiftieth Anniversary of the Battle of Gettysburg," *Vermont at Gettysburg, July 1863 and Fifty Years Later* (Rutland, VT, 1914), 26; Frank Kenfield pension file and Compiled Military Service Record (CMSR), National Archives and Records Administration, Washington, D.C. (NARA).

9 "Cayuga's Veterans Off to Gettysburg," *Auburn Daily Advertiser*, Jun. 30, 1913.

"New York-Gettysburg 1863-1913," while the lower featured embossed likenesses of Meade and Lee, along with crossed cannons, muskets, and sabers. Most of the states participating in the reunion had commissioned their own distinctive badges. Maine's consisted of a horizontal bar with the state's name, joined by a red, white, and blue ribbon to a medallion of the state's seal. The Ohio badge was also a three-piece affair, with the state seal, a flag ribbon, and another bronze piece in the shape of the state, on the latter of which were embossed the words "Ohio Survivors of the Battle of Gettysburg July 1863." The Virginians had three distinct badges, with different colored ribbons to indicate the veteran's branch of service: blue for infantry, yellow for cavalry, and red for artillery. All bore an image of Robert E. Lee.

Robert L. Drummond, a veteran of the 111th New York, was among those boarding the train in Auburn. He was mustered into service on September 2, 1864, and captured less than two months later, along with 86 other men of the regiment, outside Petersburg. They were taken first to Libby Prison and then transferred to Salisbury, North Carolina, where 41 of them died over the course of four months. "The sufferings of our soldiers in the prisons of the South have never been told," Drummond said, "because no language is strong enough to describe them." Fortunately, he himself "had inherited an iron constitution from a Scotch parentage, which had never been injured by late nights and intemperate habits; had strong faith in my country and in my God, and, seeing that the Confederates were bound to kill me, with true Scotch stubbornness, was determined, God willing, to live."[10] After the war he established a law practice in Auburn, served nine years as district attorney of Cayuga County, and became an active member of both the 111th New York Infantry Regimental Association and the Prisoners of War Association.

Perhaps those whom nature had not favored with Drummond's Scottish durability took a moment to read a set of suggestions for maintaining good health during the reunion, laid down by the surgeon general of the Pennsylvania National Guard and widely reprinted in newspapers around the country:

Get as much sleep as possible and be regular about it.

Adhere in your diet to the rations furnished by the regular army, which are ample in quantity, excellent in quality, and sufficiently varied to gratify and satisfy all tastes.

Don't indulge in intoxicating drinks. They disturb the digestion and make you more susceptible to fatigue and disease.

10 Robert L. Drummond, "Personal Reminiscences of Prison Life During the War of the Rebellion," address delivered at Hamilton College, February 22, 1901, Typescript, Robert L. Drummond Reminiscences, Division of Rare and Manuscript Collections, Cornell University (CU).

Take an extra pair of shoes with you, if possible. Nothing is more comfortable than a change of shoes and stockings. Tired feet are prevented in this way.

Don't try to meet all the old comrades at once. The camp is a big one, but you have a week before you. Take it easy.

In short, remember none of us is as young as we were fifty years ago, when we marched over the fields and hills of Gettysburg in '63.[11]

Veterans arrived in Portland, Maine, throughout the day, assembling at Union Station to board the Maine Special, which was scheduled to leave at 7:45 p.m. Eighty-four-year-old Maj. Gen. Joshua Lawrence Chamberlain was there to see them off, but "under very positive assurance of my surgeon that it would be extremely hazardous for me to undertake this journey and service in my present condition of health and strength," he reluctantly returned to his home after the train departed. Chamberlain had been ailing for months, still "very much disabled by attacks of old 'pains and penalties' of war times." The wound he had suffered outside Petersburg in June 1864, which had so nearly proved fatal, had long troubled him, and in February it was compounded by the onset of a case of bronchitis and neuritis whose pain had been "excruciating." He had managed to travel to Gettysburg in May for the fourth general conference of the Pennsylvania Commission, attended by his personal physician, Dr. Abner O. Shaw, who had served as regimental surgeon of the 20th Maine. It would prove to be his last visit to the old battlefield. [12]

In Minneapolis, Chester Durfee, Thomas Pressnell, and 45 other surviving members of the 1st Minnesota gathered at the courthouse for their annual reunion, after which they and other Minnesota veterans were treated to a banquet at the Commercial Club. Pressnell, a printer by trade when he enlisted as a private in 1861, rose to the rank of captain by the end of the war. He returned to Minnesota and worked as a compositor for several newspapers before being appointed deputy clerk of the U.S. District Court in Duluth. Durfee had enlisted in 1862 at the age of 16 (his father provided a letter stating that he was 18), following in the footsteps of his two older brothers. He was wounded on the third day at Gettysburg by a piece of shrapnel that shattered his left tibia. After the war, he worked as a railroad

11 "Veteran Vanguard Now in Gettysburg," *New York Times*, Jun. 29, 1913.

12 Jeremiah E. Goulka, ed., *The Grand Old Man of Maine: Selected Letters of Joshua Lawrence Chamberlain, 1865-1914* (Chapel Hill, 2004), 283; Diane Monroe Smith, *Fanny and Joshua: The Enigmatic Lives of Frances Caroline Adams and Joshua Lawrence Chamberlain* (Hanover, NH, 2013), 346; Letter, Joshua L. Chamberlain to Louis Wagner, Feb. 28, 1913, Commission Correspondence, RG 25.24, Box 6, PSA.

flagman in Illinois and Iowa before returning to Minnesota. The 1st Minnesota reunion party also included a Medal of Honor winner: Alonzo H. Pickle of Company K, who had been singled out "for most distinguished gallantry in action at Deep Bottom, Va., Aug. 14, 1864, when at the risk of his life he went to the assistance of a wounded officer lying close to the enemy's lines, and, under fire, carried him to a place of safety." Years later, having gone back to farming near Sleepy Eye, Minnesota, Pickle recalled, "It was nearly midnight before I succeeded in getting him inside of our lines and during that time was obliged to protect him in a ravine between the two lines of battle." Lieutenant Henry D. O'Brien, the officer he carried to safety, said of Pickle, "his reputation during all the time that he was in the service was that of a brave, exemplary soldier—and I really believe none better ever shouldered a musket. I also believe that I would have died on the field but for the assistance rendered by him, as soon after being wounded I became insensible from loss of blood."[13]

After dinner, Durfee recalled, the veterans fell in and "headed by the Morgan G.A.R. Drum Corps, we marched down 3rd Ave. to Washington Ave. . . . and through the mass of people that followed and were waiting to see us start. We boarded a train of 18 Pullman sleepers at 8:30 p.m. amid cheers and waving of hands and hats." After stopping in St. Paul to pick up a private car carrying Gov. A. O. Eberhart and his staff, the train barreled eastward through the night.[14]

For those travelling in smaller groups from more nearby points, there were no Pullmans, special trains, or bands at the station to see them off. Thaddeus Stevens Kenderdine had been named for the abolitionist Thaddeus Stevens, who was a personal and political friend of his father, a devout Quaker and successful mill owner in Bucks County, Pennsylvania. By the time he was 24, Kenderdine had driven an ox team as part of a wagon train from Leavenworth, Kansas, to Salt Lake City, Utah, worked on a ranch, travelled on to San Francisco, and returned home via the Isthmus of Panama. When the war came, he was working as a millwright in one of his family's mills. Against their father's wishes, his younger brother Robert enlisted in the Union Army and was mortally wounded while fighting with the 114th Pennsylvania of Sickles's III Corps in the Peach Orchard on the second day at Gettysburg. "For two days, in the hands of the enemy, he received no attention, or until the Union forces got possession of the field," Thaddeus Kenderdine wrote after the war. "His home companions had either died or been discharged [from the

13 Alonzo H. Pickle letter, December 31, 1894, copy in pension file, NARA; Chester Durfee pension file, NARA.

14 Chester H. Durfee, "Our Trip to Gettysburg," Vertical Files: 11-61 B: Participant Accounts, GNMP Library.

hospital], so that little information was ever received of his fate between the day of his wounding and when his father found him dying in a field hospital eight days after the casualty." Thaddeus had been drafted into the 174th Pennsylvania in 1862 and declined his father's offer to pay a substitute, "for I was getting what I wanted, and did not wish the blood of a 'sub' on my head, should my representative be the victim of a rebel bullet." The regiment spent most of the nine months of its existence on garrison duty in North and South Carolina, and he mustered out on August 7, 1863, without seeing combat. "I went from Maryland through the eastern sections of Virginia, and North and South Carolina," he recalled after the war, "but the nearest I ever got into actual conflict was at Antietam, for which battle I was four hours too late." He returned to Bucks County and became a successful coal dealer and prolific writer whose works included the four-volume *Personal Recollections and Travels at Home and Abroad* and a 138-line poem entitled "At Gettysburg."[15]

Riding the train from his home in Newton, Pennsylvania, toward Philadelphia en route to the reunion, Kenderdine "could not help but notice the indifference towards the great occasion imminent, as shown by other passengers towards the presence of three Grand Army men on this car, whose uniforms were sufficiently suggestive of the coming event. There were all of forty before we got to the city and there was not one, man or woman, who noticed them in the least. . . . In face of this, and assuming that the whole North was in the same state of indifference, it was safe to wonder if such a country was worth the cost of its salvation."[16]

Far from questioning the cost paid 50 years before, and conscious of the strain the journey to the reunion would put upon them, some veterans declared themselves ready to make one final sacrifice for a reunited nation. "This is most likely the last chance I'll have to do anything for the Union," a Kansas City man told his wife. "It's going to mean something to all the younger generation to have us old fellows get together and show there isn't any hard feeling. It will take away the last excuse for the young people to cherish any sectional hatred. It's a duty we owe the country, about the last we can fill, most of us, and I figure out I ought to do it."[17]

Another Union veteran, W. H. Rugg, who had been captured on the first day at Gettysburg and spent almost two years in Confederate prisons, had a premonition

15 Thaddeus Stevens Kenderdine, "An Echo from Gettysburg," *Personal Recollections and Travels at Home and Abroad*, 4 vols. (Newtown, PA, 1917), 4:98.

16 Thaddeus Stevens Kenderdine, "After Fifty Years, or Scenes and Incidents Connected with the Gettysburg Semi-Centennial," Part 1, *Newtown* [PA] *Enterprise*, Jul. 12, 1913.

17 "Veterans Risk Their Lives, but Not Needlessly," *Kansas City Star*, Jul. 5, 1913.

as he prepared to leave his home in Orting, Washington: "[T]he heat in the East will finish me . . . but I cannot miss this opportunity to greet the boys, even at the sacrifice of my life."[18]

*   *   *

Sunday dawned clear and hot in Gettysburg, where the annual encampment of the Pennsylvania Department of the GAR had ended on Saturday. Several hundred veterans, who had been quartered in hotels and private homes for the departmental encampment since Thursday, re-packed their bags and tramped out to the reunion camp shortly after it opened that morning. In their dark suits and neckties, their heads crowned by a variety of hats, from homburgs to panamas, they made an unlikely looking set of campers. Throughout the day they were joined by a steady stream of other early arrivals from New York, Maryland, North Carolina, and Virginia. Details of Boy Scouts met each arriving train to direct the old soldiers to the section of camp assigned to their states and carried the bags of those too worn out by the journey to do so themselves. By nightfall, there would be 21,000 men in camp.

Henry Huidekoper, who had first urged upon then-Governor Stuart the necessity of marking the Gettysburg anniversary, was among those early arrivals. As he walked along Seminary Ridge on Sunday afternoon, he encountered another man with an empty right sleeve: E. R. Wise, a veteran of the 11th Pennsylvania. Like Huidekoper, Wise had been wounded in the first day's fighting and brought to the same church-turned-field-hospital, where his arm was amputated and he "saw enough severed arms to fill an ordinary express wagon."[19]

Louis Wagner had been at the Pennsylvania GAR encampment as well but had already returned home. He had frostily informed the Pennsylvania Commission that "my arrangements are to be at Gettysburg at the session of the Department of Penna. G.A.R., reaching there on the afternoon of the 26th instant, and returning to Philadelphia on Saturday night, 28th instant. This can be my only stay in connection with this interesting Celebration." Had he remained, he would have been dismayed to see the Army of Northern Virginia's battle flag being raised on Sunday in the Confederate portion of the Maryland camp, flanked by the U.S. and state flags. A mixed Union and Confederate contingent from West Virginia

18 "Orting Veteran Dies on His Journey Home," *Seattle Times*, Jul. 10, 1913.

19 "Touching Scenes As Veterans Tour Field," *Philadelphia Inquirer*, Jun. 30, 1913.

When the reunion camp opened on Sunday, June 29, the crush of early arrivals was led by Pennsylvania veterans like these who were already in town for their state GAR encampment. *Pennsylvania State Archives*

marched in behind another shot-torn Rebel banner as men along both sides of the road raised their hats in salute.[20]

The early arrivals soon discovered one drawback to arriving on Sunday. "When I walked into the Eagle Hotel," recalled Union veteran Andrew Cowan, "I saw six gloomy looking, gray clad men—big men they were. The day was hot as hades, and Gettysburg, on Sunday, is dry as the Sahara." It was Felix Robertson, the combative Texas representative, and five of his fellow Lone Star veterans. "We are desperate men," Robertson said, "and it's strange you are not all afraid of us for we certainly do need a drink and we can't find one anywhere, thanks to your dutiful observance of the laws of Pennsylvania." Cowan invited them up to his room, "for I have a bottle of Kentucky, old enough to vote, and I will have a dozen bottles of cool sparkling water sent up for any one of you who may be W.C.T.U." The Texans left the hotel for camp just before dusk "content and smiling" and each with "a

---

20 Letter, Louis Wagner to J. M. Schoonmaker, June 17, 1913, Commission Correspondence, RG 25.24, Box 2; "Maryland Is First with Stars and Bars," *Baltimore Sun*, Jun. 30, 1913; "Maryland 500 Strong," *Baltimore Sun*, Jul. 1, 1913.

package labelled 'Old Crow' under his arm" that Cowan had managed to finagle from the hotel's proprietor.[21]

By mid-afternoon, the temperature had climbed past 100 degrees and the aid stations and field hospitals were being kept busy as men were felled by heat exhaustion and worse. A trolley accident on the Gettysburg Railway Company's line near Devil's Den and a runaway buggy on Washington Street injured seven people, including several veterans. John Reynolds of Port Chester, New York, a 69-year-old who had served in the 121st New York, and Augustus D. Brown of the 1st Maine Cavalry, 73, both died of heart failure. Brown "dropped dead while chaffing his old chums in the line waiting for food before the mess tent," leaving a widow and five grown children. He enlisted in September 1861 and served to the end of the war, suffering a gunshot wound to the right arm along the way. Reports of pickpockets in town prompted an urgent phone call to the Philadelphia police to send six detectives by the first train Monday morning to reinforce the squad of Pinkerton operatives already on the ground. Sunset brought cooler air, and that first night, according to Vermont veteran Joseph Stone, the camp was filled with non-veteran visitors. "Bands playing, autos going on all streets and you can hardly hear yourself speak, drums going, bugles blowing, cheering and so on."[22]

Around 2:00 a.m., the camp was awakened by a pair of loud explosions, and as veterans and reporters alike tumbled out of their tents to see what had happened, the air was split by the unmistakable Rebel yell out near Seminary Ridge, where most of the old Confederates were quartered. Some of the livelier ones had swabbed out two of the old cannons that marked the position of Edward Porter Alexander's batteries, charged them with black powder, and touched them off. As they did, hundreds of their comrades danced along the ridge singing "Dixie."[23]

It was going to be quite a week.

*   *   *

With the passing of the Sabbath, Gettysburg's saloons reopened on Monday morning. Normally they closed at midnight, but this week they planned to serve around the clock until the reunion was over. The rest of the town was open for business with a vengeance as well. "Every building was decked with flags and

---

21 Letter, Andrew Cowan to James L. Slayden, January 10, 1914, Vertical Files 17-5: Peace Memorial Efforts, GNMP Library.

22 "Old Foes Meet Again at Gettysburg," *New-York Tribune*, June 30, 1913; Joseph A. Stone letter, June 30, 1913, Vertical Files: 11-61-B: Participant Accounts, GNMP Library; Augustus D. Brown pension file, NARA.

23 "Peace Soldiers, 40,000 Strong, Swarm Historic Gettysburg Battlefield," *Philadelphia Inquirer*, July 1, 1913; "Guns Are Fired on Cemetery Ridge," *Richmond Times-Dispatch*, July 2, 1913.

bunting," recalled Elsie Dorothea Tibbetts, who had accompanied her Maine veteran father to the reunion. "Ropes were stretched across the streets and public square and hung with flags; and every auto, team, and shop window was decorated with national colors. It seemed as if there could not be another yard of bunting or a flag within a hundred miles." The state highway department had oiled the roads to minimize the dust raised by the thousands of automobiles that were expected to converge on the town, and as a result "the walks and steps were covered with the black, oily dirt from the streets, and littered with scraps of paper. . . . [A] dirtier place not many of us had seen before."[24]

"The stores were filled with pennants, hat bands, flags, etc., and the sidewalks downtown fairly groaned with them," noted one New Jersey veteran. "There was a ready demand for all these souvenirs, and it appeared to us boys that the storekeepers and others were making their fortunes during those few days." "The town is as upset as if the great Derby race was in progress," a Connecticut veteran complained, "and you can leave it to these frugal Pennsylvania people to make a dollar; cents don't count. They are possessed by no more patriotism than an Angora goat." According to a jaded reporter from the *Baltimore Sun*, "The minnie balls, pieces of canister and shell, remnants of old sabres, belt buckles, buttons and firearms that are being sold as the true and only originals would fill the Chesapeake Bay."[25]

"In every available space along the streets and all along the Emmitsburg road to the very edge of camp, souvenir and refreshment counters had been built," Tibbets reported. "Every description of vender that enlivens a circus ground was in evidence, and every few yards one was confronted with a penny-picture man, with cries of 'Your photo taken and finished while you wait!'"[26]

Russ Lewis, an enterprising photographer from Westminster, Maryland, had set up shop near Devil's Den and "the pile of plates rose prodigiously, making a backlog of developing and printing that took months to clear," said one of his assistants, who described a memorable encounter with one Union veteran:

A cigar-smoking hard-guy Yankee held his finger to his cheek while he drew on his stogie. When I suggested that his hand was concealing much of his face, and would thus spoil the picture, he explained:

24 Elsie Dorothea Tibbetts, *From Maine to Gettysburg, 1863-1913* (Bangor, ME, 1913), 55-56.

25 Walter H. Blake, *Hand Grips: The Story of the Great Gettysburg Reunion* (Vineland, NJ, 1913), 46; "War Veterans Meet at Gettysburg," *Hartford Courant*, July 4, 1913; "Gettysburg Receives, Dressed in its Best," *Baltimore Sun*, June 29, 1913.

26 Tibbetts, *From Maine to Gettysburg*, 57-58.

"Here I am, on Little Round Top, fightin' and yellin' at the top of my lungs, and a Reb bullet comes along and socks me right in the mouth. But what with my yellin' my mouth is wide open, so it misses my teeth and comes out my cheek. And when it heals, it don't close up tight. There's a little hole still there. If I don't plug it up with my finger I can't get no draft on my smoke. That's why."

He took a deep drag, and with lips tightly pursed, expelled the smoke through his cheek. The photograph showed this remarkable accomplishment![27]

Not all the activity was strictly commercial. The Christian Scientists had rented out the parlors of a private home on Chambersburg Street and opened a reading room for the week, while a group of suffragettes pitched a tent close by the big tent where the main events of the reunion were to take place and gathered veterans' signatures on a petition to give women the vote. An itinerant preacher stalked up and down the streets of the town, urging attendees to give up drink and tobacco. "Be clean, men," he exhorted. "Take the nasty quid out of your mouths. Don't make the Almighty stick in His fingers and snatch it." "He's a quid," muttered one passing veteran.[28]

Out on the battlefield, the *New York Times* reported, "it was a day of scouting parties. . . . Often a Confederate squad would run up against a Union squad when both were seeking to locate the place where their regiments stood, and in such cases it usually proved that they had fought each other. . . . The question heard oftenest, heard a dozen times an hour, as old men meet, is not 'Where was your brigade posted in the fight?' but "How old are you?' If the answer is 'Seventy' it is impossible to give any idea of the pride with which the answer comes 'I'm seventy-four.'"[29]

In the big tent, the survivors of Brig. Gen. John Buford's cavalry division, who had ridden into town on the track of Lee's army 50 years earlier to the day, were holding a reception for several hundred of their fellow cavalrymen, as men from George Patton's Troop A of the 15th U.S. Cavalry looked on. "As we came into town," recalled an officer of the 6th New York Cavalry, "we found on each side of the street rows of little girls, all dressed in white and singing 'John Brown's Body.' We were surprised and delighted, but we thought that was the end of it. A couple of blocks further on, however, we found another line, this time of young ladies from 12 to 20, standing on dry goods boxes, grocery boxes, or anything else that could

27 Philip Myers, "Pickett's Second Charge," Typescript, Vertical Files: 11-61-B, Participant Accounts, GNMP Library.

28 "Veterans Wilt Under the Heat," *Jersey Journal* (Hudson County, NJ), July 3, 1913.

29 "Gettysburg Honor to Girls of '63," *New York Times*, July 1, 1913.

be hastily assembled on the sidewalks to make a sort of platform. And so it went, as we rode through Gettysburg." Just then, into the tent walked "six pleasant-faced, gray-haired ladies" who had been among those lining the streets in 1863. They were escorted to places of honor on the grandstand, and Maj. Jerome Wheeler of the 6th New York stepped forward to welcome them. "If absence makes the heart grow fonder, how our hearts go out to you to-day as we look into your dear faces after an absence of fifty years," he declared, and asked if they would once again sing one of the songs with which they had welcomed Buford's troopers to Gettysburg on that long-ago day.

Mrs. Salome Myers Stewart, who had helped nurse the wounded in the aftermath of the battle, looked around doubtfully at the other five and said with a smile, "We don't think we can sing so well as we did fifty years ago," to which one of the veterans responded, "It isn't so much the singing as the singers we want." Then the band began to softly play "Rally Round the Flag," and "before those 'girls of '63' knew what they were about they had risen in their seats and had begun to sing the old favorite . . . while the old veterans stood in enraptured silence." When the women finished, the veterans broke into "wild applause" and then all joined in another chorus of the patriotic tune, which they "did not sing so well by half as the old ladies."

One 8th Illinois veteran approached the platform and told the women that back home he still had a bit of purple ribbon that one of the young ladies of Gettysburg had given him "so you can wear it in your next fight." "I've never seen her since," he said, "but I have that bit of purple ribbon yet at my home in Aurora, Ill." He paused, "hoping that the girl of his memory might rise in the assemblage to greet him once more," but no one did.

"I guess she's with the army above," he said wistfully.[30]

*   *   *

Meanwhile, from Pittsburgh and Petersburg, from Columbus and Hartford, thousands more old men were on the move toward Gettysburg.

Massachusetts veterans began arriving at Boston's South Station by train and trolley from all parts of the city and surrounding suburbs at 6:00 a.m. to board one of the day's four special trains, each with a car specially fitted up with cots and medical supplies and staffed by doctors from the state militia's hospital corps. The trains took them south as far as the Harlem River, where boats stood by to transfer them to the Jersey City terminal of the Pennsylvania Railroad. "River craft

---

30 Ibid.; "Gettysburg Vets Meet Girls of '63," *New-York Tribune*, July 1, 1913; "Gettysburg Given Over to the Blue and the Gray," *Philadelphia Inquirer*, July 1, 1913.

and factories whistled salutes to the boats that carried the veterans and thousands of New Yorkers waved greetings and farewells as the boats passed the high factory buildings, the recreation piers and the tall tenement houses."[31]

In Charlottesville, Virginia, 60 to 75 Confederate veterans—and one Union man, John Otterbacker of the 56th Ohio—assembled at city hall, where a crowd of several hundred had gathered to see them off. The local chapter of the UDC presented a refurbished flag they had originally made for the Charlottesville UCV camp 30 years earlier, and the veterans marched behind it to the railroad depot, accompanied by the Albemarle Band.

And in New York City, 3,000 veterans, including 15 members of the Medal of Honor Legion, crowded into Pennsylvania Station to board six trains bound for Gettysburg. They were, said the *New York Times*, "[g]leeful as college 'grads' returning to their alma mater for a class reunion . . . attired in the familiar uniform of the Grand Army of the Republic, with their badges pinned proudly on their breasts. Hundreds of posts were represented, some by a half dozen feeble old men, others mustering a hundred strong."[32]

From his private car on one of the new sidings in Gettysburg, James Schoonmaker was busy directing the inbound traffic. "We thought this was going to be a big affair," he told the *Pittsburgh Press*, "but it is more stupendous than we ever dreamed of. Every one of our previous estimates has been exceeded. Where we expected one train from a certain section, three are coming. . . . This means an army of people. It means work, too, but the railroads are handling the situation admirably and everything is moving as smoothly as a Dutch clock."[33]

Between midnight Sunday and midnight Monday, as 53 trains carrying another 21,882 old soldiers arrived, the clock began to show signs of running down. A train full of veterans from Pittsburgh that was scheduled to reach Gettysburg at 5:00 p.m. did not arrive until 2:30 a.m. Hundreds had to spend the night in Baltimore's Union Station, which "resembled a lodging house . . . so thick were the sleeping veterans from the south on the floors of the waiting rooms and on the benches." The South Carolina special was six hours late and when it arrived the men discovered that the tents to which they had been assigned were "pretty generally depleted of cots and bedding." Massachusetts veterans found many of their tents occupied by Boy Scouts, who had lost their own tents to arriving New Yorkers. A trainload from Bayonne, New Jersey arrived after midnight to find their

31 "Boy Scouts Crowd Out Bay State Veterans," *Boston Herald*, July 2, 1913.

32 "Veterans Off for Big Reunion," *The Daily Progress*, June 30, 1913; "3,000 on New York Specials," *New York Times*, July 1, 1913.

33 "Big Army Throngs Battlefield," *Pittsburgh Press*, June 30, 1913.

billet taken by others; they bedded down in the Ohio section, much to the dismay of the Buckeye veterans who arrived around 6:30 a.m. Fortunately, Gov. James M. Cox, who was traveling with his state's veterans, had taken the precaution of bringing along 20 extra tents. Sending one member of his staff to scare up a truck into which to load them, he went looking for a place to pitch the tents and finally succeeded in renting an oat field near the High Water Mark monument for $25. "As soon as Gov. Cox got the field," the *Washington Post* reported, "he took off his high silk hat, flung his Prince Albert coat aside, and rolling up his sleeves, directed the work of erecting the tents. In one hour he had a little camp of his own where 200 veterans will sleep tonight" and pronounced himself "extremely delighted" with the outcome. "If anybody tries to disturb us God help them," he declared.[34]

Long after midnight, men were still wandering the camp, trying to find their assigned quarters. The Boy Scouts "worked almost all night assisting these men to their tents, sometime carrying them, and toting blankets and pillows for them from the commissary tents nearly half a mile away." When they discovered that some veterans who had gotten lost in the dark as they made their way from the train station to the camp had simply dropped in their tracks from exhaustion, they organized regular search parties and "helped those they could to tents, and carried blankets to cover those they could not move." Hundreds simply bedded down as well as they could among the chairs in the big tent.[35]

"Some of us were a little sore at first to find our reservations given to other people," said the Reverend B. D. Louther, a Union veteran from Pittsburgh. One Massachusetts veteran who had spent 19 hours on a train from Boston and had arrived in camp at 2:00 a.m. to find every bed taken "spent the night in a chair and when 11:30 arrived I took a train for home." Monty Cook, another Pittsburgh veteran, was more sanguine: "It was no hardship at all. It was 3 o'clock when we got there, almost daylight and warm and balmy. When we found people in the tents we expected to occupy we naturally were gentlemen enough to not try to throw those comrades out. Then in a short time the day came and we had breakfast and a good one. Early in the day we got into our tents and everything is lovely now."[36]

As one old soldier wearily poked his head into yet another tent, hoping to find his comrades, the man within asked what regiment he belonged to. "Twenty-eighth Virginia," came the reply.

34 "55,000 Veterans Defy Great Heat," *New-York Tribune*, July 2, 1913; "South Carolinians at Gettysburg Reunion," *The State* (Columbia, SC), July 9, 1913; "Gov. Cox of Ohio Opens Camp of His Own for Buckeye Veterans," *Washington Post*, July 2, 1913.

35 "The Scouts at Gettysburg," *Boys' Life* (Sep. 1913), 16-17.

36 "Vast Reunion Crowd Increases," *Pittsburgh Press*, July 2, 1913; "Old Soldier Here After Absence of 48 Years," *Harrisburg Patriot*, July 2, 1913.

"The devil you did! Do you know what became of your regimental flag?"

"I don't. You see, I was with Armistead's brigade, the one that got into the Yankee lines when Pickett made his charge. . . . I don't rightly remember just what happened to the flag after we jumped into those Yankee batteries, but I think some of you Yankees got it."

"We did," said the tent's occupant, Thomas Pressnell of the 1st Minnesota. "We captured your flag, and we've got it now in St. Paul. The other fellows in this tent will be in in a minute, and all of them belonged to the regiment that got your flag. We've got a spare blanket here, and you'll never find your tent tonight. Come in and bunk with us."

The old Reb and his new Yank friends spent much of the night refighting the battle, and in the morning as he went off to resume the search for the Virginia section of camp, he declared, "I'm sorry we lost the flag, but if we had to lose it, I'm glad it was you fellows who got it."[37]

*   *   *

It was a long and frustrating night in the press camp as well. "The rattle of the typewriters and the telegraph instruments is continuous," noted one veteran whose tent was nearby. "It sounds as though you Johnny Rebs were peppering us with bullets on a tin roof." But with more than a hundred reporters writing thousands of words a day, a bottleneck developed at the Western Union telegraph office in the camp that first night and some stories filed between 4:00 and 6:00 p.m. did not get out until well after midnight. "Here's the telegraph company with two years' notice with six measly wires into the camp where it should have had 60," one correspondent complained. A colleague at least managed to maintain his humor in the face of adversity, telling the young woman at the counter that if his copy "did not get off in the night to just keep it; it would do for the centennial of Gettysburg."[38]

Only one woman was present among all those reporters, but her surname was familiar to every veteran in attendance. Helen Dortch Longstreet was the widowed second wife of Lt. Gen. James Longstreet, the man Lee had affectionately called "my old warhorse" but whose role in the battle of Gettysburg, postwar embrace of the Republican Party, and criticism of Lee had made him a deeply controversial, and in some quarters of the South, reviled figure. Helen Dortch had first met Longstreet when she was his daughter's roommate at Gainesville Seminary in the early 1880s.

37 "Old Soldiers Defy Gettysburg Heat," *New York Times*, July 2, 1913.

38 "Confederate Sidelights," *Jersey Journal*, July 3, 1913; "Correspondents in Battle," *Pittsburgh Post-Gazette*, July 2, 1913.

She was 34 years old and had been a newspaper reporter and editor for a dozen years when she married Longstreet, who was 76, in September 1897. Widowed in 1904, she devoted her considerable energies to vindicating the memory of her general. The reunion was an unmistakable opportunity to continue that work.

"Fifteen years out of journalism, I have come to the field where Longstreet's valor added a new glory to American arms," she wrote in the first of four dispatches that were syndicated to more than 50 papers around the country. "I brought over a stenographer with me, a young woman who isn't used to hardships. After being here for two days without food she has deserted and gone back home. . . . So I am holding the fort alone."[39]

39 "Mrs. Longstreet with Blue and Gray," *New York Times*, July 2, 1913.

Chapter 4

It Matters Little Now What the Causes Were

J ust as the sun was beginning to rise Tuesday morning, a reporter chanced to observe two veterans arguing as they returned to camp from a long and convivial night in town.

"I tell you this is the moon," said one. "Hurry, or we will lose our way when it grows darker."

"I'll bet you $10 it's not the moon, it's the sun," said the other, and he produced his money. Thus they stood arguing until another comrade, a little under the weather, came ambling along. He was called into consultation as to whether it was the sun or the moon.

"'Deed, I couldn't tell you boys," he apologized. "I haven't been in this place for 50 years."[1]

There was no question that in 1913, the United States was a nation that liked to take a drink. In the 12 months preceding the reunion, Americans consumed 143.3 million gallons of whiskey and brandy—a gallon and a half for every man, woman, and child—and 64.5 million barrels of beer. Many veterans had returned home from the Civil War with a thirst deeper and more insistent than most, and almost from the moment the armies began demobilizing in 1865, their drinking had become a source of concern in both North and South.

"Despite the earnest efforts of teetotal officers, Union soldiers binged on untold gallons of whiskey during the war—mitigating tedium in camp, cowardice on

---

1 "Little Camp-Life Incidents Among Men at Gettysburg," *Washington Post*, July 2, 1913.

the battlefield, and anguish in the field hospital," writes historian Brian Matthew Jordan in *Marching Home: Union Veterans and Their Unending Civil War.* "Now the 'deadly' drink habit stalked veterans staggering their way back home." Many would struggle with alcoholism the rest of their lives. "Whiskey brings most of them here," wrote one resident of the National Home for Disabled Volunteer Soldiers in Milwaukee in 1910, "and whiskey is taking the most of them out of here."[2]

The story in the South was the same. A member of the board of governors of a Confederate veterans home in Louisiana called it "an asylum for Inebriates," while "a Georgia trustee declared the home 'almost like a barroom,' citing more than two dozen cases of drunkenness and related incidents over a three-month period." Readers of *Confederate Veteran* were accustomed to seeing full-page advertisements from the Leslie E. Keeley Company, of Dwight, Illinois, headlined, "Don't Abuse a Man Sick with the Liquor Disease! Send Him to Us and We Will Cure Him!" "Abuse will not cure a man of typhoid fever, or smallpox, or brain fever," the ad explained. "Neither will it cure him of the liquor habit, which is a disease of the nerve cells requiring special treatment. The Keeley remedies are reconstructive tonics which restore the nerve cells to a health condition. When this is done the 'craving' disappears, because, like a cough, it is merely a *symptom* of a disease and not the disease itself." The company promised to send information "*sealed*, under absolutely *plain cover*. All communications strictly confidential."[3]

James L. Welshans, a Union veteran who traveled to the reunion from Ogden, Utah, was of the opinion that by 1913, "The tipplers and drunkards . . . were the victims of their appetites and bad habits and are nearly all gone. . . . The large majority of the veterans we now meet are sober men, respected and honored by all, nearly all of them being total abstainers." Robert Drummond declared that the camp was filled with "temperate, peaceable, God-fearing and God-serving men . . . not a drunken man upon the streets, all speaking in quiet, gentlemanly tones."[4]

2 "Drinkers and Smokers Make New Records," *Hartford Courant*, July 3, 1913; Jordan, *Marching Home*, 48, 185.

3 R. B. Rosenburg, *Living Monuments: Confederate Soldiers' Homes in the New South* (Chapel Hill, 1995), 112; *Confederate Veteran*, Vol. 19, No. 12 (December 1911), 598. Keeley was a small-town doctor and former Union Army surgeon who began advertising a proprietary cure for alcohol abuse in 1880. His license to practice medicine was revoked by the State of Illinois the following year, but that did nothing to slow the Keeley Cure's meteoric rise in popularity. By the time the governor reinstated his license a decade later, Keeley was well on his way to becoming a wealthy man, with more than 100 Keeley Institute franchises across the U.S., Canada, and Mexico. His colleagues in the medical profession, however, remained unpersuaded. Keeley, declared Dr. Charles L. Mix, professor at Northwestern University Medical School, in the July 1908 issue of the *Illinois Medical Journal*, "was a common, ordinary quack with a useless remedy which made good by advertising and catching suckers."

4 "Ogden Veterans at Gettysburg," *Ogden* [UT] *Standard*, July 9, 1913; Letter, Robert L. Drummond to Juliet Le Roy Mangum, July 4, 1913, Drummond Reminiscences, CU.

The volume of business being done by Gettysburg's saloons, however, suggested otherwise. "As you walked from the principal depot past the long line of hotels, the first thing that greeted the eye was stacks of empty beer barrels, beer kegs, empty whisky and beer bottles by the thousands," wrote John C. Delaney, another Union veteran. "All cast out of a most foul smelling cellar where temporary bars were erected in addition to the regular bar on the first floor. Those empty casks and bottles were cast out of the cellar to make room for more victims who were already six and seven deep, waiting for a chance to be poisoned." According to Pennsylvania veteran Thaddeus Kenderdine, one of the main hotels in town "had three bars running, and it was claimed that in one day $3,500 was taken in over them. . . . Going in for a look I was warned that I would have a long wait for a drink, and it looked like it. There was a dense crowd of the thirsty struggling for their turns, and whom a half-dozen bar-tenders were trying to satisfy." In their defense, a Union veteran from Pittsburgh said many of his comrades "were afraid to drink the water" in the camp, "not because it was not good, but because they were afraid to make the change from the water drank at home, fearing sickness from the change. As a result, several drank bad whisky, which put them in poor condition to withstand the hot rays of the sun." Another old soldier from Washington State declared, "The hard, limestone water was bad for us, so many preferred beer."[5]

The Texans for whom Andrew Cowan had helped procure six bottles of "Old Crow" on Sunday were not the only ones who managed to bring their own beverages into camp. The Virginians erected two tents "stocked with refreshments for the entertainment of visitors," while a Vermont veteran "brought with him a large medicine chest" that his comrades intimated contained "a medicine, which they and especially the Johnnies, enjoyed better than all others and even better than cold water." By late Monday, Lt. Col. A. E. Bradley, chief surgeon in charge of the camp's medical facilities, and Dr. Samuel G. Dixon, the state commissioner of health, were both appealing to the Gettysburg authorities "to close all the saloons and prohibit the sale of liquor in town."[6]

* * *

Tuesday marked the official opening of the reunion, but long before the formal program was scheduled to begin, three veteran musicians from the 194th

5 "Impressions of the Gettysburg Reunion," *Harrisburg Telegraph*, July 12, 1913; Kenderdine, "After Fifty Years," Part 1, *Newtown Enterprise*, July 12, 1913; "Veterans Were Well Treated," *Pittsburgh Post-Gazette*, July 6, 1913; "Gettysburg Veterans Back, Filled with Tales of Reunion," *Tacoma Daily Ledger*, July 11, 1913.

6 "Men in Gray at Reunion," *Baltimore Sun*, July 1, 1913; *Vermont at Gettysburg*, 29; "Great Army Fills Gettysburg Tents," *New-York Tribune*, July 1, 1913.

Pennsylvania roused their comrades with a fife and drum rendition of "Rally Round the Flag." Up and down the Pennsylvania and New York company streets they marched before heading over to the Confederate tents along Seminary Ridge. A South Carolina veteran called for "Dixie" and the Union men obliged, which brought scores of delighted old Rebels out of their tents to sing along. They encored with "Maryland, My Maryland" and "Yankee Doodle" before heading off to the Virginia and West Virginia sections of camp. Farther along the ridge, in the woods lining Confederate Avenue, Maryland veterans from both sides joined together for "an old-fashioned gospel song service" to start the day.

The morning hours were filled with dozens of individual unit reunions. After lunch, thousands filed into the big tent, filling every seat for the formal opening of the reunion. Only about a thousand Southerners were present, but "what they lacked in numbers they made up in lung power." In his opening prayer, the Reverend George E. Lovejoy, the GAR's chaplain-in-chief, invoked Abraham Lincoln's first inaugural: "We are brought to an hour in which prophecy pointed in the years agone; for we realize today the fulfillment of that prediction that 'the mystic chords of memory stretching from every battle field and patriot's grave to every loving heart and hearthstone over this broad land, will yet swell the chorus of Union, touched as they surely will be by the better angels of our nature.'"[7]

James Schoonmaker, the Pittsburgh railroad executive whose eleventh-hour labors had steadied an event teetering on the brink of logistical disaster, struck the keynote for the next four days:

> The honor falls to me, as chairman of the Pennsylvania Commission, of presiding at the opening exercises of a celebration unparalleled in the history of the world; an occasion on which the survivors of two mighty armies, locked in deadly conflict for three consecutive days . . . fighting for a principle as God gave them to see the right, are now, fifty years later, assembled on this historic field over which they struggled, in closest friendly relationship, citizens of one country, with one flag, made a hundred fold stronger and more enduring by their mighty deeds on this and a hundred other battlefields.
>
> It matters little to you or to me now, my Comrades, what the causes were that provoked the War of the States in the Sixties, but it matters, oh, so much . . . that our lives were mercifully spared to see the son of the old soldier of the North stand shoulder to shoulder with the son of the old soldier of the South, and under the leadership of the Generals of the South and the North, sweep San Juan Hill, sink the Spanish fleets in Santiago and

---

7 "Veterans Defy Sun," *Washington Post*, July 2, 1913; *Vermont at Gettysburg*, 96.

Located at the southern edge of camp just west of the Codori house, this massive 13,000-seat tent was the venue for each day's major events, as well as dozens of state and individual unit reunions. *Pennsylvania State Archives*

Manila Bays, and thundering at the gates of Pekin, establish our country a power second to none on earth.[8]

That a Union Medal of Honor winner would so casually dismiss the causes of the war and describe the combatants on both sides as "fighting for a principle as God gave them to see the right" was indicative of just how thoroughly the Southern catechism of the Lost Cause had become conventional wisdom in America by 1913. The writers, historians, memoirists, orators, politicians, and ordinary citizens who had labored long and hard for half a century to achieve that end had reason to be proud. The guns had barely fallen silent when Edward A. Pollard, wartime editor of the *Richmond Examiner*, began constructing one of the pillars of Lost Cause mythology: the assertion that the Southern states had not seceded to preserve slavery. In *The Lost Cause*, the first full-length Southern history of the war, published in 1866, he wrote:

> For we shall see that the distinction of North and South, apparently founded on slavery and traced by lines of climate, really went deeper to the very elements of the civilization of each; and that the Union, instead of being the bond of diverse States, is rather to be

8 *Pennsylvania Commission Report*, 95-96.

described, at a certain period of its history, as the forced alliance and rough companionship of two very different peoples. . . .

The slavery question is not to be taken as an independent controversy in American politics. It was not a moral dispute. It was the mere incident of a sectional animosity, the causes of which lay far beyond the domain of morals. Slavery furnished a convenient line of battle between the disputants; it was the most prominent ground of distinction between the two sections; it was, therefore, naturally seized upon as a subject of controversy, became the dominant theatre of hostilities, and was at last so conspicuous and violent, that occasion was mistaken for cause, and what was merely an incident came to be regarded as the main subject of controversy.[9]

"Slavery was trivialized as the cause of the war," writes Alan T. Nolan, "in favor of such things as tariff disputes, control of investment banking and the means of wealth, cultural differences, and conflict between industrial and agricultural societies." The fundamental disagreement was not over human bondage, but whether the Constitution permitted secession. "The premise . . . was that because the Constitution was silent on the issue, withdrawal from the Union was permitted. It was argued that the states had entered into a compact from which they had the right to withdraw."[10] That a prostrate, defeated, and economically devastated South would attempt to make such a case is understandable. "If we cannot justify the South in the act of Secession," said Clement A. Evans, commander of the Georgia Division the UCV, "we will go down in History solely as a brave, impulsive but rash people who attempted in an illegal manner to overthrow the Union of our Country."

In the version of history that Jubal Early and other Lost Cause partisans expounded in the pages of the *Southern Historical Society Papers* and elsewhere, Virginia was the decisive theatre, which Lee—"the best and most admirable general of the war"—bestrode like a colossus with Stonewall Jackson at his right hand. Ulysses S. Grant was a clumsy butcher commanding an army comprised of the dregs of Northern society, and the Union ultimately prevailed through the brute weight of numbers and overwhelming material resources. The Southern soldier was "invariably heroic, indefatigable, gallant, and law-abiding" and supported on

9 Edward A. Pollard, *The Lost Cause: A New Southern History of the War of the Confederates* (New York, 1866), 47.

10 Alan T. Nolan, "The Anatomy of a Myth," in Gallagher & Nolan, eds., *The Myth of the Lost Cause*, 15, 18, 13.

the home front by "[t]he planter aristocracy, the other whites, and blacks . . . [all] united in defense of the South's humane, superior culture."[11]

As Gary W. Gallagher has observed, the military part of argument was not without merit. "Robert E. Lee *was* a gifted soldier who inspired his army to accomplish prodigious feats on the battlefield. The Army of Northern Virginia and other Confederate forces consistently fought against serious disadvantages in numbers and materiel. A number of Northern newspapers as well as some soldiers in the Army of the Potomac joined Confederates in complaining about Grant's 'hammering' tactics in 1864. . . . The distortion came when Early and other proponents of the Lost Cause denied that Lee had faults or lost any battles, focused on Northern numbers and material superiority while ignoring Confederate advantages, [and] denied Grant any virtues or greatness."[12]

The "nothing to see here" approach to the role of slavery in bringing on the war, however, was nothing short of fantasy. From the Southern states' debates over leaving the Union to the plain language of the secession ordinances themselves, there is no equivocation. "Our position is thoroughly identified with the institution of slavery," said Mississippi's "Declaration of Immediate Causes" for secession, which went on to accuse the North of advocating "negro equality, socially and politically" and promoting "insurrection and incendiarism in our midst." The Georgians were equally clear: "For twenty years past, the Abolitionists and their allies in the Northern states, have been engaged in constant efforts to subvert our institutions, and to excite insurrection and servile war among us." And in case anyone had missed the point, Alexander H. Stephens, vice president of the new Confederate States of America, told a large crowd in Savannah, Georgia, on March 21, 1861, that the new government's "foundations are laid, its cornerstone rests, upon the great truth that the negro is not equal to the white man; that slavery, subordination to the superior race, is his natural and moral condition"; therefore, the Confederacy was "the first Government ever instituted upon principles in strict conformity to nature and the ordination of Providence, in furnishing the materials of human society."[13]

The man who followed Schoonmaker to the stage to address the veterans at the reunion's opening ceremony was an accomplished spinner of the Lost Cause spell. With his snow-white hair and mustache, immaculate gray uniform, and military bearing, Bennett H. Young was the very picture of a gallant old Confederate officer.

11 Gary W. Gallagher, "Jubal A. Early, the Lost Cause, and Civil War History: A Persistent Legacy," in Gallagher & Nolan, eds., *The Myth of the Lost Cause*, 39; Nolan, "Anatomy of a Myth," 17.

12 Gallagher, "Jubal A. Early, the Lost Cause, and Civil War History," 43.

13 Charles B. Dew, *Apostles of Disunion* (Charlottesville, VA, 2001), 12-14.

A native of Jessamine County, Kentucky, he had ridden with Col. John Hunt Morgan's cavalry on his daring July 1863 raid into Indiana and Ohio. Captured and imprisoned in Camp Douglas near Chicago, he escaped and in October 1864, the 21-year-old lieutenant led a small band of Confederates out of Canada to raid St. Albans, Vermont, in the South's deepest strike into Union territory.

Young, a commissioned Confederate officer, and 21 raiders robbed the town's three banks of more than $200,000 and killed one citizen in the ensuing melee, but their attempt to burn the town fizzled when the bottles of "Greek fire" they hurled at the American House hotel, the hardware store, and other establishments on the main street proved incapable of igniting the rain-soaked buildings. The raiders escaped back over the border, where they were promptly arrested by Canadian authorities. In a series of trials that stretched all the way through the surrender of Lee's army the following April, it was determined that Young and his men were acting under orders from the government in Richmond and that the raid was a sanctioned act of war, not a common criminal offense; therefore they would not be extradited to the United States. Northern public opinion, however, remained so outraged by the temerity of the St. Albans raid that post-war amnesty proclamations issued by President Andrew Johnson specifically excluded the raiders. Young spent almost three years in exile in Ireland, where he studied law at Queens University in Belfast, before he was finally able to return to the United States.[14]

He settled in Louisville, Kentucky, and within five years, according to biographer Oscar A. Kinchen, "he was numbered among the great lawyers of the city. It was said of him that in summing up his arguments before a jury he had few equals and that crowds of onlookers would gather at the courtroom to hear him speak at any of his important trials." He developed a deep and abiding interest in collecting and studying the stone implements and other artifacts of prehistoric "mound builders" in Kentucky, whom he judged to be "a superior race" that ultimately had been conquered by "a more primitive and warlike people from the north." These mound builders, Young wrote, had been "a separate race" from the American Indian, "one whose attainments and works stamp him as a man of greater patience . . . higher aims, more domestic and gentle in his habits and methods of life than the race that usurped his possessions and robbed him of his home and peace." For Young and his readers, the parallels with more recent history were obvious.[15]

---

14 For a good overview of the St. Albans raid and its aftermath, see Cathryn J. Prince, *Burn the Town and Sack the Banks* (New York, 2006).

15 Oscar A. Kinchen, *General Bennett H. Young: Confederate Raider and a Man of Many Adventures* (West Hanover, MA, 1981), 82, 94-95.

In October 1864, 21-year-old Bennett H. Young led the daring Confederate raid on St. Albans, Vt. In 1913, he was commander-in-chief of the United Confederate Veterans with a prominent speaking role at the reunion. *Pennsylvania State Archives*

Young threw himself with equal fervor into Confederate veteran affairs, speaking at the first meeting of the UCV in Nashville in 1889 and rising through the ranks of both the Kentucky division and the national organization. He was a prime mover in rallying political and financial support for the Kentucky Confederate Home and served as the first president of its board of trustees. A powerful and polished orator, Young was a highly sought-after speaker at Confederate reunions, memorial ceremonies, monument dedications, and other Lost Cause ceremonial occasions. According to *Confederate Veteran* editor S. A. Cunningham, "no other could so move the Confederate heart as this Kentuckian." In his history of the Kentucky Confederate Home, Rusty Williams wrote that Young "had learned all the movements of the Lost Cause symphony, and it was a tune he could play by heart. Behind the lectern, Young was scholar, storyteller, teacher, and poet. When he chose to turn on the charm, it flowed in irresistible waves; when he intended pathos, women sobbed and men reached for their handkerchiefs."[16]

Young's remarks on Memorial Day at Cave Hill Cemetery in Louisville offer a fair example both of his oratorical skills and his bedrock convictions:

16 Ibid., 104; Rusty Williams, *My Old Confederate Home* (Lexington, KY, 2010), 85.

The sword in and of itself never made any cause right, and the outcome of battles does not affirm the truth of political or even religious questions. We of the South accepted the result because we could not help ourselves. Defeat does not change our political views. The men who composed the Southern armies surrendered none of their convictions at Appomattox or Greensboro. They acquiesced wisely, honestly, and philosophically when powerless to resist further. They did not admit the incorrectness of their interpretation of the Constitution. The defeat of their armies, the triumph of their foes changes neither their faith nor the belief in the Southern mind that secession was an inalienable right of States.[17]

In May 1912, Young was elected commander-in-chief of the UCV, a position to which he would be re-elected three times. He now stepped to the front of the platform in the big tent and declared, "Comrades, I can give you something that no one else in the world can give you, and, in recognition of the splendid hospitality of this great Commonwealth, extended from the Governor, we propose to give him the Rebel Yell."

With that, a dozen other Confederate officers on the stage and hundreds of the rank and file in the audience leapt to their feet and let loose the unmistakable, blood-curdling cry. As its echoes died away, Young addressed the crowd. "I am more than half a thousand miles from my home," he began, "but all the same I am at home. In this land everywhere is my home. This country of ours, this glorious America, belongs to us all, whether we be men of the North or men of the South, whether in the great war we followed the Confederate red and white or the Union red, white and blue. The scenes at Gettysburg today furnish the completest evidence of the greatness as well as of the perpetuity of the American Republic."[18]

As citizens of a reunited nation, Young claimed for his fellow Confederates the same prerogatives enjoyed by the Union victors. "You had great soldiers," he said, "you had hundreds of thousands of men whose hearts were touched with the truest instincts of patriotism. Cherish the memories of your great leaders and captains. . . . Build them monuments wherever you will, laud their courage and their virtues as you may, write in unnumbered volumes the story of their achievements, and enshrine in your hearts the sacrifices of the millions who fought and thought as you fought and thought. We only claim the same right as to our dead comrades."[19]

Young sketched out some of the major engagements of the first two years of the war, but touched only briefly on Gettysburg, which along with Chickamauga

17 "Gen. Bennett Young at Cave Hill Cemetery," *Confederate Veteran*, Vol. 20, No. 8 (August 1912), 372.

18 *Pennsylvania Commission Report*, 105.

19 Ibid., 108.

in the west had "left the outcome full of doubt and uncertainty," notwithstanding the by-then firmly established conventional wisdom that those three days in July had been the climactic struggle of the war. The reason for taking this rhetorical tack soon became clear. The battles that followed Gettysburg, like Spotsylvania and Cold Harbor, "demonstrated that there was no lessening of the vigor of the men on either side; that it was no longer a question of courage, no longer a question of whether the soldiers on one side or the other would fight; but the real question was, how long could the Confederates hold out against the unfailing supplies of the Government, where neither money, men, nor supplies appeared to have a limit?"[20]

"We believe we failed," Young declared, "not because we were wrong, but because you men of the North had more soldiers, better food, longer and better guns, and more resources than the men of the South." Defeat had brought Reconstruction, when "[l]aws were enacted that challenged the equality of the men of the South; but, tried in the crucible of reason, liberty, and patriotism, they have all been repealed. Every State has equal rights, every man has equal privileges. The war has left no badge of inferiority."[21] That last point was crucial, for Young wanted it clearly understood that he and his fellow Confederates felt no shame for either their cause or their defeat:

The splendor and importance of this occasion are immeasurably enhanced by the fact that no explanations are sought or expected. . . . If any Southern man who comes here clad in the gray uniform so dear to him and those of his blood believed he would be expected even in thought to question the memories connected with the heroic past, he would go out from these tents and quickly march away. The Confederate comes here with his heart still loyal to the South and to those who made the four years of the Confederate nation's life resplendent with heroism, glory, and noblest sacrifice.

You would not have wanted us to come otherwise, you would have despised us as cowards had we done so. We thank God you didn't ask us to express apologies or regrets. Nor do we ask you to express any regrets in the main for what you did. We both have fought for principles and you won, not because we lacked courage but because we lacked further resources.[22]

Precisely what those contending principles had been remained unspoken and Young averred, without any apparent sense of irony, that the people of the reunited

20 Ibid., 111.

21 Ibid., 106.

22 "'Rebel Yell' Awarded Governor Tener at Veterans' Exercises," *Philadelphia Inquirer*, July 2, 1913; *Pennsylvania Commission Report*, 107-108.

nation "will tolerate no injustice, submit to no impairment of any citizen's rights, but will ever demand that the highest good for all shall be the cardinal principle upon which the government rests."[23]

*   *   *

With temperatures once again approaching 100 degrees, the heat in the big tent was intense, and more than two dozen veterans had to be taken away for treatment by the camp medical staff. "It ought to be made a criminal offense to say 'Is this hot enough for you?'" grumbled one old Confederate. But though the tent was full, the opening exercises themselves "stirred but passing interest in the hearts of the men of Meade and Lee," according to one of the *Philadelphia Inquirer*'s reporters on the scene. "[T]he vast majority . . . spent the day out on the familiar old battlefield or in the tents of their comrades."[24]

The *New York Times* agreed. "There was a formal opening in the big tent, with speeches by Secretary of War Garrison and others, but that wasn't the event. The event was the hunting up of the man who shot you, if you could find him, and if you couldn't, then hunting up of the man whose regiment fought yours. There was an amazing number of such reunions."[25]

John M. Morris of Columbus, Ohio, was a veteran of Capt. Frank Gibbs's Battery L, 1st Ohio Light Artillery. On July 2, 1863, the 19-year-old Morris had helped manhandle the battery's 12-pounder Napoleons into position near the northwestern base of Little Round Top on either side of the Wheatfield Road. "Our front was hardly clear when the irregular, yelling line of the enemy put in his appearance," Gibbs wrote in his official report, "and we received him with double charges of canister. . . . So rapidly were the guns worked that they became too hot to lay the hand on." Fifty years later, Morris returned with two of his battery mates, Ben Reed and John Summers, and "found no trouble in locating not only the position of the Battery, but of each individual gun. The scenery looked familiar. Just like looking at an old picture that you have not seen for years. While we were there, two Confederate Soldiers came over from where their lines was, shook hands with me, and one of them said, 'Were you in this Battery?' I said that I was! 'Well,' said he, 'SHAKE. I belonged to the Brigade that charged your Battery twice. I'm from Georgia.' I told him I was glad to meet him and that I thought they did some

---

23 *Pennsylvania Commission Report*, 111.

24 "Death List Much Greater in Veterans' Camp Than Given Out, Is Rumor," *Philadelphia Inquirer*, July 2, 1913; "Impressions from Gettysburg," *The Daily Progress*, July 9, 1913.

25 "Old Soldiers Defy Gettysburg Heat," *New York Times*, July 2, 1913.

pretty good charging. 'Yes and we all thought you did some pretty good shooting,' said he, 'and we tried to give you your money's worth.' And they surely did."[26]

Some veterans had made specific arrangements to meet at the reunion. Frank H. Cobb of the 1st Regiment of Berdan's Sharpshooters had first encountered the 11th Alabama's William H. Sanders in 1863 while on picket duty along the Rappahannock River near Fredericksburg when Sanders went down to the river to swap tobacco for sugar and coffee. A year later, Cobb was seriously wounded in the leg at the Wilderness and captured by the 11th Alabama, and their paths crossed again as Sanders, by then the regimental surgeon, saw to the Yankee's treatment. After the war, Sanders set up a medical practice in Mobile, and Cobb went home to Hudson, Michigan, where he worked as a railroad clerk. The wound had shattered his right femur, leaving it almost two inches shorter than the left, and Cobb had to walk on the ball of his foot with his right heel some two inches above the ground. More than 10 years later, fragments of bullet and bone continued to work their way to the surface, causing the wound to ulcerate.

Sanders and Cobb corresponded for a time after the war, but eventually fell out of touch. Then in March 1913, as the reunion drew near, Sanders, who by now was living with his daughter in Cooksville, Mississippi, wrote to the postmaster of Hudson: "I knew F. H. Cobb during the war, of First Michigan [sic] Sharpshooters, who was wounded the 7th day of May, when charged the 11th Alabama Regiment. His right thigh was broken. We took him in our lines. (Had the assistant surgeon set his leg.) . . . If any of the family are living at Hudson, I will thank you to hand them this letter. I expect to attend the Reunion at Gettysburg, July 1, 2, 3, 1913, and want to meet some of them, if Mr. Cobb is dead. If not at Hudson and you know where they live, please mail this to them. Please find stamps to mail and answer. You will greatly oblige an old soldier who befriended Cobb during the war." Cobb was very much alive, as it turned out, and the two resumed their correspondence, and made plans to meet at Gettysburg, where "they spent two days and part of the third walking over the . . . battlefield."[27]

Eighty-two-year-old Thomas Taylor Munford, who had led cavalry brigades under Stonewall Jackson and J. E. B. Stuart, and 76-year-old Capt. George N. Bliss of the 1st Rhode Island Cavalry had also arranged to meet and ended up

26 *The War of the Rebellion: A Compilation of the Official Records of the Union and Confederate Armies*, 128 vols. (Washington, D.C., 1880-1901), Series 1, Vol. 27, Part 1, page 662; John M. Morris, "Notes of the Trip to Gettysburg 1913," Aug. 13, 1913, transcribed by Donald E. Darby, SUVCW, https://suvcw.org/sites/default/files/2023-03/pr001.pdf, accessed June 9, 2023.

27 "Hudson Civil War Veteran and His Confederate Friend at Former's Home," *Adrian* [MI] *Daily Telegram*, July 22, 1913; "Hudson Veteran Gets Letter From Confederate Who Befriended Him 50 Years Ago on the Firing Line," undated newspaper clipping in Frank Cobb pension file, NARA.

talking for hours together. "General Munford was stronger than I expected to find him," Bliss wrote to his wife. "He said the excitement of the occasion stimulated him like wine." Michigan veteran Andrew Fairchild had corresponded for several months before the reunion with his old comrade, George Wrider. "He arrived first," Fairchild recalled, "and waited for a day . . . before I arrived. When I came to headquarters he was standing at the door asking every company that went in if Andrew Fairchild was there. I stood beside him for several minutes before telling him who I was. When I did he took my hand, the tears streaming down my face, and asked me if I was certain who I was. I satisfied him as to my identity and we spent many happy hours together on the battlefield."

The Hennighausen brothers had fought on opposing sides. Both born in what is now Germany, one was living in Baltimore and the other in Richmond when the war came. Louis answered the first Union call to arms, enlisting in a three-month militia unit from the District of Columbia in April 1861. At the expiration of that enlistment, he joined the 46th New York; he was commissioned as a second lieutenant and subsequently was promoted to first lieutenant. His older brother Carl enlisted in the 15th Virginia, whose Company K was filled with German-born men. Now 79, Carl took the train up to Baltimore to meet his 72-year-old brother and the pair were driven to Gettysburg by their nephew.[28]

Many others met serendipitously. Charles Warren, who had taken part in Pickett's Charge as a 14-year-old orderly in the 28th Virginia, found the Union gunner who had knocked him senseless with a rammer in the hand-to-hand fighting at the Angle. Harry Simmons of the 17th Georgia, who had been wounded on July 2 in the fierce fighting around the 4th New York Battery's guns near Devil's Den, met Hugh Martin, a member of one of the gun crews "who had assisted in removing me to a place of safety. We simply could not be separated after that, and were together much of the time at Gettysburg." Another Confederate walked up to Irving Ewing and asked, "Aren't you from the Sixth Michigan Cavalry?" When Ewing said that he was, the man continued, "Don't you remember trading a sack of sugar and coffee with a Johnny for some tobacco? Well, I am the man." "We were in encampment on one side of the Rapidan River," Ewing recalled, "and the Johnnies were on the other side and one called me across and asked if I did not want to exchange some sugar for tobacco. I agreed, and we both left our arms on the river banks and waded our horses out to the middle of the stream where the exchange was made."[29]

A Union veteran from Harrisburg was reunited with three fellow members of the 81st Pennsylvania whom he had not seen since the Grand Review in Washington in May 1865, while a Virginia veteran who had lived in Missouri since the close of the war found a tent full of his old comrades from Company A of the 11th Virginia. "It's sure a treat for sore eyes," he said. "I never expected to see you boys again." E. V. Kauffman of the 10th Virginia was able to return a bible to the friends of a man killed at Spotsylvania Courthouse. J. D. Irwin of North Carolina was walking through the camp when he heard a veteran from New York inquiring about the 20th North Carolina. "I introduced myself to him and after talking a while he asked me if we lost our flag the first day. I told him we lost it but later recaptured one-half of it. He slapped me on the shoulder and said, 'Old fellow, I have the other half.' I invited him to my tent and we had a long talk. He said he would send me the flag when he got home. His name is Henry M. Fitzgerald, now living in Chicago. So I hope to reunite our flag soon."[30]

Any misgivings Irwin and his comrades might have had concerning the reception they would receive at the reunion quickly evaporated. "The Rebel gray is a popular color in Gettysburg," reported the *New York Times*. "Any man who wears it is sure of a tumultuous greeting. . . . All through the streets to-day the same picture was being repeated every moment—some old man in gray coming along and being instantly pounced upon by half a dozen men in blue and being borne off in triumph. It is a real reunion, the genuine article." Ann Tayloe Lomax, attending the reunion in place of her father, Maj. Gen. Lunsford Lindsay Lomax, who had died just a month before the camp opened, agreed. "The town's opened its arms to the old Confederates," she wrote to those back home. "They get twice the ovation and you'll see one old Confederate in gray and dozens of [Union] veterans surrounding him."[31]

One of the most dramatic and widely reported reunions involved Audubon C. Smith of the 56th Virginia and Albert N. Hamilton of the 72nd Pennsylvania. Smith had enlisted three days after his 18th birthday, in the first, heady months of the war, and was one of the hundred or so men from Armistead's and Garnett's

---

29 "Shakes Hands Over Cannon with Foe of 50 Years Ago," *Salt Lake Herald*, Aug. 31, 1913; Blake, *Hand Grips*, 123; "Met 'Reb' He Traded Sugar for Tobacco 50 Years Ago," *Flint Daily Journal*, July 19, 1913.

30 "Survivors of Pickett's Charge Revisit Scenes," *Philadelphia Inquirer*, July 1, 1913; "A Remarkable Story Concerning a Captured Flag," *Webster's Weekly*, July 8, 1913.

31 "Old Soldiers Defy Gettysburg Heat"; Letter, Anne Tayloe Lomax to mother, undated, Virginia Historical Society (VHS).

Two old Rebels share a quiet moment. *Pennsylvania State Archives*

brigades who broke through the Yankee lines at the Angle during Pickett's Charge. Shot through both shoulders, he was taken prisoner, and after being paroled spent months convalescing, first in Chimborazo Hospital in Richmond, then back home in Louisa County. After the war, he became a dentist in Green Springs, married, and raised two daughters. Hamilton was 23 when he enlisted in Philadelphia in September 1862, collecting a $25 bounty. He made it through the war unscathed, serving first in the 72nd Pennsylvania and then the 183rd, in which he was promoted to sergeant. When peace came, he returned to Philadelphia and his prewar occupation of house painter, and married. In 1875, his wife, Elizabeth, took their four-year-old daughter and moved back in with her parents due to Hamilton's "intemperate habits and failure to provide for herself and child." Two years later, he tried to kill her, shooting her in the middle of Morris Street on a warm August evening as horrified neighbors looked on. Hamilton was "a bad, good-for-nothing man," according to one of Elizabeth's friends, "frequently drunk and always drinking." A surgeon's certificate filed with his pension application in 1892 described him as "a poorly nourished, excitable man" with 20/50 eyesight. Eight years later, Elizabeth Hamilton successfully petitioned the Pension Office to have one-half of his pension paid to her because of his desertion and non-support, but when she died in 1911, he lost no time in writing to request that they "kindly fix my papers to state that I may receive my full pension."

Now, as Smith walked along the Angle with a group of fellow Confederates, he described what had befallen him 50 years earlier. "Right here," he said, "we leaped across. I had reached a yard beyond the wall, I guess about there, when I was hit and fell. I remember only that a man in blue came toward me five minutes later, when our army had broken in retreat, and lifting me up, gave me a drink of water and carried me off on his shoulders. When I returned to consciousness, I was in a Yankee field hospital."

As Smith told his story, a group of Union veterans was approaching, paying equally rapt attention as Hamilton recounted his own story of the third day's fight. "They got about to here, and then we beat them back. And it must have been right about here that a Johnny fell, almost into my arms. I lifted him up and gave him a drink of water, and a few minutes later put him on my shoulders."

When Smith heard those words, he took Hamilton by the shoulders and peered intently into his face. "Why, good God, mister," he cried, "you're the man who saved my life!" Whether or not Hamilton's weak, rheumy eyes actually confirmed it, he played along, and the two embraced, to the cheers of their companions and the delight of the reporters who chanced to be nearby, whose gushing copy turned an attempted murderer and inveterate drunk into one half of a heartwarming tableau of reconciliation.[32]

Not all attempts at reunion ended successfully, however. New Hampshire veteran Charles Paige complained that, given the sheer number of veterans present, "it was next to impossible to find anyone you might be looking for." Porter Farley of the 140th New York agreed. "Registration books were not brought to the camp until Wednesday so that many of the old soldiers who wanted to see the friends they had fought with in the battle were unable to do so. It would have been better if each state had had its own register and every man on his arrival had been asked to enroll his name, regiment and company in the proper place. This would have made it convenient for the men to find their comrades, since each of the tents bore a large number and the streets were all numbered."[33]

John Fordyll of the 7th West Virginia brought with him the sword he had taken from a captured Confederate officer. Though he did not know his name, each day

32 "Old Soldiers Defy Gettysburg Heat"; "55,000 Veterans Defy Great Heat"; "Sun Is Scorching on Battlefield," *Richmond Times-Dispatch*, July 2, 1913; Albert N. Hamilton pension file and CMSR, NARA.

33 Charles C. Paige, "Reflections on the Gettysburg Jubilee of July 1-4, 1913," Wendell W. Lang, Jr. Collection, U.S. Army Military History Institute (USAMHI), Carlisle, PA; "Says Veterans Fared Well at Great Reunion," *Rochester Democrat & Chronicle*, July 7, 1913.

Fordyll walked out to the spot where it had happened, hoping to encounter the officer once again and return it to him. Jacob Heater of the 33rd Virginia had a bit more to go on—a canteen whose owner's name and regiment, Monroe D. Prindle, 211th Pennsylvania, were printed on it—but no better luck.

J. D. Cottrell was a veteran of Company D of the 48th New York, known as the "Die-No-Mores" because of the large number of seminary students in their ranks and their propensity for hymn singing. He came to the reunion hoping to meet once more his old sergeant, whom he had carried wounded from the battlefield at Fort Wagner and had never seen again. As Cottrell walked up and down the company streets in the New Jersey section of camp, calling out in a booming voice, "Has anybody seen John G. Abbott of the 'Die No Mores'?" a man stuck his head out of a tent and demanded, "What do you know about John G. Abbott?"

Cottrell explained his quest, and the man said, "Comrade, I am John G. Abbott's oldest brother. I am Chaplain William Abbott, of Asbury Park, of the 23rd New Jersey. . . . My brother died in a New York hospital from wounds received at [Fort] Wagner. I've wanted for fifty years to thank the man who was kind to him on the field, and I thank God for this opportunity."

"Dead! Dead, did you say?" Cottrell muttered dazedly. 'Dead!" Then he smiled. "No, he ain't dead—he's gone home, you mean. Gone home to die no more!"[34]

By mid-afternoon, it was 102 degrees and hundreds of veterans sought relief at the aid stations and field hospitals. "[M]any were overcome for a while but the boy scouts had them before they struck the ground and give them first treatment, at the same time blow a whistle and the ambulance was there in an instant," noted George Duke of the 104th Pennsylvania in a letter to his daughter. "We couldn't even stumble but what one of those boys was there to help us," an Indiana veteran concurred. "The Scouts did 'first aid' work . . . on the grounds and in the crowded streets of the town, even when 'off duty,'" *Boys Life* noted proudly. "Time and again they took care of prostrated or injured persons, winning applause from men and women who had stood around, not knowing what to do." The *Gettysburg Compiler* reported that "fully two thirds" of the heat prostrations "were caused by the mixing of liquor with the heat." For Christopher Yates, a 78-year-old Union veteran from Latrobe, Pennsylvania, the heat proved fatal; he was the fourth veteran to die in camp. Allen D. Albert, a longtime employee of the pension office in Washington who had survived two wounds during the war and toiled for three

34 Blake, *Hand Grips*, 81-82.

years writing a history of the 45th Pennsylvania, was the first to die in town, felled by a cerebral hemorrhage.[35]

Most of the encampment was "on ground that has been baked as hard as a brick and dried into dust" with scarcely a tree to be found. But as Elsie Tibbetts observed, "west of the Confederate camp along Confederate Avenue and up across the Emmitsburg Road in Zeigler's grove and the National Cemetery, where the foliage of the trees and bushes was thick enough to keep the ground beneath from getting warm it was fairly cool. At least there was air and no danger of sunstroke if one could manage to get there safely, and to these places of relief thousands of veterans from all parts of the camp flocked in the early morning, and many wisely stayed there all day."[36]

Those who visited the South Carolina section of camp found a palmetto tree next to the state flag at the head of the street, brought by W. A. Clark of Columbia. People began asking for pieces as souvenirs, so with Clark's permission, the veteran serving as the "color guard" began cutting streamers from the tree's leaves. "Old soldiers all over the place were [soon] seen with these souvenirs stuck in their button holes or pinned to their coats. The streamers were cut until the tree was bare of branches." Over in the Maryland camp, the Confederate battle flag "was the centre of much interest" among veterans and non-veteran visitors alike. "Many young ladies had cameras with them and snapped the blue and gray as they stood together" around the flag. Not everyone, however, was pleased to see the Rebel banner on display. According to Vermont veteran Frank Kenfield, "many of the boys that wore the blue, took exception to the Confederate flag, and considered it an insult to that emblem of Liberty for which they fought four long years to sustain." When a New Jersey veteran saw the North Carolina state flag being flown, he began cursing and declared that it ought to be buried, at which J. Dallas Griffin of the 63rd North Carolina "told him he had better try to bury it, and if he did try he would be buried before the flag was buried."[37]

Tense moments such as these were the exception, however. John Morris of Ohio paid a visit to the Southern side of camp and "was very pleasantly surprised at the cordial manner in which I was treated, and enjoyed my two hour visit over

35 Letter, George Duke to daughter, July 6, 1913, Vertical Files: 11-61-B: Participant Accounts, GNMP Library; "The Scouts at Gettysburg," *Boys' Life* (Sept. 1913), 16-17; "The Great Peace Camp," *Gettysburg Compiler*, July 9, 1913.

36 "Blue and Gray Mingle in Historic Gettysburg," *Los Angeles Times*, June 30, 1913; Tibbetts, *From Maine to Gettysburg*, 81-82.

37 "Palmetto Tree at Gettysburg," *The State*, July 11, 1913; "Maryland 500 Strong," *Baltimore Sun*, July 1, 1913; "Maryland Is First with Stars and Bars," *Baltimore Sun*, June 30, 1913; *Vermont at Gettysburg*, 29; "Gettysburg Reunion," *Chatham Record* (Siler City, NC), July 9, 1913.

Despite some controversy and confusion before the reunion began about whether Confederate battle flags would be permitted in camp, a number of veterans proudly displayed them, including these South Carolinians. *Pennsylvania State Archives*

there very much." A New Hampshire veteran went to "the Confederate quarters and found on the whole a good-looking and well-behaved set of men. I bought a Virginia badge of their quarter master."[38]

On balance, a *Washington Post* reporter thought, the old men "are showing remarkable stamina. Not until sheer exhaustion compels them to drop in their tracks will they give up, and one of the hardest tasks imposed on the physicians is to force the men into ambulances before it is too late. Men of 89 and 90 years are marching around like boys in their teens." Despite the fact that it was "hotter than Tophet" as one young civilian visitor tramped from the Angle to the Wheatfield with a veteran of the 32nd Massachusetts, "This old fellow of 74 took every fence like a colt and was as fresh as a daisy." An army medical officer told of treating a 96-year-old Massachusetts veteran who told him apologetically, "Major, I wouldn't have had to come to you if I hadn't been on a little bat [in other words, a bender] last night."[39]

38 Morris, "Notes of the Trip to Gettysburg"; Paige, "Reflections on the Gettysburg Jubilee."

39 "Gov. Cox of Ohio Opens Camp of His Own for Buckeye Veterans," *Washington Post*, July 2, 1913; "Tented Gettysburg Swept by Storm," *New York Times*, July 3, 1913; Letter, Claude G. Leland to wife and sons, July 2, 1913, American Historical Manuscript Collection, New-York Historical Society (NYHS).

These two Union veterans brought along a small cannon and enlivened the camp with frequent salvos, much to the dismay of Lt. George S. Patton, Jr. *Pennsylvania State Archives*

Second Lieutenant Patton, already put out by the fact that he and his fellow Regulars had been reduced to "doing park policeman work," took a less charitable view. "They are a disgusting bunch dirty and old and of the people who 'God loves,'" he wrote to his wife. "One old hound has been beating a drum ever since he got here. Two others have a small cannon which they fire as often as possible. As one of my men said yesterday the best of them were only damned militia men and did not no [sic] much."[40]

*   *   *

[40] Letter, George S. Patton to Beatrice Banning Ayer, July 1, 1913, in Blumenson, ed., *The Patton Papers*, 255.

Night again brought some small relief from the heat. "A lot of the boys shifted their cots to the outside of their tents in the company street so's to keep cool and that helped some," noted Jacob Raab, a veteran of the 14th Brooklyn. "Occasionally the cry of a hound or an owl was carried across on the wind," Walter Blake of the 6th New Hampshire observed. "The dim outlines of trees reared themselves against the sky, shadows flitted past camp fires and disappeared in the great gloom. The grass glistened under the electricity in the early evening dew. Lanterns flashed in and out among the tents; in the distance they looked like hundreds of fireflies flitting about."[41]

Landis Travis spent a pleasant evening in town with two of his five daughters, who had accompanied him to the reunion from Westmoor, Pennsylvania. They agreed to meet again at the young ladies' hotel the next morning and Travis walked back to camp around 9:00 p.m. On Wednesday morning he rose early, washed his face and hands in the basin outside his tent, and set out for town. Travis had served through all four years of the war in the 191st Pennsylvania and the 5th Pennsylvania Reserve Infantry, and spent nine months as a prisoner of war, suffering from malnutrition, scurvy, and the rheumatism that would trouble him for the rest of his life. A comrade who saw Travis in the hospital not long after his release from the Confederate prison camp in Salisbury, North Carolina, said, "He was a mere skeleton . . . and scarcely able to walk." Since the war he had worked as a railroad fireman and engineer, for the last 42 years with the Lehigh Valley Railroad. According to the *Wilkes-Barre Times-Leader*, "His relatives warned him against making the trip to Gettysburg, but he was desirous of seeing the field on which he fought fifty years ago."

He was crossing the town square around 8:00 a.m. when he dropped dead on the sidewalk outside the Gettysburg Hotel. Thaddeus Kenderdine happened by not long after. "In the lobby lay a dead soldier, just brought in from the pavement where he had been felled by heatstroke, a corner of a newspaper barely covering his face. . . . A gaping group were looking at the corpse, which was waiting the coming of the dead-wagon."[42]

Under a three-column, page-one headline that proclaimed, "Death List Much Greater in Veterans' Camp Than Given Out, Is the Rumor," the *Philadelphia Inquirer* that morning reported the veterans' suspicions "that the list of death victims had not been fully told":

41 "Veteran Raab Back from Gettysburg," *Jersey Journal*, July 3, 1913; Blake, *Hand Grips*, 107.

42 "Heat Proves Fatal to Local Veteran at Gettysburg," *Wilkes-Barre Times-Leader*, July 2, 1913; Kenderdine, "After Fifty Years," Part 1, *Newtown Enterprise*, July 12, 1913.

The rumors were coupled with the admission of a prominent medical man in the camp that there had been up until 3 o'clock this morning no less than nineteen deaths, and that it was fully expected that by this evening there would be twenty more added to the gruesome list. In corroboration of the medical man's statement, it was admitted by the Pennsylvania Railroad, in whose charge the coffins were brought to Gettysburg, that nineteen of the long dead boxes had so far been turned over to the authorities of the camp.

It is believed that the suppression of the death list would be undertaken simply to prevent a panic or fright among the thousands of veterans, who might succumb more easily should the high mortality be made known.[43]

Some New Jersey veterans who were convinced they had seen two men die in their section of the camp "were astonished when they saw no mention of it in the papers, and came to the correspondents' camp to ask why no notice had been printed." They and the *Inquirer*'s "prominent medical man" notwithstanding, Travis was only the sixth veteran to die since Sunday; a tragedy, to be sure, but far fewer than the toll of 10 per day for which the organizers had steeled themselves. Given the numbers being hauled away in ambulances each day overcome by heat or other ailments, however, it was understandable that some were mistaken for fatalities by their comrades.[44]

But the *New York Times* was having none of it:

[T]he alarmist talk about the prospective death rate is without foundation. . . . Pity for these supposedly enfeebled and tottering old men is out of place. They are an astonishingly sturdy and husky lot of old men, as they show by tramping all day over hills that would break the heart of a younger and more delicate generation. They stand straight and have big voices, and walk with a swing, and many of them are not yet gray. . . .

But it cannot be said too often or too strongly that the talk about high death rate and danger is the invention of persons who never have lived in the open air before and don't know anything about it. It is hot, to be sure, but the heat is a dry heat that doesn't hurt anybody. . . . Men who never slept in a tent before are wailing about the discomforts of it, but none of these wailers is a soldier.[45]

43 "Death List Much Greater in Veterans' Camp Than Given Out, Is the Rumor," *Philadelphia Inquirer*, July 2, 1913.

44 "Trenton Veterans Having Big Time," *Trenton Times*, July 3, 1913.

45 "Old Soldiers Defy Gettysburg Heat."

Chapter 5

Sickles and Mrs. Longstreet

Of the 14 corps commanders present at Gettysburg in 1863—11 in the Army of the Potomac and three in the Army of Northern Virginia—only one was still alive in 1913: Maj. Gen. Daniel E. Sickles of the Union's III Corps, a man whose continued presence among the living was a rebuke to anyone who believed longevity was the gods' reward for a man of probity, honor, and sobriety. Born into wealth in New York City in 1819, Sickles "matured into a suave, mustachioed, and pathological liar."[1] From a young age, he reveled in the bare-knuckle Democratic politics of Tammany Hall, which dovetailed well with his other interests, including gambling, drinking, and a whore named Fanny White, who accompanied him to Albany when he was elected to the state assembly in 1847. Five years later, at the age of 33, he married Teresa Bagioli, the beautiful 16-year-old daughter of a family friend, but neither matrimony nor subsequent fatherhood materially altered Sickles's active social life, including his relationship with White, who had risen in the world to become the proprietress of a high-end bordello on Mercer Street in New York City.

In 1856 he was elected to Congress and leased a house on Lafayette Square in Washington, where he and Teresa entertained lavishly, and where Teresa soon made the acquaintance of Philip Barton Key, U.S. attorney for the District of Columbia and son of Francis Scott Key, composer of "The Star-Spangled Banner." By the winter of 1857–58, they had begun an affair, which became increasingly indiscreet as the months rolled on. Sickles, preoccupied with both congressional business

1 Allen C. Guelzo, "Mad Dan," *The Civil War Monitor*, Vol. 3, No. 2 (Summer 2013), 50.

and his own extramarital activities, was blissfully unaware of what was happening under his nose until an anonymous letter arrived in late February 1859. Stunned, he asked a close associate to make some discreet inquiries, which confirmed the worst. Sickles confronted Teresa and forced her to write an excruciatingly detailed confession, the general outlines of which would somehow become known publicly within a week.

The next day, he saw Key, unaware that the game was up, strolling across Lafayette Square, and rushed out of the house armed with a pair of pistols. Crying, "Key, you scoundrel, you have dishonored my bed—you must die!" Sickles pulled out a derringer and fired, but his shot only grazed Key's hand. The two grappled and then, as a dozen stunned witnesses looked on, Sickles broke free, drew a second pistol, and fired two more shots, striking Key in the thigh and the chest, the latter wound proving fatal.[2]

To call the ensuing murder trial sensational would be an understatement. Sickles's legal team, which included future Secretary of War Edwin M. Stanton, presented a defense based upon the then-novel claim of temporary insanity and prevailed. Sickles was acquitted and three months later reconciled with Teresa, an action that outraged public opinion even more than his murder of Key. "He prudently decided not to tempt public contempt by running for re-election," historian Allen Guelzo writes, "and he might have dropped soundlessly into the footnotes of American political history if not for the Civil War. As a loyal Democrat, Sickles was likely expected to fall in with the fellowship of New York City's Lincoln-haters: August Belmont, Fernando Wood, and Manton Marble. Instead, Sickles bound himself to President Abraham Lincoln and the Union cause and set about recruiting the five-regiment Excelsior Brigade." Lincoln, always anxious to shore up Democratic support for the war, was only too happy to embrace Sickles, the quintessential political general. By July 1863 he was a corps commander and the highest-ranking non-West Pointer in the Army of the Potomac.[3]

Sickles's III Corps arrived at Gettysburg too late to play a part in the first day's fighting, and Maj. Gen. George G. Meade, the Army of the Potomac's commander, ordered him to anchor his right to the II Corps and extend the Union line south to Little Round Top. Throughout the morning of July 2, however, Sickles became increasingly dissatisfied with his position along Cemetery Ridge—in truth, little more than a gentle rise in the III Corps' sector—and was alarmed at the prospect of Confederate forces posting artillery on the slightly higher ground along the Emmitsburg Road, several hundred yards in his front. By early afternoon, his

2 W. A. Swanberg, *Sickles the Incredible* (New York, 1956), 54.

3 Guelzo, "Mad Dan," 51.

agitation was so great that, on his own initiative, he ordered his entire command forward to a new line that ran along the Emmitsburg Road, with its right flank in the air, then bent southeast along the west branch of Plum Run to Devil's Den, a quarter mile from Little Round Top where his left was supposed to be anchored. The center of this new line was some 1,500 yards forward of the rest of the Union position along Cemetery Ridge. When Maj. Gen. Winfield S. Hancock, commander of the II Corps, saw Sickles's men advancing to their new line, he is famously said to have observed that the spectacle was "beautiful to look at, but gentlemen they will not be there long."[4]

When Meade was told what Sickles had done, the army commander was furious. Sickles vainly argued the necessity of occupying the higher ground. "General Sickles, this is in some respects higher ground than that to the rear," Meade agreed acidly, "but there is still higher ground in front of you, and if you keep on advancing you will find constantly higher ground all the way to the mountains." But little could be done; Confederate artillery was already shelling Sickles's line, and Lafayette McLaws's and John Bell Hood's divisions of Longstreet's Corps were about to come boiling out of the woods on Seminary Ridge to commence what Longstreet would later call "the best three hours' fighting ever done by any troops on any battle-field."[5]

Those three hours—in the Wheatfield and the Peach Orchard, along the Emmitsburg Road and in the Devil's Den—shattered the III Corps. Meade had to pour in reinforcements from the II and V corps to prevent the Union left from collapsing under the weight of Longstreet's assault. Sickles's right leg was shattered as well, by a Rebel shell fragment, and was amputated above the knee.

"General Sickles, misinterpreting his orders, instead of placing the Third Corps on the prolongation of the Second, had moved it nearly three-quarters of a mile in advance—an error which nearly proved fatal in the battle," wrote Maj. Gen. Henry Halleck in his official report of the battle. "The enemy attacked this corps on the 2nd with great fury, and it was likely to be utterly annihilated, when the Fifth Corps moved up on the left, and enabled it to reform behind the line it was originally ordered to hold."[6]

"I know, and have heard, of no bad conduct or blundering on the part of any officer, save that of Sickles, on the 2nd of July," Lt. Frank A. Haskell, a member of Brig. Gen. John Gibbon's staff, wrote to his brother, "and that was so gross,

4 James A. Hessler, *Sickles at Gettysburg* (El Dorado Hills, CA, 2009), 131.

5 Guelzo, "Mad Dan," 54; James Longstreet, "Lee in Pennsylvania," in Alexander K. McClure, ed., *The Annals of the War Written by Leading Participants North and South* (Philadelphia, 1879), 424.

6 Hessler, *Sickles at Gettysburg*, 254.

and came so near being the cause of irreparable disaster that I cannot discuss it with moderation. I hope the man may never return to the Army of the Potomac, or elsewhere, to a position where his incapacity, or something worse, may bring fruitless destruction to thousands again."[7]

As Sickles was being carried from the battlefield on July 2, he knew his reputation and military career were hanging by a thread, and he knew what needed to be done to salvage them. The next day, as Union and Confederate forces squared off for the climactic assault known to history as Pickett's Charge, Sickles, escorted by a squadron of cavalry, three aides, a doctor, and 40 infantrymen to serve as stretcher bearers, set off for Washington. They arrived on Sunday morning, July 5, and that afternoon an aide announced that President Lincoln had come to see him, as Sickles had surely hoped he would.

"Pitifully weak though he was, and perfectly aware that he might die, there was no man in the world Sickles would rather have seen at that moment than the President," wrote Sickles biographer W. A. Swanberg. "He well knew that Meade might have some unpleasant things to say about his forward move at Gettysburg. . . . Dan Sickles could carry himself cooly amid shot and shell, and could light a perfecto [cigar] while his shattered leg was spouting blood, but his courage was not of the sort that could gracefully admit error." According to Lt. Col. James Rusling, Sickles's chief quartermaster, who was present, "He certainly got his side of the story of Gettysburg well into the President's mind and heart that Sunday afternoon; and this doubtless stood him in good stead afterward."[8]

Rusling offers no details concerning what that side of the story sounded like, but it's a reasonable bet that it was a rough first draft of the tale Sickles would tell, with growing confidence and fresh layers of fabrication, for the next half-century: Meade had been timid, indecisive, oblivious to the Confederate threat on his left, and more interested in retreating before Lee than engaging him. It was Sickles, through bold, aggressive action, who had saved the day, and by extension, the Union itself.

"It is understood in the army that the President thanked the slayer of Barton Key for *saving the day* at Gettysburg," Haskell fumed. "Does the country know any better than the President, that Meade, Hancock, and Gibbon were entitled to some little share of such credit?"[9]

Sickles would do his best to ensure that the country remained in the dark on that point, using every weapon at his disposal: planting doubts about Meade

7 Frank A. Haskell, *The Battle of Gettysburg* (Sandwich, MA, 1993), 117.

8 Swanberg, *Sickles the Incredible*, 222; Hessler, *Sickles at Gettysburg*, 237.

9 Haskell, *The Battle of Gettysburg*, 122.

directly in the ears of Lincoln and Stanton; feeding friendly reporters his version of the battle; making sure that allies like Maj. Gen. Daniel Butterfield, who cordially despised Meade (a feeling the Pennsylvanian reciprocated), were called to testify before the Joint Congressional Committee on the Conduct of the War; and in a series of articles about the battle, whose pseudonymous author "Historicus" is generally thought to be Sickles himself, the first of which was published in the *New York Herald* a week after Meade testified before the committee. But this war of innuendo and character assassination was the only additional fighting Sickles would do. Though he longed to return to his beloved III Corps, Meade was implacably opposed, and the war ended without Sickles receiving another command.

Sickles's post-war career was characteristic of the man. He returned to New York and Tammany politics, built a successful and lucrative law practice, and was appointed minister to Spain, where he was rumored to have had an affair with Queen Isabella II. He was a regular attendee at veterans' events and served for 26 years as chairman of the New York Monuments Commission, which was charged with memorializing the contributions of New York troops on the battlefields of Antietam, Gettysburg, and Chattanooga. Reelected to Congress in 1892, he helped pass the legislation that created Gettysburg National Military Park. His political opponents still liked to remind people of his checkered history, and when the *New York World* called him a pimp in print, Sickles threatened to sue for libel, causing that prolific diarist and keen observer of the New York scene, George Templeton Strong, to wearily observe, "One might as well try to spoil a rotten egg as to damage Dan's character."[10]

Through it all, he continued to propound "his side of the story of Gettysburg" to anyone who could be made to listen, and by the 1880s he had picked up an unlikely ally: his July 2 opponent, Lt. Gen. James Longstreet.

*   *   *

The man Lee called his "old war horse" may have lacked the dashing persona of J. E. B. Stuart and could boast no single, legendary feat of arms to match Stonewall Jackson's Shenandoah Valley campaign or the flank attack at Chancellorsville, but day in and day out through four years of war he had been one of the Army of Northern Virginia's hardest fighting generals, and certainly Lee's most trusted corps commander after the death of Jackson, the rock upon whom he depended. That, indeed, was the reputation with which Longstreet emerged from the war, but his views on post-war political realities, combined with Lost Cause partisans' need to craft a narrative that absolved Lee of any hint of blame for the South's defeat,

---

10 Hessler, *Sickles at Gettysburg*, 312.

soon tarnished that reputation so severely that a century and a half later it has not yet been fully restored.

The transformation began in March 1867, when the *New Orleans Times* asked a number of prominent ex-Confederates for their views on the Military Reconstruction Acts passed that month by Congress. "We are a conquered people," Longstreet responded with characteristic bluntness, urging his fellow Southerners to "accept the terms as we are in duty bound to do, and if there is a lack of good faith, let it be upon others." In itself this was unexceptionable, but three months later Longstreet released a second letter to the press in which he counseled not simply patience, but active cooperation with the Republican Party, which he saw as the only way for white Southerners to maintain sufficient power and influence to control the black vote. "It is all important that we should exercise such influence over that vote, as to prevent its being injurious to us, and we can only do that as Republicans. . . . [I]t seems to me that our duty to ourselves and to all of our friends requires that our party South should seek an alliance with the Republican party." As he wrote to R. H. Taliaferro, "My politics is to save the little that is left of us, and to go to work to improve that little as best we may."[11]

For most Southerners, however, there was no more hated group than the "Black Republicans" who now were imposing the hard hand of Radical Reconstruction upon them, and Longstreet received death threats after the publication of this second letter. The fact that only a few days after it appeared in print he finally received the federal pardon that he had applied for 18 months earlier savored of self-serving opportunism, an impression reinforced when he endorsed Republican Ulysses S. Grant for president the following year and was nominated for the post of surveyor of the port of New Orleans, at a salary of $6,000 per year, less than a week after Grant took office.

According to William Garrett Piston in *Lee's Tarnished Lieutenant: James Longstreet and His Place in Southern History*:

> If Longstreet's contemporaries had been able to judge him in a vacuum, his pragmatic approach to Reconstruction might have been appreciated, if not endorsed. But Longstreet's actions occurred at a time of intense emotional turmoil throughout the South. To explain how a righteous cause, blessed by God, could fail, former Confederates . . . cultivated what historians usually call the Lost Cause myth. . . . By making defeat seem honorable, the Lost Cause rationale heightened the South's already high concept of honor. Consequently, no

11 Jeffrey D. Wert, *General James Longstreet: The Confederacy's Most Controversial Soldier* (New York, 1993), 410-411; William Garrett Piston, *Lee's Tarnished Lieutenant: James Longstreet and His Place in Southern History* (Athens, GA, 1987), 106.

group of men ever incurred greater dishonor in the eyes of their peers than the minority of white Southerners who supported the Republicans.

"When Longstreet joined the Republicans instead of rallying to the Lost Cause," Piston notes, "he exposed not only his present motives but his Confederate past to attack."[12]

So long as Lee was alive, criticism of Longstreet focused on those present motives. But after Lee's death in October 1870, partisans of the Lost Cause, led by Jubal Early, began to develop a new line of attack. In a speech at the newly renamed Washington and Lee College in January, 1872, Early claimed that on the night of July 1, 1863, Lee had said that he intended Longstreet's Corps to attack the Federals at dawn the next day. Had Longstreet done as their chief desired, Early declared, rather than delaying his assault until late afternoon, Gettysburg would have been the decisive Confederate victory that secured Southern independence.

Longstreet did not respond publicly to the first appearance of this patent fabrication, nor for years thereafter, as Early and allies such as the Reverend William N. Pendleton, Lee's former chief of artillery, who had good reason to deflect attention from his own performance at Gettysburg, continued to insist that Longstreet had bungled Lee's plan for a dawn attack on July 2. But as Piston observes, "Early's words took on great power and the ring of authority because he told Southerners exactly what they wanted to hear. His version of Gettysburg, which blamed Longstreet, provided an explanation for the Confederacy's defeat which neither entailed the loss of God's Grace nor questioned the superiority of Southern civilization. He chose as his scapegoat a man already intensely unpopular, who was not identified with any one state and who could therefore be attacked without insulting the memory of soldiers from any part of the South."[13]

By the late 1870s, however, Longstreet could stand no more. He published a pair of articles in *McClure's*, later reprinted in *The Annals of the War Written by Leading Participants North and South*, in which he quoted extensively from letters of members of Lee's staff to thoroughly demolish the myth of the intended dawn attack. Had he stopped there, he might have done much to repair the damage to his wartime reputation, but he went on to offer a critique of his commander's performance at Gettysburg. "There is no doubt," Longstreet wrote, "that General Lee, during the crisis of that campaign, lost the matchless equipoise that usually characterized him, and that whatever mistakes were made were not so much matters of deliberate judgment as the impulses of a great mind disturbed by

---

12 Piston, *Lee's Tarnished Lieutenant*, 109-110.

13 Ibid., 119-120.

unparalleled conditions." Far from putting the controversy to rest, Longstreet's articles ignited a new wave of vituperative responses from Early, Pendleton, and others, much of it in the pages of the *Southern Historical Society Papers*. Longstreet fired back. During a trip to Antietam in 1893, he gave a long interview to Leslie J. Perry, a Union veteran and one of the compilers of *The War of the Rebellion: Official Records of the Union and Confederate Armies*, which ran in *The Washington Post*. In it, Longstreet gave what he undoubtedly felt was a balanced assessment of his old commander, which only served to further infuriate his critics. "Gen. Lee was a large-minded man, of great and profound learning in the science of war," Longstreet told Perry. "In all strategical movements he handled a great army with comprehensive ability and signal success." But after his stunning and audacious victory at Chancellorsville, "he came to have unlimited confidence in his own army, and undoubtedly exaggerated its capacity to overcome obstacles." That confidence, combined with an innate pugnacity, led to an "impatience to strike, once in the presence of the enemy, whatever the disparity of forces. . . . This trait of aggressiveness led him to take too many chances—into dangerous situations." He also pulled no punches in his assessment of his post-war nemesis. "Early's mental horizon was a limited one, and he was utterly lost beyond a regiment out of sight of his commanding general. How Gen. Lee could have been goaded into sending him down the valley with an army in 1864 I never clearly understood. I was away from the army that summer wounded. Early had no capacity for directing. He never could fight a battle; he could not have whipped Sheridan with Lee's whole army."[14]

Longstreet and Sickles met for the first time in 1888 during the celebration of the 25th anniversary of the battle of Gettysburg. It was the beginning of an unlikely friendship between two of Gettysburg's most controversial figures. Four years later, they were the guests of honor at a St. Patrick's Day dinner in Atlanta, a long and convivial evening during which a healthy amount of Irish whiskey was consumed. Sickles recalled that toward the evening's end he said to Longstreet, "Old fellow, I hope you are sorry for shooting my leg off at Gettysburg. I suppose I will have to forgive you for it some day." To which his old adversary replied, "Forgive me? You ought to thank me for leaving you one leg to stand on."[15]

The following year, they joined other high-ranking veterans from both sides, including Maj. Gen. Oliver O. Howard, Brig. Gen. William Mahone, and Brig. Gen. Edward Porter Alexander, to once again visit the battlefield, where Longstreet told a reporter from the *New York Times*, "Had not Sickles been so far out we

---

14 Longstreet, "Lee in Pennsylvania," 432; "Gen. Longstreet as a Critic," *Washington Post*, June 11, 1893.

15 Hessler, *Sickles at Gettysburg*, 337.

would have taken the Round Tops without firing a shot, and shelled the Union Army out of its position along Cemetery Hill. Even had Sickles prolonged the line of the Second Corps, his left flank would not have been heavy enough to resist an attack. . . . He was fighting as much for time as for position, and had the fight begun at the same hour, with Sickles' left covering the Round Tops, we would have had no trouble whatever in working to his rear and outflanking him." In a letter to Sickles himself, which the old reprobate made sure was reproduced and widely distributed, Longstreet wrote, "I believe it is now conceded that the advanced position at the Peach Orchard, taken by your corps and under your orders saved that battlefield to the Union cause."[16]

Sickles attempted to return the favor, penning a lengthy introduction for *Lee and Longstreet at High Tide*, Helen Longstreet's 1904 memoir and defense of her general, who died just months before it was published. Sickles characteristically managed to turn the occasion to his own advantage as well: "Longstreet was unjustly blamed for not attacking earlier in the day, on July 2. . . . I can answer that criticism, as I know more about the matter than the critics. . . . Every regiment and every battery that fired a shot in the afternoon was on the field in the morning, and would have resisted an assault in the morning as stubbornly as in the afternoon. . . . On the other hand, if Lee had waited an hour later, I would have been on Cemetery Ridge in compliance with General Meade's orders, and Longstreet could have marched, unresisted, from Seminary Ridge to the foot of Little Round Top, and might, perhaps, have unlimbered his guns on the summit."[17]

*   *   *

In November 1912, an audit of the New York Monuments Commission's books found more than $28,000 unaccounted for and suspicions turned, naturally, to its 92-year-old chairman, who was known to be in straitened financial circumstances, had no explanation for the discrepancy, and about whom rumors of financial improprieties had swirled before. (In 1904, sculptor James Kelly, who created the 6th New York Cavalry monument at Gettysburg, claimed that he had traced $60,000 of the commission's money to Sickles's private account.) Down in Georgia, Helen Longstreet heard of his distress and declared that she would "raise money among the ragged, destitute, maimed veterans who followed Lee to pay the amount demanded if the New York officials will allow sufficient time. . . . The Republic, whose battles you fought, will not permit your degradation."

16 "On Gettysburg Field Again," *New York Times*, May 1, 1893; Swanberg, *Sickles the Incredible*, 376.

17 Helen D. Longstreet, *Lee and Longstreet at High Tide* (Philadelphia, 1904), 21-22.

"The service rendered by the widow of my illustrious adversary, Lt. General Longstreet, touches my heart deeply," Sickles replied. "May God bless her and the generous and gallant Southern veterans who respond to her appeal."[18]

A warrant was issued for his arrest in January 1913, but Sickles remained free on bond while his friends worked frantically to keep him out of jail. To generate cash, he rented out apartments on the upper floors of his Fifth Avenue home, including one to New York's newly elected governor, William Sulzer, a Tammany man. In the midst of it all, Sickles found time to send a letter to the New York sheriff who had served the warrant in which he expounded on the criticism of his performance at Gettysburg, even enclosing a copy of Longstreet's letter on the subject. "You will see from the statement of General Longstreet that I won the great and decisive battle of Gettysburg," he wrote to the undoubtedly perplexed lawman. Finally, in early May, wearying of Sickles's delaying tactics and the negative publicity the case was generating, the state attorney general called off the dogs. "Sickles never did 'make good' on the full shortage," notes James A. Hessler, author of *Sickles at Gettysburg*. "He had spent the previous fifty years cultivating his war-hero image. In the end, that image combined with his ability to rally supporters saved him from the worst consequences of his chronic financial irresponsibility." It must have been with no small sense of relief that Sickles set out for Gettysburg and the reunion. "The old warrior certainly has sympathy in his misfortunes," the *Boston Globe* editorialized, "and the knowledge that he has the regard of the Boys in Blue may serve to remove some of the bitterness from his cup."[19]

Sickles arrived in Gettysburg on Sunday afternoon to find a cheering crowd of veterans and other visitors surrounding the Western Maryland station. The train, which was carrying several thousand other New York veterans, was going to continue on the spur that ran all the way out to the camp, but Sickles and his entourage, including his housekeeper, several non-veteran friends, and the Reverend Joseph H. Twichell, a former army chaplain who had been by his side

18 Hessler, *Sickles at Gettysburg*, 372-374; Letter, Daniel E. Sickles to Helen D. Longstreet, February 18, 1913, Daniel Edward Sickles Papers, Box II:2, Reel 4, Library of Congress (LOC).

19 Hessler, *Sickles at Gettysburg*, 375-376; "Editorial Points," *Boston Globe*, June 29, 1913. Sickles also had the sympathy of the central figure in a case as notorious in the first years of the new century as his own slaying of Philip Barton Key a half-century earlier. Harry K. Thaw, the obsessive, mentally unstable millionaire who murdered architect Stanford White in 1906, sent a letter to chairman James Schoonmaker of the Pennsylvania Commission from his cell in New York's Matteawan State Hospital for the Criminally Insane, in which he enclosed $1,000 in cash with which to help pay off the old general's debts. The *Philadelphia Inquirer* pronounced Schoonmaker "dumbfounded" and reported that he planned "to return the money to Thaw with a letter informing him that the Pennsylvania Commission is interested in General Sickles only to the extent of extending to him the courtesies of the State while he is within its borders and that it could not undertake to be the custodian of such a fund." See "Harry Thaw Goes to General Sickles' Aid," *Philadelphia Inquirer*, July 3, 1913.

when his leg was amputated, disembarked at the station. Sickles was helped into a waiting automobile and, accompanied by an escort of 24 troopers from the 15th U.S. Cavalry, was driven to the Rogers house on Emmitsburg Road, where he was to be the honored guest of the veterans of Carr's Brigade. In a twist that would be wildly implausible in any other man's life but was merely par for the course in Sickles's, the next day an 82-year-old resident of the Confederate Soldiers' Home in Pikesville, Maryland, arrived on the morning train from Baltimore. A veteran of Breathed's Battery of horse artillery in J. E. B. Stuart's command, he had been wounded twice, captured at Madison Court House, and spent more than a year as a prisoner of war. His name was John Francis Key, and he was the grandson of the Star-Spangled Banner's composer: the nephew of the man Sickles had murdered five and a half decades earlier.

Like Mrs. Longstreet, Sickles had agreed to provide his impressions of the great event, which would be syndicated to newspapers throughout the country; in the three dispatches he filed, he lost no opportunity to burnish his own name. He attributed the Army of the Potomac's ability to hold its position on Cemetery Hill at the end of the first day's fighting "to my arrival late in the afternoon with the first division of my corps." He complimented Maj. Gen. John F. Reynolds of the I Corps in terms that were clearly meant to reflect on another Union general as well: "He was beloved by his men, which is the final test of a competent commander." He took potshots at his old nemesis Meade: "At the end of the second day, General Meade was still pessimistic. He still believed it would be better to retreat and fight at Pipe Creek. . . . I personally have always entertained doubts whether Lee would have followed us to Pipe Creek and offered battle."[20]

He began his July 2 piece with characteristic modesty:

The thronging hordes who have motored and walked and trolleyed to my camp today have swept there [sic] hats off and hailed it as "Sickles Day."

And so I have always regarded July 2nd.

It was on this day a half-century ago that God gave me strength to serve my country and my Maker, better than I had ever been able to serve them before.

It was upon this day in '63 that I lost my leg and did my little part by the mercy of God to preserve the Union. . . .

Meade never had been in favor of giving battle at Gettysburg and I knew that he would order me to leave my position and move to Pipe Creek, where he intended to battle. . . .

---

20 "Sickles Contrasts Battlefield of '63 with Present Scene," *Philadelphia Inquirer*, July 2, 1913; "Sickles Tells of His Bitter Fight on July 2nd, 1863," *Philadelphia Inquirer*, July 3, 1913.

Let me call attention right here to the fact that if I had not taken the initiative our left would have been lost. Longstreet said I won the battle by my advance move. Sheridan said so, and Grant indorsed the former's opinion.[21]

Mrs. Longstreet added her endorsement as well, in her signature purple prose: "The tragic figure of this great reunion is the grim warrior whose life blood on these wind-swept fields, on the fateful July day 50 years ago, cemented forever the indissoluble union of indestructible States." Ignoring the prominent role that he had played in planning the reunion in order to heighten the pathos of the moment, she declared, "Sickles, perhaps was not formally bidden. He was not placed on the program. He was probably not expected. But he came because he could not help coming." She continued:

It was his victory. It is his field. The dim-eyed boys in gray and the maimed heroes in blue gather about him and touch his hands reverently. They have forgotten the trials and tribulations of the twilight years of the citizen. Sickles is in the saddle once more. Ancient history lingers over the name and deeds of the warrior who conquered the Orient and contended with mighty Caesar for the empire of the world. At last, conquered, betrayed, murdered, Pompey lay unburied under the sad Egyptian stars, on the desolate Egyptian strand. Caesar stood beside the lifeless body and wept.

Today a nation may weep for its forgetfulness of the commander who won Gettysburg for the Union.[22]

The *Philadelphia Inquirer*, weary from five decades of defending hometown hero George Meade against Sickles's slanders and exasperated by an editorial in the *New York Sun* "in which not only does Meade's name not once appear, but the lame and impotent conclusion is averred that 'it was a corps commanders' battle," fired back:

Sickles had been ordered thrice to maintain the line to Little Round Top. He moved forward to the Emmitsburg Road against orders, as he expressly avowed, and because he believed that this was for the best—although it nearly wrecked the plans of Meade. To this extent only was it a corps commanders' battle on the second day. But to remedy this disobedience of orders Meade took entire command and sent to all parts of the field, bringing to the point of danger troops from nearly every position of the army . . .

21 "Sickles Tells of His Bitter Fight on July 2nd, 1863."

22 "As Mrs. Longstreet Sees It," *Baltimore Sun*, July 2, 1913.

Had not a man of Meade's caliber been in command there might have been another defeat. . . .

This is a day to honor Meade, whose abilities and services have been all too greatly dimmed by subsequent events over which he had no control and by personal jealousies exercised against him and favoritism shown others to an extent which nearly broke his proud heart, though he never uttered a public murmur.[23]

Every day a steady stream of visitors from both armies made their way to the Rogers house to pay their respects to Sickles. Patrick McManus, who at age six had emigrated with his family from their home near Enneskillen, Ireland, and at 19 enlisted in the 71st New York, was one of them. "What joy welled in my heart when I beheld my old commander," he said. "Standing at attention I saluted and to the grizzled old hero I said: 'God bless you, General Sickles, my old commander. I am Pat McManus, one of your old soldier boys.'" At which Sickles exclaimed, "Little Paddy McManus, the brave young Irish lad, who was so good and thoughtful of his mother—come here and let me take your hand. . . . [I]t does my heart good to meet you after fifty long years."

Sickles then told those gathered around how McManus, with a premonition of his death before the battle of Chancellorsville, had given the chaplain $20 and asked that he see that it was delivered to his widowed mother in Newark, New Jersey. McManus was wounded but survived the battle, and the chaplain returned the money to him, saying, "There, Paddy my boy, take the money home to your dear old mother yourself, and may God bless and keep you."

At least that is how McManus related the encounter to a reporter for the *Trenton Times*, though he elided a few details in the telling. He had actually been wounded near the North Anna River in May 1864, not at Chancellorsville, where he had been captured and spent four months as a prisoner of war. After the war, he worked as a hatter, and later as a guard at the New Jersey State Prison. The reporter also noted, without further editorial comment, that McManus was "a writer of clever poetry, most of his verses being on the Civil War. He took the New York *Herald's* cash prize of $100 for writing the best war story a year or two ago."[24]

Thaddeus Kenderdine's impression of Paddy's old commander was somewhat different. "Among a host of others I shook hands with him," he wrote, "but with reservations; the greeting being more like that with a corpse, so helpless he seemed as he lay back in his Morris chair trying to smoke. He had a suite of four with

23 "Meade at Gettysburg," *Philadelphia Inquirer*, July 2, 1913.

24 "Gallant Old Gen'l 'Dan' Sickles at Gettysburg Reunion Praised Brave 'Pat' M'Manus of Trenton," *Trenton Times*, July 9, 1913; Patrick F. McManus pension file and CMSR, NARA.

Major General Daniel E. Sickles, the last surviving corps commander who fought at Gettysburg, signs an autograph for one of the countless visitors who flocked to see him at the reunion. *Library of Congress*

him, trained nurses and their aids. One of the nurses was fanning him, while the other, with an aid's help, was trying to light his cigar. . . . I pitied him as he lay back in his chair in the door yard, a curious throng constantly on the stare around him, a passerby from his old command coming through it now and then to shake his limp, passive hand and listen to the mumbling words from the heat-oppressed, weary man."[25]

If age and health kept Sickles largely confined to the front porch of the Rogers house, Helen Longstreet seemed to be everywhere, interviewing veterans, gathering colorful impressions of the great event, and always reminding readers of her late husband's role. "All the fighting worthy of the name for the Southern cause at Gettysburg on July 2 and 3, 1863, was made by Longstreet," she declared. "General Longstreet was the hardest fighter in the Confederate service. He was easily the superior of Lee as an offensive tactician. The great Virginian, in his impatience to strike, once in the presence of the enemy, sometimes lost his equipoise. Military critics agree that Lee perhaps had no equal on either side as a defensive fighter. Lee had proved himself well nigh invincible before his invasion of Pennsylvania, and when reconciled to the single purpose of defensive fighting. But of the art of war comprehended in offensive fighting, Lee was not a master and this defect wrecked the Southern cause on the rocks of Cemetery Ridge half a century ago."[26]

She made her way to the Rogers house and at her approach, Sickles "arose and bowed deeply. He took the greatest pleasure in the dramatic situation and the utmost satisfaction in being permitted on this anniversary and at that spot of spots to tell Longstreet's widow what a splendid and noble enemy her husband was. Of course, he took the first opportunity of pointing out . . . with his crutch that particular place in the wheat field lying before them where that ball shattered his leg." Later, as she walked back up the Emmitsburg Road toward the great camp, she fell in with Sarah, "a little woman with faded eyes" who told her, "I just couldn't help coming. Jim was killed along here somewhere. I think it must have been about here." When Mrs. Longstreet asked if Jim had been the woman's husband, she quickly replied, "Oh no, he was just my sweetheart, but I told him that I would wait until he came back. I won't have much longer to wait now. He did not come back to me, but I am going to him." Sarah was not alone in making her pilgrimage to Gettysburg. "The unidentified graves of the dead seem to attract these women," a *Richmond Times-Dispatch* reporter observed, "and one sees them standing by hours looking at these unmarked mounds in the walk leading around the graves of the unknown. . . . In front of one of these tablets was seated an old

25 Kenderdine, "After Fifty Years," Part 2, *Newtown Enterprise*, July 19, 1913.

26 "As Mrs. Longstreet Sees It," *Baltimore Sun*, July 5, 1913.

woman, her hair snow white, her form bent with age. Somewhere among those nameless mounds was the grave of one she sought."[27]

"The hardship, the suffering, the agony of the women who waited in the war homes of the nation may never be told," Mrs. Longstreet wrote. "Some day a grateful Government will erect a monument that will pierce the blue heavens from Gettysburg's stateliest, sunniest slope, and on it will stand the figure of one in whose courageous soul every battle was fought and every victory won—the women who placed the flag of her faith in the hands of her best loved and sent it to the front when the first gun was fired on Fort Sumter."[28]

Helen Longstreet was not alone in advocating a memorial to the women of the Civil War, an idea that had been discussed off and on for at least 20 years. Just days before the opening of the great reunion, Alfred B. Beers, commander-in-chief of the GAR, had told those attending the Department of Pennsylvania's annual encampment that he supported building a monument at Gettysburg "to the wives, mothers, sisters and sweethearts who suffered untold anguish at home while husbands, sons, brothers and lovers fought and died for the cause in which they unhesitatingly took up arms." Union veteran Walter Blake thought Congress should appropriate money "to erect on the most beautiful spot in Gettysburg a monument which should commemorate adequately the heroism of the mothers of '61 to '65." The final two pages of his book about the 1913 reunion described in detail the elements that should be part of this monument and its dedication ceremony, including a nationwide moment of silence. "As a mark of respect, at the moment when this climax of sculpture is unveiled, let every wheel in the factories of the nation be still, let the business of the country cease, and men everywhere in this fair land . . . stand with uncovered heads as they pay tribute to the holiest thing which God ever created, a mother-heart." In October 1913, a Congress with a somewhat more modest vision decided to kill two birds with one stone and passed a bill appropriating $400,00 toward the construction of a new headquarters for the American Red Cross in Washington, which would also serve as a memorial to the women of the Civil War. The appropriation represented a bit less than half the total project cost, the remainder of which was to be raised from private donations. Construction began in 1915 and was completed in 1917. Inscribed above the

---

27 "55,000 Veterans Defy Great Heat," *New-York Tribune*, July 2, 1913; "Mrs. Longstreet with Blue and Gray," *New York Times*, July 2, 1913; "Reunion Is Held by Army Nurses," *Richmond Times-Dispatch*, July 3, 1913.

28 "Mrs. Longstreet with Blue and Gray."

columns that frame the main entrance to the building are the words, "In memory of the heroic women of the Civil War."[29]

While Mrs. Longstreet toiled with the other reporters, Robert Lee Longstreet, who like his stepmother had been born in the same year as the battle, was shepherding his nephews, James Longstreet Welchel and John E. Welchel, around the famous field. "I would be derelict in memory to my father," the Spanish-American War veteran said, "did I not attend the present reunion with my only sister's children, both of whom are imbued with the military spirit." Three of Meade's granddaughters and two of Pickett's grandsons also attended the reunion.

"My only regret in connection with the present celebration," said Longstreet, "is that my father did not live to be present. Thirty years ago he, with General Sickles of the Federal Army, and several comrades from both sides met at Gettysburg and held a small reunion. They prophesied that some day such a great reunion as is now about to take place would be seen. It is my belief that then was started the movement which has resulted in this great patriotic celebration."[30]

29 "Confederacy's Flag Flies at Gettysburg," *Baltimore Sun*, June 28, 1913; Blake, *Hand Grips*, 212-214.

30 "Sons and Grandsons of Gen. Longstreet," *Atlanta Constitution*, June 30, 1913; "Maryland Is First with Stars and Bars," *Baltimore Sun*, June 30, 1913.

Chapter 6

Remembering and Reshaping the Past

As Landis Travis set off that Wednesday morning on what would prove to be his final walk, other veterans were lining up at the camp's field kitchens to fill their tin plates with a breakfast of fried eggs, bacon, hash browns, applesauce, and freshly baked bread and butter. "I don't reckon the folks at home will believe me when I tell them how fine I've been treated here," said C. P. Deering of the 28th Virginia. "You can't get at any hotel such food as we've had." Breakfast was served each day from 6:30 to 8:00 a.m., dinner from noon to 1:30 p.m., and supper from 5:30 to 7:00 p.m. The fare was hearty—beef stew, roast mutton, hamburger steaks in gravy, all washed down with tin cups full of hot coffee and iced tea—and plentiful. "We had good things to eat and plenty of it," said Michael J. McGuire of the 15th Alabama, who had been captured in that regiment's fierce fight with the 20th Maine on Little Round Top, "and the man who went to the reunion and says he didn't get enough to eat was simply a hog."[1]

There were a few dissenters, especially among the Connecticut veterans for some reason. "The coffee is abominable," one wrote. "The food would shock a pirate." According to the *New-York Tribune*, "Telegrams state that many of the Connecticut delegation are leaving in disgust, complaining of dirty cooks, filthy dishes and unsanitary conditions which they fear will make them all ill if they remain." And Jessie P. Rich of the School of Domestic Economy at the University

1 "Pickett's Charge Fifty Years After," *New York Times*, July 4, 1913; "M. J. McGuire Tells of His Trip to Gettysburg," *Montgomery Advertiser*, July 7, 1913.

The camp's 173 field kitchens served up vast quantities of food during the reunion. This group of veterans is joined by one of the Regulars who were responsible for the smooth operation of the camp, as well as a friend hoping for some leftovers. *Pennsylvania State Archives*

of Texas thought the menus ill-suited for septuagenarians in the suffocating heat of a Gettysburg July. "Fried foods are hard to digest, and all fatty foods are heat producers," she told the *Dallas Morning News*. "There were no fresh fruits . . . to give the cooling acids or needed laxative for these sedentary people."[2]

Jacob Raab of the 14th Brooklyn disagreed. "The boys who take care of their stomachs get along alright," he declared. "If they give way to the hospitality shown them they get their innards all wrong and so have only themselves to blame." A Confederate veteran was blunter in his dismissal of the critics. "Some seemed to think the food should have been ordered direct from the Waldorf Astoria," he said. "It is not to be expected that all the idiots are dead."[3]

2 "Report Camp in Bad Shape," *New-York Tribune*, July 4, 1913; "Criticism Made of Menu at Gettysburg," *Dallas Morning News*, July 13, 1913.

3 "Veteran Raab Back from Gettysburg," *Jersey Journal*, July 3, 1913; "Impressions from Gettysburg," *The Daily Progress*, July 9, 1913.

Nonetheless, the heat, the crowding, the lack of bathing facilities, and the aches and pains inevitable for men in their eighth decade spending nights under canvas on army cots, were combining to cause some veterans—the *New York Times* estimated 10,000 in all by Wednesday—to pack up and head for home. "I told my wife I'd be back on the fifth," said Tony Bauer of GAR Post 97 in Wilkes-Barre, Pennsylvania, "but she will be glad to see me tomorrow. She told me before I left that it was too much for an old man like me. I told her I was an old soldier, but it's too much for an old soldier, even."[4]

For the press, of course, there was no question of going home before the last veteran decamped on Saturday, and though the first night's bottleneck at the Western Union office had been unclogged, the scramble for stories and bits of camp color to fill each day's budget of copy was relentless. The *Jersey Journal* found a Delaware veteran contentedly smoking a pipe with a sparrow perched upon the stem and reported that "since he was 12 he was able to tame squirrels and quail in a few hours" and had done so many times to entertain his comrades during the war. A Yank and a Reb were said to have purchased a hatchet in a local hardware store and buried it on the battlefield, either at Devil's Den or the Angle, depending on which account one read. Harry Hall, a color bearer in the 114th Pennsylvania—Robert Kenderdine's regiment—drew plenty of attention as he walked through camp in his Zouave uniform: bright red trousers, blue jacket, and a red fez. Slightly less colorful was Alexander Hunter of Virginia. When the Associated Press erroneously reported that the Confederate battle flag would be barred from the encampment, Hunter had declared, "If the battle flag is obnoxious, the ragged gray uniform must be equally so. They go together, one and inseparable. . . . As for myself, I feel that all the soul, all the sentiment, all the entente cordial of the reunion has been shattered by that 'no battle flag' order. No Gettysburg for me." But come he did, dressed in "the identical suit and hat which he wore at Gettysburg fifty years ago. The suit is in rags and has a bullet hole through one of the sleeves. He carries all his accoutrements used at Gettysburg and wears a Union belt taken from a foe at Gettysburg."[5]

Several reporters turned up claimants to the title of youngest veteran, including 65-year-old W. K. Benjamin from New York and 64-year-old William Schoenleber from Pennsylvania, but the winner was 61-year-old Col. John L. Clem of the Regular Army, known to posterity as "the Drummer Boy of Shiloh" for his

4 "It's Too Much for An Old Soldier Is New Countersign," *Harrisburg Patriot*, July 1, 1913.

5 "Veterans Wilt Under the Heat," *Jersey Journal*, July 3, 1913; "Tented Gettysburg Swept by Storm," *New York Times*, July 3, 1913; "Blinded by Rain," *Los Angeles Times*, July 3, 1913; "Zouave Uniform," *Adams County News*, July 5, 1913; "Battle Uniform," *Adams County News*, July 5, 1913; Alexander Hunter, letter to the editor, *Baltimore Sun*, June 28, 1913.

youthful exploits in that battle. There was less controversy about the oldest veteran present. Micajah Weiss, who had served as a teamster in the 141st Pennsylvania, was variously reported as being 110 or 112 years old. A farmer and lumberman for most of his life, Weiss "never used tobacco in any form, though he had a glass of whiskey whenever he felt like it." He had outlived three wives and was driven to Gettysburg from his home in Sullivan County, New York, accompanied by his fourth, a 70-year-old "earnest woman of German descent, who speaks but broken English." Not surprisingly, when the car arrived it was mobbed "by a dozen special correspondents and fully half the camera men on the field," who did not rest until they could bring Weiss and Clem together for a photograph.[6]

No fewer than 30 press photographers were present in camp and according to the *Harrisburg Telegraph*, they "have probably covered more ground than any of the other newspaper men here, for they have been ordered to all parts of the battlefield, national cemetery, the town of Gettysburg, historic homes and a dozen other places, but their collection of photographs will be the most valuable things on the grounds." The composition of those images sometimes called for a little effort and imagination on the part of the photographers. "The old soldiers have been made to do foolish things, too, as they say, for the life of the newspapers of the country. Press photographers have placed them in all kinds of poses from the now familiar hand shake to a position dancing an old fashioned jig. But after all they seem to enjoy their experiences and when newspapers are brought into the grounds they are sought after almost as much as cold water. When they find their pictures they immediately place big orders for mailing to show the folks at home what these 'young scamps' have been doing to them."[7]

A *New York Times* reporter was fortunate enough to come upon H. W. Berryman, a veteran of the 1st Texas, who had brought to the reunion a letter he had written to his mother on July 9, 1863, and carefully preserved for half a century. "Dear Mother, Sister, and Family," it began, "It is the will of God that Newt and myself are permitted to write you all again, bearing the news to you of our good health, but it is not so with all. Poor Mort Murphy was killed in making one of the most gallant charges ever made by the First Texas." It went into that day's story verbatim. A correspondent from the *Richmond Times-Dispatch* discovered the camp's lost and found, located under the stands in the great tent, where "crutches seem to be the most losable of all the veterans' possessions. There are at least a

---

6 "Pickett's Charge Fifty Years After"; "Veteran Aged 112 Autos 240 Miles," *Philadelphia Inquirer*, July 3, 1913; "Comrade, Aged 110, Arrives on Field Tired but Happy," *Harrisburg Patriot*, July 2, 1913; Micajah Weiss pension file, NARA.

7 "Veterans Like to be Photographed," *Harrisburg Telegraph*, July 3, 1913.

Micajah Weiss, variously reported to be 110 or 112 years old, and Col. John L. Clem, 61, were respectively the oldest and youngest veterans at the reunion. *Pennsylvania State Archives*

hundred piled up in the bureau, with only a dozen or so applicants for them. Those who come to redeem their lost crutches seldom can recognize them, and most of them go away with somebody else's." Also waiting to be reclaimed: a wooden leg and several sets of false teeth. "A Vermont veteran came in yesterday, asking for his teeth, which he had dropped from his pocket after he had removed them for comfort. He looked over the collection, but could not identify any set as his. He wanted to try them on, so as to establish his right to possession, but his request was refused." The daily *Gettysburg Times* was filled with ads for lost watches, walking sticks, cameras, railroad tickets, and occasionally a more eye-catching item such as this: "LOST: John Runner, Marcus, W. Va.; brown checked suit, brown felt hat, mustache and chin whiskers; about 5 feet 8 inches tall; G.A.R. badge, Co. E, 15th Virginia Reg't. If found, have him report at West Virginia Headquarters." Runner's name does not appear among the reunion's death toll, so it may be hoped that he was ultimately reunited with his comrades.[8]

When it came to stories of heartwarming reunions between foes parted for 50 years, the time-honored reporter's rule of thumb, "too good to check," seemed to be in full force. A Pennsylvania veteran claimed to have met the Reb who had cut off his arm—with a bayonet—in hand-to-hand fighting at the "High Water Mark." Orlando Douglass, a North Carolinian, told James Schoonmaker that he distinctly recalled taking a shot at him during the battle, while I. N. Roberts, a Confederate from Missouri, said he had met a Yank "who declared he recognized me as the Reb who had shot at him three times during the fight here. I apologized to him for my poor marksmanship and said I was sorry that I had not done a better job."[9]

Other reporters, through a combination of carelessness, credulousness, and ignorance of history, swallowed even taller tales, which they dutifully relayed to their readers. Hugh Mellen of the 147th New York described being wounded early on the morning of July 1 and taken to a makeshift field hospital on the second floor of the Western Maryland Railroad station in town, from a window in which, "several hours later, I think it was about 10 o'clock, I saw General Reynolds shot from his horse . . . on the Chambersburg pike about 100 yards from the station." Mellen may have seen a Union officer unhorsed near the depot, and Reynolds was indeed killed around 10:00 a.m., but he was felled by a Confederate bullet on McPherson's Ridge, almost a mile away. James Kirkland of the 53rd Virginia averred that he had been shot seven times during Pickett's Charge, finally falling

8 "Tented Gettysburg Swept by Storm"; "Camp at Gettysburg is Full of Oddities," *Richmond Times-Dispatch*, July 4, 1913; advertisement, *Gettysburg Times*, July 3, 1913.

9 "Took Off His Arm," *Adams County News*, July 5, 1913; "Missed His Shot," *Adams County News*, July 5, 1913; "Pathetic Night Scene in Veterans' Great Reunion," *Pittsburgh Press*, July 1, 1913.

just before reaching the wall at the Angle, while another Confederate told the *Richmond Times-Dispatch* that upon revisiting that same wall (which the reporter described as being "below Little Round Top") for the first time since the battle, he had been struck blind. "I have made my peace with God," he said, "and I have made my peace with the Yankees, whom I once damned, and I am a supremely happy man. This darkness, this inability to see again my beloved Southland, is terrible, but I accept it."[10]

The *Philadelphia Inquirer*, however, outdid them all with the story of "William H. Whitney of Carthage, N.Y., [who] has witnessed in his life the two most famous events in modern warfare. The first was the desperate charge of Pickett's men at Gettysburg, and the second the verse-famed charge of the Light Brigade at Balaklava." The reporter described in breathless detail how Whitney enlisted "as a boy" in the 6th New York and served through the end of the war. "But the lust for battle grew upon him again and with the outbreak of the struggle between Russia and the allied British and French powers he sailed for Liverpool and joined a division commanded by Sir DeLacy Evans. Whitney served in the hottest battles of the Crimea. He was at Sevastopol, Balaklava and Adan, and joined in the terrific assault upon the redoubts at Redan."[11]

There was just one small problem, of course. The Crimean War had ended in 1856.

With marks such as this reporter wandering the field, it was only natural that some veterans would decide to have a bit of fun with them. And so it transpired that the *Philadelphia Inquirer* (the absence of by-lines makes it impossible to determine whether the same scribe who misplaced the Crimean War was responsible) related "the meeting of the two George W. Anthonys, who pumped bullets at each other in the battle of Fredericksburg and today walked arm in arm under the banner of peace."

> Strangely enough, both Anthonys live in cities of the same name. One is a wealthy merchant in Burlington, N.J., and served in the One-hundred-and-tenth Pennsylvania Infantry. The other is a lumber dealer in Burlington, N.C., and was a member of the Sixth North Carolina. Through letters becoming mixed because of the similarity of name and address, they learned of each other's existence recently, and today the "Johnny" Anthony hunted up Anthony the "Yank," and for the rest of the morning the man in gray and the man in blue sat under an American flag at Parker Grubb Post headquarters and swapped

---

10 "Touching Scenes as Veterans Tour Field," *Philadelphia Inquirer*, June 30, 1913; "Seven Times Wounded," *Boston Globe*, July 2, 1913; "Blindness Comes on Battlefield," *Richmond Times-Dispatch*, July 4, 1913.

11 "Veteran of Two Bitter Wars at the Reunion," *Philadelphia Inquirer*, July 3, 1913.

war yarns of the great battles in which they faced each other as deadly enemies half a century ago. Later, with equal magnanimity, the Northern Anthony visited his Southern friend in the Confederate camp and there they held another reception among the men in gray.[12]

It was, indeed, a postal mix-up that had led George Anthony of the 6th North Carolina and George Anthony, who had enlisted as drummer boy in the 110th Pennsylvania at age 16, to discover each other's existence, but that discovery had been made five years earlier, and they met for the first time in December 1908. After relating this slightly edited version of the truth to the *Inquirer*'s man, the two concluded it was still somewhat lacking in the drama demanded by an occasion of such historic importance. So they renamed themselves "John Carson" and ambled over to the press tents, where they announced that they had met for the very first time *that day*, completely by accident, near the High Water Mark monument on Cemetery Ridge, and discovered the remarkable coincidence of their names and hometowns. That this version of their story moved on the Associated Press wire and appeared in papers around the country was no doubt a source of great satisfaction to them.[13]

Fifty years on, the urge to embroider one's war record just a bit was difficult to resist. "I ain't seen a Reb yet who didn't charge Round Top and take it all by himself," one Southerner observed to a Pennsylvania veteran. "No, and I ain't seen a Yank who didn't break up Pickett's charge by his own self," the Union man replied.[14] Finley Peter Dunne, a popular American humorist of the late nineteenth and early twentieth centuries, poked some gentle fun at the many individual reunions reported to have occurred on the battlefield, through the voice of his most famous creation, Mr. Dooley, a saloonkeeper on Chicago's South Side. In a nationally syndicated piece published two weeks after the reunion, Mr. Dooley opined thus:

> Th' other day a lot iv ol' lads that had fought at th' battle iv Gettysburg wint back to look over th' field an' pint out to each other th' place where they'd shtud durin' Pickett's charge. They'd meet together an' wan ol' fellow wud go up to a perfect sthranger an' say: "Ain't ye the Jawnny Reb that I had th' saber dool with on th' hill?" An' says th' other: "Well, I vow if ye ain't th' Yank that I carried on me back to th' ol' barn afther I'd martally wounded ye." "Sure I am; an' d'ye remember how whin ye lay dyin' I crawled on me hands an' knees

12 "Two Anthonys Meet After Fifty Years," *Philadelphia Inquirer*, July 3, 1913.

13 "Same Name, Same Lives," *New York Times*, December 6, 1908; "Odd Coincidence," *Adams County News*, July 5, 1913; "Scorching Heat Drives 6,000 Veterans Home," *Buffalo Evening News*, July 1, 1913.

14 "'Go As You Please' in Camp," *Kansas City Star*, June 30, 1913.

to th' well an' fetched ye wather in a goord?" An' so they go on gossipin', an' it don't make anny diff'rence if this is th' first time in their lives they've iver clapped eyes on each other, th' feelin' is just th' same. An' they hobble away an' have a toddy or maybe a sunsthroke together.[15]

As Dixon Wecter observed 30 years later in *When Johnny Comes Marching Home*, "The civilian . . . with his preoccupations that looked so puny against the horizons of Gettysburg, tempted the soldier's satire, just as the former's idle curiosity about blood and battle provoked the telling of tall tales. . . . A couple of generations later, doughboys in France would sometimes avow their ambition after the war 'to go home and out-lie the G.A.R.' It was the veteran's ageless right."[16]

The *Richmond Times-Dispatch*'s editorial page took a dimmer view. "[I]t is morally certain that there are many at Gettysburg now as veterans of the battle who never saw Gettysburg before. There are braggarts who now wear the blue and who now wear the gray, who have done most of their fighting since the termination of hostilities. Camp followers and home guards have been ripened by the passage of time into captains who charged into the cannon's mouth. Colonel Mosby said at a reunion of the Mosby Rangers a year or so ago that he met there several 'rangers' that he never saw before, and doubtless the same thing is true across Mason and Dixon's line."[17]

*   *   *

The doings in the big tent, which leaned heavily toward windy orations by politicians and professional veterans, offered less scope for human interest reporting but were no less revealing in their own way. On Wednesday morning, two dozen individual regiment and state reunions took place, while the afternoon was devoted to Military Day, the second of the four larger themed exercises—along with Veterans Day on Tuesday, Governors Day on Thursday, and National Day on Friday, July 4—arranged by the Pennsylvania Commission.

One theme that ran strongly through the four days of speechmaking was the enormous historical importance of the reunion, which veteran and non-veteran observers alike thought was destined to be remembered forever alongside the battle itself and Lincoln's dedicatory address at the National Cemetery four months later. "Once again is Gettysburg the center of the world's attention," proclaimed Secretary of War Garrison during Tuesday's opening ceremonies. Governor Tener thought

---

15 "Mr. Dooley on Peace," *Lexington* [KY] *Leader*, July 20, 1913.

16 Dixon Wecter, *When Johnny Comes Marching Home* (Westport, CT, 1944), 131.

17 "Very Close to Gettysburg," *Richmond Times-Dispatch*, July 3, 1913.

the reunion was "unmatched in all of recorded time; for nowhere in history have men who opposed each other in mighty battle thus come together in peaceful reunion fifty years thereafter, all content with the result of the struggle and grateful that in defeat or victory, there was left no stain upon American manhood, and no question as to the bravery or devotion to duty of the American soldier." Mrs. Longstreet felt that the "sunny July days of 1913 are scarcely less momentous in the splendor of their promise than the stormy days of 1863, which decreed that the young nation which rose without shame should fall, but fall without dishonor."[18]

"[T]hese splendid statues of marble and granite and bronze shall finally crumble to dust, and in the ages to come, will perhaps be forgotten," intoned Dr. Nathaniel Cox, chairman of Indiana's Gettysburg Reunion Commission, during a meeting of the state's veterans in the big tent on Wednesday, "but the spirit that has called this great assembly of our people together, on this field, shall live forever. . . . There is no record in all history, where half a century afterwards, the survivors of opposing armies met on the same field in friendship, affection and brotherly love, rejoicing with each other, that peace has already come to our beloved land. That great patriot who loved his country and his fellowman, who stood on these hills a half century ago, and dedicated this hallowed ground in simple language that will live forever, had a vision of this scene, when he uttered these prophetic words, 'This nation, under God, shall have a new birth of freedom, and that government of the people, by the people, and for the people, shall not perish from the earth.'"[19]

Speakers repeatedly returned to the tenets of the Lost Cause myth. They stressed that each side had fought for the right as they understood it, with the South taking arms to defend states' rights and not slavery, and referred only in passing to emancipation as an important outcome; the emphasis was on restoration of the Union, to which the onetime foes were all now said to be equally devoted. "Those who honestly believed that the United States was a voluntary association of independent sovereign states, met in irrepressible conflict those who honestly believed that the United States was an indissoluable union of otherwise independent states," noted Secretary of War Garrison. "Each side, with all the earnestness of those whose hearts, minds and consciences are committed to an ideal, sought to mold the Government to their respective views. There was no earthly tribunal before which this great issue could be tried and determined." And now they had returned to Gettysburg, according to Governor Tener, "not to commemorate a victory, but rather to emphasize the spirit of national brotherhood and national

18 *Pennsylvania Commission Report*, 98, 101; "As Mrs. Longstreet Sees It," *Baltimore Sun*, July 2, 1913.

19 *Pennsylvania Commission Report*, 115.

unity, which, in the years since the close of that War, has enabled this Republic to move forward and upward, until today she leads the nations of the earth in all that makes for the advancement and uplift of the human race."[20]

One of the few speakers who did broach the subject of slavery was the Reverend Newell Dwight Hillis, pastor of Plymouth Church in Brooklyn, Henry Ward Beecher's old pulpit, and even he reduced slavery to a subordinate role in bringing on the war. In his remarks during the New York Day celebration of that state's veterans on Thursday, Hillis said, "Thoughtful men distinguish between the occasion of war and the cause of the conflict. The occasion of an explosion is a spark, but the cause is in the powder and the air. . . . The occasion of the Rebellion was slavery, but the cause of the war was the attempt to overthrow a government conceived in liberty, and dedicated to the proposition that all men are free and equal. . . . [T]he occasion of the war was slavery, but the cause of the war was the love of the Union." Edward A. Pollard would have nodded approvingly. In Hillis's telling, slavery seemed more like an impersonal force that had held half the nation in thrall rather than the product of human agency. "Slavery was a cancer that had fixed itself upon the vitals of the South, and God anointed the soldier to be the surgeon to cut away the deadly disease, that liberty might recover her youth and beauty."[21]

North Carolina veteran John C. Scarborough, who spoke during Wednesday's Military Day program, offered yet another pillar of the Lost Cause, the contented slave:

> We were afraid that the negroes would rise behind us. That is the way we felt in North Carolina. . . . But now I want to say that our fears were all misplaced. Because the negro was as quiet and safe and as thoroughly imbued with the idea of the principle that was involved, and was as loyal to the South as he was to his master and his mistress, and as they were loyal to the cause. The negro knew what the war was for. My father's negroes knew what it was for, and every other man's negroes knew what it was for, and they knew if the North succeeded that they would be free. Through all the war there was not a negro that stirred from the field, unless he was requested to do so, and not a negro ever raised his hand against a master or mistress in our State or in any of the Southern States, and thus our fears were misplaced.[22]

20 Ibid., 99-100, 101.

21 "Address of Rev. Newell Dwight Hillis, D. D.," *Fiftieth Anniversary of the Battle of Gettysburg 1913: Report of the New York State Commission* (Albany, NY, 1916), 36, 29.

22 *Pennsylvania Commission Report*, 125. The South's enslaved people may not have risen in open rebellion, but tens of thousands risked everything to escape, enlist in the Union army, and return to fight for the freedom of those they left behind. And as David Blight writes, "Lost to near oblivion

In *Baptized in Blood*, Charles Wilson Reagan writes,

> Southerners refused to admit that God's displeasure with the peculiar institution was the cause of Southern defeat. They never abandoned the belief that slavery was a divinely ordained institution, or the idea that Southerners had helped Christianize the Negroes, which seemed to be God's plan in bringing Africans to America. . . . [W]hen it became apparent that the slaves would be freed, many Southerners assumed that God was displeased not with the institution itself, but with the Southern agents of divinity. As Robert L. Dabney said immediately after defeat, God had taken from Southerners, and given to Northerners, the responsibility for civilizing and Christianizing the heathen Negro."[23]

By the turn of the twentieth century, it was widely accepted that during the Reconstruction years, Northerners had approached that responsibility not only with reckless haste but also with a vindictive spirit toward the white population of the South. "Carpet-bag rule, with the negro as its facile and ignorant instrument, inaugurated a new system of debauchery and crime," wrote Thomas Nelson Page, a Virginia lawyer and prolific author of short stories that idealized antebellum plantation life. The popular historian James Ford Rhodes, in his seven-volume *History of the United States from the Compromise of 1850*, declared, "No large policy in our country has ever been so conspicuous a failure as that of forcing universal negro suffrage upon the South." That conclusion would be reinforced by Columbia University's William A. Dunning and his numerous acolytes until, as David Blight writes, "The victors of Southern redemption over Yankee carpetbaggery and treachery held as high a place in national memory as the victors at Gettysburg or Appomattox." And so in 1913, after praising the foes who had "fought bravely and well upon this historic field," Robert Drummond could go on to urge his fellow veterans of the 111th New York "to recognize before the whole world their splendid efforts to raise a devastated country from its ruin and ashes, their long fight to wrest their land from the hands of those who had taken possession of it for the purposes of greed and gain; and we are ready to admit that in their lives and their respective states and localities, the soldiers of both the blue and the gray became good citizens all worthy in the best and highest sense of the word American." "The reconstruction days were the real war," a Mississippi veteran told Mrs. Longstreet as he pumped a drink of water for her behind the Rogers house.

---

in white memory by the early twentieth century were the countless wartime testimonies of planters about the 'defections' and 'betrayals' of their most trusted slaves." David W. Blight, *Race and Reunion: The Civil War in American Memory* (Cambridge, MA, 2001), 287.

23 Charles Wilson Reagan, *Baptized in Blood: The Religion of the Lost Cause, 1865-1920* (Athens, GA, 1980), 68-69.

"Nothing saved us from utter ruin but the Ku Klux Klan, and I am proud to say that I was a member of it."[24]

Scarborough, the North Carolina veteran who now served as his state's superintendent of public schools, assured the crowd in the big tent that the work so imprudently begun during Reconstruction remained unfinished. "The colored man is here," he said, "because of the greed of the white man. Therefore, now that he is free, we must treat him with a view to making a good citizen out of him. You of the North sympathize with the people of the South, and are helping us bear the awful burden. We owe it to the negro. God Almighty has helped us in our trial and aided us in dismissing all the hate from our hearts. God has helped the Southerner and will help this great Nation. He will vouchsafe His blessing to make us stand in the forefront." Most of his listeners probably nodded in agreement. For 20 years or more, through minstrel shows and magazine features and popular literature like Joel Chandler Harris's Uncle Remus stories, the Northern public had become accustomed to thinking of Southern blacks as a strange and foreign people, and of Southern whites as possessing a unique ability to understand and deal with them. "I never went South without being impressed by the fact that no Northern man who has not been South can even faintly appreciate the relation between the whites and the colored people," declared Northern travel writer Julian Ralph. "Where the negro has thrived it has invariably been under the influence and by the assistance of a stronger race," Page assured his readers in an 1892 essay. "In the cities, where they are in touch with the whites they are, I think, becoming more dignified, more self-respecting, more reasonable; in the country where they are left to themselves I fail to see this improvement." And if the application of influence and assistance sometimes required the support of sterner measures, like the scores of lynchings that took place each year, Northerners needed to understand that "the only thing that stands between the negro race and the people of the North today is the people of the South."[25]

"As ethnic tensions and immigration problems swelled in the northern states," writes historian Nina Silber, "especially in the 1890s . . . [and] as middle-class northerners confronted the political challenge of accepting new immigrants, and perhaps even overseas colonials, as voters and citizens, they showed greater

24 Thomas Nelson Page, "A Southerner on the Negro Question," *The North American Review*, Vol. 154, No. 425 (April 1892), 406; *Blight, Race and Reunion*, 358; "Old Hundred and Eleventh," *Auburn* [NY] *Democrat Argus*, July 4, 1913; "Old Soldiers Defy Gettysburg Heat," *New York Times*, July 2, 1913.

25 "Plea for Big Navy as Rainstorm Rages," *Philadelphia Inquirer*, July 3, 1913; Nina Silber, *The Romance of Reunion* (Chapel Hill, 1993), 140; Page, "A Southerner on the Negro Question," 403, 410.

sympathy for the South's problem and for southern whites' professed interest in uplifting and educating the black electorate, and even, in some cases, for limiting black suffrage."[26]

Governor Samuel M. Ralston of Indiana sounded a related theme echoing yet another element of the Lost Cause narrative: that the Civil War had been a clash of men of the same heritage and blood, men of equal valor, Americans all, and this was both the reason it had lasted four bloody years and a source of common, justifiable pride to the combatants on both sides. "This field on which we look was once the scene of as great a display of human bravery as the world ever witnessed," he said during a special program for his state's veterans in the big tent. "The test of American courage is the test of American endurance. And in these valleys, up these slopes, and upon these heights that test was made. It was a fearful test. It was made in a war to the death between men of the Anglo-Saxon race. It was made in a contest between men of the same country—heirs of the same traditions—men who loved liberty, and held high ideals of personal honor—men of character as well as courage. . . . Now, this same field is to afford the world its greatest object lesson in peace. The centuries leading to and beyond the pyramids never held anything like it." At the New York Day event, veteran John Leathers of the 2nd Virginia extolled "the glory and valor of American manhood, no matter on which side it was displayed." "The valor displayed in the war," echoed Speaker of the House Champ Clark, "was not Northern valor; it was not Southern valor; but I thank Almighty God it was American valor."[27]

Newspaper editorialists also took up the theme. "They were not the armies of rival nations maddened by greed or made arrogant by an abuse of power," said the *Lowell Sun*. "They were men of the same race, professing the same nationality, meeting in all the eagerness of youth and enthusiasm to fight for a principle which each side interpreted differently but which each interpreted sincerely." "The valor of the Confederates, the genius for battle of the leaders, the spirit to do and, if need be, to die, of their officers and men," added the *Cincinnati Enquirer*, "but brightens the renown, heightens the fame of the heroes of the North who withstood the attacks of such splendid soldiers, who repulsed the rushes and charges of such valiant troops."[28]

---

26 Silber, *The Romance of Reunion*, 141.

27 *Pennsylvania Commission Report*, 117; "Address of Maj. John H. Leathers," *New York State Commission Report*, 50; "Blue and Gray Act Pickett's Charge," *New-York Tribune*, July 4, 1913.

28 "The Semi-Centennial," *Lowell* [MA] *Sun*, July 3, 1913; "Gettysburg 1863-1913," *Cincinnati Enquirer*, July 6, 1913.

As usual, few reached the rhetorical heights scaled by Helen Longstreet. "The mettle that wrestled and triumphed here is the mettle that for twelve centuries has kept the hope of the Anglo-Saxon undimmed," she wrote in a column filed on July 3. "It bore fruit in the Magna Charta. It flashed from the arms of Cromwell's Ironsides. It unsheathed the sword of Washington. It thundered in Patrick Henry's eloquence. The mettle that met on this field fifty years ago has been tested throughout the long centuries in the cause of human liberty. It was Anglo-Saxon against Anglo-Saxon on a field where Chevalier Bayards met the 'Charge of the Light Brigade' of American history."[29]

In this, too, the ideas expressed at the reunion echoed larger themes at work in American culture. In the context of the growing influence of Darwinian theories and the racial hierarchies that could easily be interpolated from them, Nina Silber argues, "a cult of Anglo-Saxonism developed, stressing the unique Anglo-Saxon traits that would make for national and international greatness. . . . As many racial theorists explained, Anglo-Saxons had already demonstrated their fitness for democracy and self-government in history; in the nineteenth century, they likewise proved their readiness to expand across and govern much of the globe. By the 1890s white Americans often defined their sense of national will, no longer seen as a legalistic entity, as the working out of the Anglo-Saxon destiny." Many Southerners, as Charles Wilson Reagan has pointed out, went a step further, contending that "the South was quintessentially American," due in no small measure to "the purity of Southern blood." Episcopal Bishop Theodore DuBose Stratton was a case in point. "The South above any other section represents Anglo-Saxon, native-born America," Stratton claimed. For this reason, concluded another divine, the Reverend R. Lin Cave, "The preservation of American government is in the hands of the South, because Southern blood is purely American." Or as Confederate veteran Julian S. Carr put it just a month before the opening of the reunion in his dedicatory remarks for the statue on the University of North Carolina campus that would come to be known as "Silent Sam," "The present generation, I am persuaded, scarcely takes note of what the Confederate soldier meant to the welfare of the Anglo Saxon race during the four years immediately succeeding the war, when the facts are, that their courage and steadfastness saved the very life of the Anglo Saxon race in the South—When 'the bottom rail was on the top' all over the Southern states, and to-day, as a consequence the purest strain of the Anglo Saxon is to be found in the 13 Southern States—Praise God." Carr went on to share with the crowd his fond recollection of the day, not long after he returned home at the war's end, when he had "horse-whipped a negro wench

29 "Says Famed Charge Was Longstreet's," *New York Times*, July 4, 1913.

until her skirts hung in shreds, because upon the streets of this quiet village she had publicly insulted and maligned a Southern lady."[30]

*   *   *

Nowhere in this lovingly constructed Civil War memory of a titanic clash of Anglo-Saxons was there a place for the more than 180,000 free African Americans who had fought to restore the Union and emancipate nearly four million enslaved people. The Southerners who had questioned the reunion's organizers during the planning phase about "whether negro members of the G.A.R. would participate" need not have been overly concerned. Unlike the concerted efforts undertaken to encourage Confederate veterans to attend the great event, there was no comparable focus on turning out black Union veterans. Even if there had been, by 1913 there were far fewer of them alive than their white counterparts on either side, as Donald R. Shaffer documents in *After the Glory*. An African American man's life expectancy in the late nineteenth century was a full 10 years less, on average, than that of a white man. "More than half of the white men who had joined the Union and Confederate armies and navies were still alive in 1890," Shaffer writes, "but less than 30 percent of African-American veterans survived." By 1913, their numbers had dwindled still further.[31]

Those who did attend are all but invisible in both the press coverage and the documentary record of the reunion. Fifty or so came from Thomas Hamilton Post 56 of the GAR in Trenton, New Jersey; a dozen from David R. Stevens Post 520

---

30 Silber, *The Romance of Reunion*, 136; Reagan, *Baptized in Blood*, 167; Julian S. Carr, "Unveiling of Confederate Monument at University, June 2, 1913," Julian Shakespeare Carr Papers #141, Southern Historical Collection, Wilson Library, University of North Carolina at Chapel Hill (UNCCH). Silent Sam's dedication was part of a wave of Confederate monument building in the first two decades of the twentieth century. According to Gaines Foster, more than 300 memorials to the Confederate soldier and the Southern dead were erected in courthouse squares and other public spaces between 1900 and 1912, compared with fewer than 200 in the first 35 years after the war, the vast majority of which had been sited in cemeteries; see Foster, *Ghosts of the Confederacy: Defeat, the Lost Cause, and the Emergence of the New South* (New York, 1987), (273). In 1907, Jeb Stuart and Jefferson Davis joined Robert E. Lee on Monument Avenue in Richmond; Stonewall Jackson followed in 1919. New Orleans erected statues of Davis and P. G. T. Beauregard in 1911 and 1915, respectively, while Memphis chose to honor Nathan Bedford Forrest—pre-war slave trader, post-war leader of the Ku Klux Klan, and the man responsible for the Fort Pillow massacre—in 1905. Whether they memorialized the unknown dead or honored the leaders of the Lost Cause, these statues served as marble and limestone reminders that in the Jim Crow South, the bottom rail had been decisively returned to what men like Carr considered its proper place. As Memphis attorney and Confederate veteran T. B. Turley told the crowd at the dedication of Forrest's monument, "The principles of the cause for which Forrest fought are not dead, and they will live as long as there is a drop of Anglo-Saxon blood on the face of the earth."

31 Donald R. Shaffer, *After the Glory: The Struggles of Black Civil War Veterans* (Lawrence, KS, 2004), 55. Shaffer's account is indispensable for anyone seeking to understand the experience of black veterans.

in Harrisburg, Pennsylvania; and an unknown number from New York City's Thaddeus Stevens Post 255. The *Richmond Times-Dispatch* reported that "one long street in this camp is devoted entirely to negro soldiers" and the *Kansas City Star* said the organizers "placed the camp for colored soldiers on the west [sic] side of the camp, thereby eliminating the possibility of friction." But the maps contained in the final report of the Pennsylvania Commission do not identify a section set aside for black veterans. Elsie Tibbetts, the Maine woman who accompanied her father to the reunion, said that 200 of the cooks and kitchen helpers working in the camp "were negroes, and as it happened were assigned to the streets occupied by Maine and the other northern states." It is possible that a reporter mistook their two dozen tents, arrayed in a line at the very eastern edge of the camp along the Emmitsburg Road—as far away from the Southern section as possible—for an encampment of black GAR members.[32]

Only about 10 percent of the men who came to the reunion bothered to sign one of the register books that were set up around the camp, and of those who did, fewer than half a dozen were veterans of black units. They included Henry Charles of Company F, 55th Massachusetts; Alfred Williams, Company K, 29th Connecticut; and Josephus Prince and Robert C. Coleman of the 5th Massachusetts Cavalry, a unit that actually spent its entire service dismounted and employed as infantry. On the handful of occasions that black Union veterans did appear in newspaper coverage of the reunion, they remained nameless, faceless caricatures: "Every evening they get out in their street, tune up a banjo, and begin to sing all the old plantation melodies," reported the *Richmond Times-Dispatch*. Nor was there any recognition of the fact that their service included fighting, and dying, alongside any of those Anglo-Saxons. "They, too, had their stories to tell," Tibbets wrote in her account of the reunion, "tales of the 'Underground Railway,' desperate escapes, and journeys to the north, and how they had returned in blue uniforms to help in a hundred ways the boys who were fighting their cause. But these gray old darkies still love their masters, and among their stories were many of the old plantation days 'befo' de war.'"[33]

Black veterans appear in just two of the hundreds of photos of the reunion that have been preserved in the State Archives of Pennsylvania. Two can be seen in a group sitting on the steps of the Pennsylvania Memorial. Another, perhaps

32 "Harrisburg Veterans Off for Gettysburg," *Harrisburg Patriot*, July 1, 1913; "Trenton Veterans Having Big Time," *Trenton Times*, July 3, 1913; "1,200 from New York City," *New York Times*, June 30, 1913; "Camp at Gettysburg is Full of Oddities," *Richmond Times-Dispatch*, July 4, 1913; "But Pity the Poor Visitor," *Kansas City Star*, June 29, 1913; Tibbetts, *From Maine to Gettysburg*, 43.

33 Registers of Participants, Fiftieth Anniversary of the Battle of Gettysburg, RG-25.29, PSA; "Camp at Gettysburg is Full of Oddities"; Tibbetts, *From Maine to Gettysburg*, 74.

This photo of a crowd of veterans around the Pennsylvania Memorial is one of the rare images from the reunion in which African American veterans can be seen. The two men are seated on the steps in the foreground. *Pennsylvania State Archives*

from Harrisburg's Stevens Post, stands in a crowd of white veterans, all waiting to check into the Pennsylvania section of the great camp. One member of that post who did attend the reunion bore the appropriately warlike name of Cassius H. Mars. He had been a 20-year-old waiter when he enlisted in the 41st United States Colored Infantry in September 1864, mustering in at Camp William Penn. After he was mustered out a year later in Texas, Mars returned to Harrisburg and for the next 50 years worked as a waiter, a laborer, and a custodian at Blough Brothers, a manufacturer of ladies' and children's clothing. In his application for an increase in his veteran's pension in 1907, he cited disabilities including rheumatism, kidney trouble, heart trouble, lumbago, impaired vision, and paralysis of the right side. (He got his increase, from eight dollars a month to $12.) Mars was a charter member of Stevens Post, as well as a trustee of the Harris A.M.E. Zion Church. He and his wife, Flora, had one daughter, but by 1913 he was a widower.[34]

34 Cassius H. Mars pension file, NARA. The other members of Post 520 who attended, according to the June 30 edition of the *Harrisburg Patriot*, were George W. Thomas, William Dixon, James Stokes,

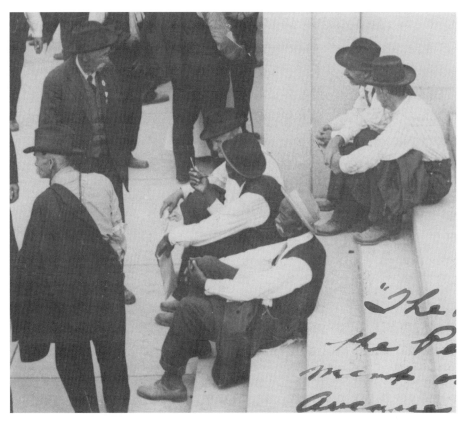

This detail isolates the two African American veterans in the crowd at the Pennsylvania Memorial. *Pennsylvania State Archives*

Barbara Gannon located another photo of two black veterans at the reunion, tucked away in the Edgecombe County Library in Tarboro, North Carolina, which she included in *The Won Cause*, her study of black and white veteran comradeship in the GAR. But with the exception of two brief references to black veterans' reactions upon hearing a reenactment of the Rebel Yell, "no other details of the Gettysburg reunion, including the activities of African American GAR members, were reported" by any of the black newspapers preserved in the Library of Congress.[35]

Several sources mention the presence of former slaves who had been the body servants of Confederate officers, including one of General Pickett's. When a group

William White, Charles James, George Gibson, Samuel Hall, James A. Auter, Stephen Ziegler, David Stephens, and Mr. Brooks.

35 Gannon, *The Won Cause*, 184, 188.

This photo of Pennsylvania veterans arriving in camp (more tightly cropped than the version on page 58), depicts an African American veteran on the far left looking toward the camera. A second, wearing a bowler hat, stands with his back to the photographer between two white veterans on the right. *Pennsylvania State Archives*

of Tennessee veterans came upon several who were sleeping on piles of straw in the big tent, having no quarters of their own, "they took them into their own camp, set aside a tent for them, and in every way displayed their gratitude to the old slaves." Thaddeus Kenderdine encountered another, Washington Wingate, whose master had been killed at Gettysburg. "He was afterward sent after his captain's body, whose burial place he knew, and took it home. He remained here till after the battle, taking care of wounded officers. He had with him a certificate from a Confederate veterans camp testifying to his services in the army as servant and nurse. Wingate impressed me as one of those faithful family slaves we hear so much about, and which many Southern whites speak so favorably of."[36]

Union veteran Walter H. Blake had his own story to tell about African American veterans at the reunion:

36 "Camp at Gettysburg is Full of Oddities"; Kenderdine, "After Fifty Years," Part 2, *Newtown Enterprise*, July 19, 1913.

Mention of the colored comrades recalls a very pretty little incident that occurred on a New Jersey camp street one day. It was an incident that made some of the Northern boys sit up and take notice.

A giant of an old negro, Samuel Thompson, from Mount Holly, was resting under some shade trees, when along came a crowd of old Confederates.

"Howdy do, Boss!" saluted the old colored man.

Of the score of Johnny Rebs every one returned the salute of the old negro. Then one gaunt boy in gray went up and extended his hand frankly.

"We-all are glad to see you," he promised, "an' we-all want to shake hands with you, nigger, an' to say as we have some niggers at home just as big as you."

"'Deed you has, Boss, 'deed you has," laughed the old darkey, and EVERY ONE of the Southerners stepped up and followed the example of their comrade, shaking hands with their dark-skinned brother, and slapping him with a kindly slap. No color line here.[37]

No, indeed.

*   *   *

A bit past 2:00 p.m., with the temperature again topping 100 degrees, the skies darkened and the wind began to blow out of the west, "filling the air with a blinding cloud of gray dust from the hard, sun-baked ground" and growing stronger and stronger until it began to balloon the big tent and topple chairs in the upper tier of the stands. The crowd grew uneasy and some began to move toward the exits. Amidst the crack of thunder and flash of lightning, Andrew Cowan, master of ceremonies for Military Day, urged them to remain calm, and instructed the band to play. Most returned to their seats as the skies opened and the rain came down in sheets. Out on the battlefield, many veterans were caught in the downpour. "They huddled for shelter on the lee side of the big boulders of Devil's Den, while the lightning played around them, crashing into trees and streaking the sharp edges of the big stone piles with strange light." "Veterans of three score and ten moved like youngsters just of age as they hauled down tent sides and looped fastening after fastening over stakes. . . . Out on Seminary Ridge aged men literally ran along Confederate avenue, and then hopped stone walls and climbed through underbrush to gain the safety of tents."[38]

37 Blake, *Hand Grips*, 66-67.

38 "Plea for Big Navy as Rainstorm Rages"; "Tented Gettysburg Swept by Storm"; "Terrific Storm Brings Relief to Gettysburg," *Philadelphia Inquirer*, July 3, 1913.

Just before the storm struck, the men of the 124th New York had been preparing to set out for Devil's Den to hold their regimental reunion. The unit, recruited from Orange County in southern New York and known as the "Orange Blossoms," had suffered almost 40 percent casualties at Chancellorsville. Posted along Houck's Ridge to support four guns of Capt. James Smith's battery on the second day at Gettysburg, the 124th traded volleys with the 1st Texas before fixing bayonets and charging in an attempt to break the Confederates' momentum. Both their colonel and major were killed in the charge along with scores of enlisted men, and by the end of the day the regiment was commanded by a captain; the highest-ranking man in Company G was a corporal. Fifty years later, the spectators waiting for them in Devil's Den "heard around the bend of the road leading to the Peach Orchard the approach of an ancient fife and drum corps. . . . With the first huge drops of rain the music of the fife and drum corps ceased. . . . What happened when the storm passed over is not recorded. The visitors finally left the scene. They asked diligently along the road back to the camp after the old men who had approached to the tune of the drum corps, but no one could be found who had seen them. They are not sure now they were not the victims of a ghostly demonstration."[39]

For more than half an hour the storm swept the camp. "The rain fell in torrents and turned the streets of the camp into rivers of mud," recalled Walter Blake. "Thousands of the old boys were caught away from their tents and drenched to the skin before they could reach cover. . . . The tempest brought great relief, however, for the mercury dropped like a drilled man and after its passage there was comfort under canvas."[40]

Once the storm passed, "the streets very quickly assumed the appearance of a ship on washday. Thousands of pieces of wearing apparel were strung on lines to dry out while the veterans lay on their cots." Many passed the time by dashing off a postcard or working on a longer letter to the folks back home. Since Monday, Gettysburg's post office had been handling up to 100,000 post cards a day, in addition to other mail. After being stamped by the cancelling machine, it was all dumped into huge sacks and sent on to York, Harrisburg, and Baltimore for sorting. The postal service dispatched a squad of "twenty-four expert railway mail clerks" to Harrisburg, where they set up shop in a special mail car for five days to process the deluge.[41]

---

39 "7 Stabbed as 'Vet' Defends Lincoln," *New-York Tribune*, July 3, 1913.

40 Blake, *Hand Grips*, 90-91.

41 "Busy Day for New Englanders," *Boston Globe*, July 3, 1913; "At the Post Office," *Adams County News*, July 12, 1913.

A Virginian finds a quiet moment to write to the folks back home. Virginia provided three distinct badges for its veterans. All featured an image of Robert E. Lee on the drop, but the ribbons varied: blue with stacked muskets for infantry; yellow with crossed sabers for cavalry; red with crossed cannons for artillery. This veteran's badge identifies him as an artilleryman.

Library of Congress

Clearing skies were also the cue for dozens of local boys and women to appear and begin searching for relics of the battle that had been exposed by the rain. "It seems that a harvest of bullets is always collected after a heavy storm has washed away some of the surface," reported the *New York Times*, "and this is a recognized Gettysburg industry." It was also a favorite pastime of the veterans during the reunion, "for while hundreds of these can be bought at five cents each the veteran would rather spend hours in the broiling sun to find one so that when he returns home he can say, 'I picked that up in the Peach Orchard, 50 years after the battle.'"[42]

*   *   *

Chester Durfee and his comrades from the 1st Minnesota were safely under canvas in the Confederate part of the camp when the storm struck. They had been visiting there much of the day with "several Confederates that we had met face to face in that charge of July 2nd." Durfee and the other surviving members of Company K had already spent time "going down through the field and in the woods and the same dry creek [Plum Run] that we charged over when we met the Confederates on that eventful evening. During the fifty years since the young timber has grown up to quite large trees, and the underbrush is now quite thick," Durfee wrote in the journal he kept during the reunion, "but we were able to locate our line and place of attack."[43]

"That charge of July 2nd" to which Durfee referred so matter-of-factly was one of the most gallant and extravagant sacrifices made by a single regiment during the war. As the broken remnants of Sickles's III Corps came streaming back toward Cemetery Ridge on the afternoon of July 2, all that stood between the pursuing Confederate brigade of Brig. Gen. Cadmus M. Wilcox and the Union rear was the 1st Minnesota. With three of his companies on detached duty, Col. William Colvill, the regiment's commander, had just 262 men in line when Maj. Gen. Winfield S. Hancock, the II Corps commander who seemed to have a penchant for arriving in the right place at the right time, galloped up and cried, "My God! Are these all of the men we have here?" Hancock had sent for reserves to strengthen a line behind which the fleeing III Corps troops could rally, but they were still minutes away, and three regiments of Wilcox's Alabamans did not seem inclined to wait for their arrival. Something had to be done to delay them. "What regiment is this?" Hancock demanded of Colvill. "First Minnesota," came the reply. The general pointed toward one of the regimental flags leading Wilcox's line and ordered, "Advance, Colonel, and take those colors!"

---

42 "Tented Gettysburg Swept by Storm"; "Good Health, High Spirits," *Boston Globe*, July 4, 1913.

43 Durfee, "Our Trip to Gettysburg."

"I immediately gave the order, 'Forward, double quick,'" Colvill wrote, "and under a galling fire from the enemy, we advanced."

"We charged down into these woods with 262 men," Durfee recalled in 1913, "and in ten minutes we had done what we had been ordered to do, and all but 47 was left on the ground killed or wounded."[44]

The Alabamans were checked. The line held.

Amidst the speechmaking and wide-eyed newspaper accounts of improbable reunions, it was all too easy for a nation enthralled by the grand spectacle of the reunion to gloss over the staggering human toll of Gettysburg. But as Durfee's words suggest, it was never far from the thoughts of the veterans themselves. At the National Cemetery, where each grave had been decorated with the crossed flags of the United States and the state of Pennsylvania, GAR men scanned the headstones intently. "I find the names of seven comrades of my company right here," said one, his voice choking as he turned his head to hide his tears. Near the 44th New York monument on Little Round Top, Claude Leland, a Spanish-American War veteran who came to Gettysburg to experience the great reunion, met George K. Redmond, a 20th Maine veteran who "had never been back until today." Redmond had enlisted at 19 in Embden, Maine, and while he had come through the battle of Gettysburg unscathed, he suffered a gunshot wound in the left shoulder at Cold Harbor the following year, and a second wound in the left ankle less than four months later at Peebles Farm that ultimately led to his discharge. "When I took him over the brow of the hill away around to the extreme left of the Union line and he caught sight of the stone embankments he helped build and the granite shaft just where the colors stood, it was too much for him, he broke down and cried like a child," Leland wrote to his wife. "I read all the names on the monument to him." A Union veteran told a group of Confederates as they stood together on Cemetery Ridge, "When you fellows came up here that time there was a deep depression just over there where I'm pointing, and a lot of you got huddled in there, and my company just poured shot into you and slaughtered you like flies." As a Confederate veteran stood gazing out across the scene of Pickett's Charge, he told Mrs. Longstreet, "I just sometimes can't help feeling powerful sad when I think of them brave boys who had to die out there for nothing."[45]

---

44 Harry W. Pfanz, *Gettysburg: The Second Day* (Chapel Hill, 1987), 410-411; Richard Moe, *The Last Full Measure: The Life and Death of the First Minnesota Volunteers* (New York, 1993), 269; Durfee, "Our Trip to Gettysburg."

45 "Veterans Forget the Hot Weather," *Watertown* [NY] *Daily Times*, July 3, 1913; Letter, Claude Leland to wife and sons, July 2, 1913, NYHS; George K. Redmond pension file and CMSR, NARA; "Pickett's Charge Fifty Years After"; "Mrs. Longstreet with Blue and Gray," *New York Times*, July 2, 1913.

The *Charleston News and Courier* was one of the few newspapers in 1913 to look unblinkingly at the reality of Gettysburg. "Let us feel, if we can, the grief that settled down upon thousands of hearts in the North and in the South when the lists of the dead were published in the newspapers," the paper editorialized. "At Gettysburg men butchered one another. At Gettysburg thousands died in utmost agony. At Gettysburg good and gentle women were widowed and the happiness of homes was destroyed. Let us try to see the thing as it was—to see it in all its crimson horror and all its ghastly cruelty."[46]

Seven women who had seen that crimson horror up close, former army nurses, held a reunion of their own that week at the home of one of their number, Salome Myers Stewart, on Baltimore Street. The gathering included Clarissa F. Dye of Germantown, Pennsylvania; Cornelia Hancock of Philadelphia; Margaret Hamilton of Wakefield, Massachusetts; Mary Stevens of Peabody, Massachusetts; Annie Irving of Newburg, New York; and Helen Cole, who had travelled all the way from Sheboygan, Wisconsin. Hamilton had been a girl of 17 when the war came. It took almost a year to overcome the opposition of her parents, but in 1862 she left her home in Rochester, New York, to become an army nurse and served through the end of the war. Charles R. Hamilton of the 19th Maine was one of the wounded men she tended after the battle of Gettysburg. They married after the war and raised five daughters together, but by the time of the reunion she had been a widow for more than a dozen years.

Stewart—still Miss Myers in 1863—was a Gettysburg native whose home had been turned into a temporary field hospital during the battle. Asked by a dying soldier to write a letter to his brother, she began a correspondence that led to their marriage three years later. The union was a short-lived one, however; by 1868, Stewart was a widow with a young son. She returned to Gettysburg and never remarried.[47]

As the decimated Confederate brigades fell back following the repulse of Pickett's Charge, Clarissa Dye and two other nurses had volunteered to go down into the field in front of the Union lines to aid the hundreds of wounded there. "They were only boys," Dye recalled a half century later, "just boys, few of them had any uniform. We found them lying among the trees, most of them already beyond any aid we could give. We bent over them and when we found one whose last spark of life had not fled, we three did what we could to save him."[48]

---

46 "What We Are Celebrating," *Charleston News and Courier*, July 1, 1913.

47 "Army Nurses Here," *Adams County News*, July 5, 1913; "Touching Scenes as Veterans Tour the Field"; "Wed Soldier She Nursed," *Boston Herald*, July 2, 1913.

48 "Reunion Is Held by Army Nurses," *Richmond Times-Dispatch*, July 3, 1913.

Four of the former army nurses who came to the reunion. From left to right: Clarissa F. Dye, Cornelia Hancock, Salome Myers Stewart, and Mary Stevens. *Pennsylvania State Archives*

Hancock, whose *Letters of a Civil War Nurse* paints a vivid picture of the hardships, suffering, and determination of the women and men who struggled to deal with the carnage of the war, was the daughter of Quaker parents whose abolitionist beliefs outweighed their nonviolence. Her only brother enlisted in the Union Army in 1862, and when her brother-in-law, a Philadelphia doctor, summoned her to Gettysburg to help with the thousands of maimed and dying young men the armies had left behind, she did not hesitate. She arrived on the evening of July 6 and went to one of the churches that had been converted into field hospitals. "Hundreds of desperately wounded men were stretched out on boards laid across the high-backed pews as closely as they could be packed together," she recalled. "The boards were covered with straw. Thus elevated, these poor sufferers' faces, white and drawn with pain, were almost on a level with my own. I seemed to stand breast-high in a sea of anguish."[49]

"You will never be forgotten by us," an anonymous soldier wrote to Hancock several weeks after the battle, "for we often think of your kind acts and remember them with pleasure. Please excuse a Soldier for taking the liberty to write to you,

---

49 Cornelia Hancock, "A Young Quakeress Goes to War," in Henrietta Stratton Jaquette, ed., *Letters of a Civil War Nurse: Cornelia Hancock, 1863-1865* (Lincoln, NE, 1998), 4.

for although we are Soldiers we know how to appreciate a kind act." She also received a silver medal "worth twenty dollars" on which was inscribed "Miss Cornelia Hancock, presented by the wounded soldiers 3d Division 2d Army Corps" and "Testimonial of regard for ministrations of mercy to the wounded soldiers at Gettysburg, Pa – July 1863."[50]

"[She] gave her best days and strength in the Second Corps Field Hospital," declared Union veteran Robert Drummond in 1913, "and with her own fair hands and by her own sweet voice had nursed and comforted the wounded and the dying upon those awful days in July 1863. As a white-haired, gentle, but aged woman she moves about among those brave men [at the reunion], standing together with the peace of the Hereafter upon their faces, and now and then picks out and calls one by name who she helped back from the dead, upon the night of July 3d on the bloody field of Gettysburg."[51]

In a war in which disease killed twice as many men as combat and a stay in a field hospital was as likely to result in infection or death as recovery, the bonds between those who recovered and the ones who nursed them back to health were strong. It was those bonds that led one of Drummond's comrades from the 111th New York to walk into the North Carolina camp and ask a Confederate officer if he could help him find Green Eller of the 34th North Carolina, who "had been very kind to him while sick and near unto death from his wounds in a Confederate hospital."

"Why my dear boy," the officer replied, "I knew him well, he was one of our own boys from my own county, but I am grieved to tell you that he passed over the river five years ago." At that news, "my poor companion's face took on a troubled look," Drummond wrote, "and strong man that he yet is . . . he sank down upon a seat on the ground, buried his face in his hands and wept as though his heart would break."[52]

For some, a song was enough to evoke memories of loss and suffering. Wandering down 39th Street in the camp one evening, New Jersey veteran Walter Blake "noticed a crowd of comrades gathered around a big, florid German veteran" and urging him to sing. "I had passed on down the street, but as the first line of: 'Oh, where is my wandering boy to-night?' came from the big fellow's lips I stopped. A comrade ahead of me stayed. Then another, in company with two ladies. By ones and twos, in little groups, in dozens and in scores, we stopped and turned about to listen to that wonderful voice. Soon there were several hundred

50 Ibid., 12-13.

51 Drummond to Mangum.

52 Ibid.

within the sound of the singer's voice, and from the great throng came no sound. Only the clear, sweet, musical song of the singer was to be heard on the still night air. Then came the convulsive sob of a woman."

The words were those of a popular hymn, first published in the 1870s, and associated with the temperance movement:

> Where is my wandering boy tonight,
>
> The boy of my tenderest care,
>
> The boy that was once my joy and light,
>
> The child of my love and prayer? . . .
>
> Go for my wandering boy tonight;
>
> Go search for him where you will;
>
> But bring him to me with all his blight,
>
> And tell him I love him still.

"A comrade near me bent his head and buried his face in his hands," Blake said. "Strong men struggled with obstinate lumps in their throats; some wept. . . . It was a strange scene. A scene I shall never forget."[53]

*   *   *

Despite the pleas of Dr. Dixon, commissioner of the state health department, and the officers in charge of the army's field hospital in camp, Gettysburg officials had thus far shown no interest in throttling back the roaring, round-the-clock business being done by the town's saloons. According to the *New-York Tribune*, "the intimation came from the county courthouse that no drastic action would be taken unless the necessity was greater than appeared to be the case at present."[54]

Necessity appeared Wednesday evening in the form of two Virginians in their mid-thirties who had accompanied their fathers to the reunion. Malcolm Griffin was an attorney from Roanoke, Virginia, the son of Maj. Samuel Griffin, who had fought in the 2nd Virginia Cavalry under T. T. Munford, and since the war had become a prominent attorney and judge in Roanoke. His companion was William Byrd Henry, originally from Wise County, Virginia, and the son of Maj. Robert Randolph Henry, whose wartime service had included stints on the staff of Maj. Gen. Richard H. Anderson and Brig. Gen. William Mahone. (*A Narrative History*

---

53 Blake, *Hand Grips*, 49-50.

54 "Doctors Amazed at Veterans' Endurance," *New-York Tribune*, July 2, 1913.

of Wise County actually attributes the much-reported, possibly apocryphal hatchet-burying incident to R. R. Henry and an unnamed Union veteran.) The younger Henry had recently hung out his shingle in Camden, New Jersey, after practicing law for eight years in New York, where he was also active in the Democratic Party and had stumped for Woodrow Wilson during the 1912 presidential election. He had seen his father off on a train back to Tazewell, Virginia, earlier in the day, and by 7:00 p.m. he and Griffin were unwinding in the packed dining room of the Gettysburg Hotel.[55]

Across the table from Henry was a Union veteran, H. N. Baker of Alexander, Pennsylvania. The two younger men engaged him in conversation, and nearby diners later said that "from the start of supper they could see that the two men were deliberately trying to pick a fight with the old Union soldier." There was "general talk about the war" and Baker "was just dilating to the women in his party on the beauty of the character of Lincoln" when Henry leaned across the table and said, "Lincoln was nothing but a damned nigger." At this, the Union veteran seized a heavy glass tumbler from the table and hurled it at Henry.

"Immediately, there was an uproar" and Henry "jumped to his feet, drew a knife and began slashing at those nearest to him. Tables were upset and bottles, glasses and other missiles flew through the air." As women screamed and other diners scrambled to get out of the way, two waiters and a bellhop were stabbed as they tried to subdue Henry and Griffin. A state trooper who had heard the commotion rushed in from the street and struck Henry with his blackjack, but the young Virginian shook off the blow and stabbed the trooper in the arm and chest before making a dash for the door. When he reached the sidewalk, several other troopers swarmed him and put him under arrest. In all, seven men were stabbed, including Griffin, who apparently was the victim of an errant slash from his friend.[56]

Henry was locked up in the county jail, where he vigorously protested his innocence, claiming that he had been minding his own business when someone reached over his shoulder and stabbed his friend. "I did not see his face, and when I jumped up all was confusion," he said. "I hit someone and knocked him down. It was the man who stabbed Griffin. The knife flew from his hand and I picked it up. Instantly there were cries of murder and someone yelled 'Kill him!' They meant me."[57]

55 "Another Battle at Gettysburg," *Richmond Times-Dispatch*, July 3, 1913; "Henry's Father Commands Brigade," *Baltimore Sun*, July 4, 1913.

56 "7 Stabbed as 'Vet' Defends Lincoln"; "Abused Lincoln, Seven Stabbed in Gettysburg," *Philadelphia Inquirer*, July 3, 1913; "Another Battle at Gettysburg"; "Young Southerner Stabs Seven Men," *Salt Lake Tribune*, July 3, 1913.

57 "Eight Stabbed at Local Hotel," *Adams County News*, July 5, 1913.

The headlines the next day—"7 Stabbed as 'Vet' Defends Lincoln" (*New-York Tribune*), "Abused Lincoln, Seven Stabbed in Gettysburg" (*Philadelphia Inquirer*), "Another Battle at Gettysburg" (*Richmond Times-Dispatch*), "Young Southerner Stabs Seven Men" (*Salt Lake Tribune*)—were not the sort to encourage post-reunion tourism to Gettysburg, and the town fathers found themselves weighing the bird-in-the-hand of more than 53,000 thirsty visitors already on the ground against the dampening effect further incidents like this one could have on future business. Coupled with further entreaties from Dr. Dixon, these prudential concerns led Judge Samuel McCurdy Swope of the County Court to issue an order the next day to all saloon keepers, instructing them "to close their barrooms at 11 o'clock each night during the remainder of the week" and forbidding them "to sell liquor to intoxicated men."[58]

---

58 "Pickett's Charge Fifty Years After." When Henry's case came to trial in November, he pleaded guilty and his attorney, J. D. Swope (son of Samuel McCurdy Swope, one of the three judges presiding) asked that the sentence be suspended. According to the *Gettysburg Compiler*, "This request was accompanied by written petitions of the injured to the same effect. The injured men had sued Henry for damages and these cases it is understood were settled by payment of a total of about $1500 and parties then joined in request for suspension of sentence." Virginia Governor William Mann sent a letter in support of suspending the sentence, as did Pennsylvania's assistant deputy attorney general. Faced with this united front, the court agreed to suspend Henry's sentence and directed him to pay all costs, which the paper reported totalled more than $300. ["Regular November Court," *Gettysburg Compiler*, Nov. 12, 1913.]

Chapter 7

The High Water Mark Once More

According to the official program, Thursday was to be Governors' Day, with speeches by Vice President Thomas Marshall, Speaker of the House Champ Clark, and the chief executives of 11 states. Nine Pennsylvania regiments were scheduled to hold reunions, and there was a special program for more than 8,000 New York State veterans slated for 4:30 p.m. in the big tent. For the reporters on the ground and the newspaper-reading public around the country, however, none of that mattered. If July 2 had been "Sickles Day" (at least in the mind of Dan Sickles) then July 3 was "Pickett Day" to Americans both North and South.

For the first two days of July 1863, the Army of Northern Virginia and the Army of the Potomac had slugged it out across the farm fields and through the orchards and woods surrounding Gettysburg. Lee had attacked his foe's right and left flanks, inflicting and absorbing terrible casualties without achieving a decisive result. On July 3, he was determined to land one more blow, this time against the Union center on Cemetery Ridge; a breakthrough could open the road to Washington, and perhaps ultimate victory for the Confederacy. He massed 11 brigades—about 13,000 men—for the assault. The force consisted of three brigades from Longstreet's Corps, Virginians all, from Maj. Gen. George E. Pickett's fresh division, and eight from Lt. Gen. A. P. Hill's Corps: four from the division of Brig. Gen. Henry Heth, now under the command of Brig. Gen. James Johnston Pettigrew, and two each from the divisions of Maj. Gen. Richard H. Anderson and Maj. Gen. Dorsey Pender. In all, 18 Virginia regiments, 15 North Carolina regiments, six from Alabama, and three each from Tennessee and Florida would take part in the assault, under Longstreet's overall command. The section of the

Union line upon which the blow would fall was held by a little less than 6,000 men from Brig. Gen. Alexander Hays's and Brig. Gen. John Gibbon's divisions of the II Corps, arrayed behind a low stone wall that ran roughly north-south, with two right angle jogs that pushed its southern portion about 80 yards west of the northern leg.

The assault was to be preceded by an artillery bombardment unlike anything yet seen in the war: more than 140 guns would pound the Union center in an attempt to silence the opposing batteries before the Rebel infantry stepped off. The ferocity of the hour-long barrage, followed by the advance of thousands of infantrymen in carefully dressed lines of battle moving with apparently inexorable resolve across almost a mile of open ground toward the Union position, fixed the moment indelibly in the minds of men on both sides. "The regimental flags and guidons were plainly visible along the whole line," wrote one Union officer, and "the guns and bayonets in the sunlight shone like silver." The sight of the advancing infantry "stirred all the highest and deepest emotions of our nature, of admiration for the splendid bearing and courage of our Southern men," Brig. Gen. Lafayette McLaws reported proudly. General Hays thought the Rebels came on "as steady as if impelled by machinery," while a Pennsylvania enlisted man later recalled with admirable (if perhaps retrospective) equanimity, "It was a grand sight and worth a man's while to see it."[1]

It was a sight that ended up being worth many a man's life as well. On and on they came, minute by agonizing minute, as Union artillery tore gaps in the advancing gray lines. A handful from the 37th North Carolina in Pettigrew's Division briefly made it to the wall near the Bryan barn but were quickly overwhelmed and captured. Farther south, just below the jog in the fence known to history as "the Angle," a hundred or so of Pickett's men, led by Brig. Gen. Lewis Armistead, breached the Union line and created a tenuous lodgment. At that moment, thought Frank Haskell of Gibbon's staff, "the fate of Gettysburg hung upon a spider's single thread!"[2] Then Armistead fell mortally wounded as Union infantrymen wheeled from their positions just south of the crisis point and rushed to contain the breakthrough before the mass of Confederates still struggling on the far side of the wall could exploit it. The ensuing close quarters fight was brief but brutal, at times hand-to-hand, and in a matter of minutes all the men who had breached the Union line were either dead, wounded, or captured, and those who had been stopped short of the wall began falling back toward Seminary

---

1 Guelzo, *Gettysburg*, 407; Carol Reardon, *Pickett's Charge in History and Memory* (Chapel Hill, 1997), 19.

2 Haskell, *Battle of Gettysburg*, 91.

Ridge. The battle of Gettysburg was effectively over, and with it, the last large-scale Confederate invasion of the North.

Numerous mistakes were made in the execution of Lee's plan of attack. Faulty fuses had caused a significant portion of the ordnance fired in the preliminary barrage to sail over its intended targets and explode (or not) in the rear of the Union lines. On the right, Brig. Gen. Cadmus Wilcox's Alabama brigade and Col. David Lang's three regiments of Floridians did not advance until the issue at the Angle was nearly decided, while Col. John Brockenbrough's small Virginia brigade, which had seen hard fighting on the first day against Henry Huidekoper's 150th Pennsylvania as well as the 2nd and 7th Wisconsin, was asked to anchor the left of the line. It melted away under withering fire before reaching the Union position. But the most significant reason for the failure of the assault was probably the one Longstreet had cited as he tried in vain to convince Lee that the commander's plan of attack was fatally flawed. "I have been a soldier all my life," Longstreet told him. "I have been with soldiers engaged in fights by couples, by squads, companies, regiments, divisions and armies, and should know, as well as anyone, what soldiers can do. It is my opinion that no fifteen thousand men ever arrayed for battle can take that position."[3]

Victory, it is said, has a thousand fathers, but defeat is an orphan, and it was not long before the men of the Army of Northern Virginia, as well as those on the Confederate home front, began casting about for a doorstep other than Lee's upon which to deposit this one. Major Jedediah Hotchkiss, best known as Stonewall Jackson's brilliant mapmaker, noted in his diary that "we drove the enemy from their works, but our supports were not near enough and the enemy rallied and regained them. Pickett's div. took the hill on the right, but Pettigrew failed to sustain him." Colonel Edward Porter Alexander, Longstreet's chief of artillery, agreed that the assault failed "when Pettigrew's Divn. on Pickett's left broke and fell back under fire." The same opinion ran down through the ranks, especially among the Virginians. William H. Cocke of the 8th Virginia claimed that Pettigrew's North Carolinians had run "like sheep" while James Dearing, an artilleryman, wrote that "Gen'l Heth's Division started on his [Pickett's] left but never reached their works. . . . From the fact of not being able to hold the heights Pickett took we were disappointed in the fruits of our Campaign."[4]

---

3 George R. Stewart, *Pickett's Charge: A Microhistory of the Final Attack at Gettysburg* (Boston, 1959), 22.

4 Reardon, *Pickett's Charge*, 32-34.

The Richmond press, whose frontline reporting set the tone for coverage of the war across the South—many of its stories were "clipped" and reproduced verbatim in papers throughout the Confederacy—soon weighed in. On July 23, the *Richmond Enquirer* ran a long dispatch from its correspondent, Jonathan Albertson. "I have never seen since the war began (and I have been in all the great fights of this army) troops enter a fight in such splendid order as did this splendid division of Pickett's," Albertson wrote. But he thought Pettigrew's line, which he mischaracterized as being filled with "raw troops" who had never been under fire, "wanted the firmness of nerve and steadiness of tread which so characterized Pickett's men, and I felt that these men would not, could not stand the tremendous ordeal to which they would soon be subjected." He watched "Pickett's brave Virginians" breach the Union line and "the Yankees fly; the enemy's batteries are, one by one, silenced in quick succession as Pickett's men deliver their fire at the gunners and drive them from their pieces. I see Kemper and Armistead plant their banner in the enemy's works; I hear their glad shout of victory! . . . While the victorious shout of the gallant Virginians is still ringing in my ears, I turn my eyes to the left, and there all over the plain, in utmost confusion, is scattered this [Pettigrew's] strong division. Their line is broken; they are flying, apparently panic stricken, to the rear."[5]

According to historian Carol Reardon in *Pickett's Charge in History and Memory*, the coverage of the July 3 assault in the Richmond press "left the kind of lasting images most first impressions imprint." In addition to providing "authoritative validation of army gossip that already had identified the culprits responsible for the great defeat and Pickett's steep losses," it began the transformation of the destruction of Pickett's Division from a battlefield disaster to a sublime and noble sacrifice without parallel in the war. "From the time men first met men in deadly strife," wrote one of Albertson's colleagues, "no more unflinching courage was ever displayed by the veteran troops of the most martial people than the battle of Gettysburg witnessed in the determined valor of Pickett's division." While "many a Virginia home will mourn the loss of some noble spirit, yet, at the name of Pickett's division, and the battle of Gettysburg, how the eye will glisten, and the blood course quicker, and the heart beat warm, as among its noble dead is recalled the name of some cherished one. They bore themselves worthy of their lineage and their State. Who would recall them from their bed of glory?—each sleeps in a hero's grave."[6]

---

5 Ibid., 55. All four regiments of Pettigrew's Brigade—the 11th, 26th, 47th, and 52nd North Carolina—had fought fiercely on July 1, and the 11th and 26th had taken heavy casualties while driving the Iron Brigade's 24th Michigan and 11th Indiana from McPherson's Ridge.

6 Ibid., 56-57, 61.

With the passage of time, the battle took on ever greater significance in the public's eye. "By 1870," Reardon writes, "that clump of trees on Cemetery Ridge where Northern defenders stopped Southern attackers and seemed to put the two armies on the road to Appomattox had won unique designation as 'the high water mark of the Rebellion.'. . . The seductiveness of the notion that somehow this one moment marked the war's turning point quickly blurred the historical reality that very few soldiers who survived the charge and its repulse actually had felt that way."[7] It was a notion that was assiduously burnished by the survivors of Pickett's Division and, to a lesser extent, the veterans of Brig. Gen. Alexander S. Webb's Philadelphia Brigade who had defended the stretch of wall where Armistead and his men broke through. In February 1887, a group of Pickett's veterans met in Richmond to formally organize the Association of Survivors of Pickett's Division. They began a lengthy correspondence with the Gettysburg Battlefield Memorial Association (GBMA) about their desire to hold a reunion that summer on the battlefield, at which they wished to dedicate a monument on Cemetery Ridge, marking the point they reached after piercing the Union lines. That same month, the Philadelphia Brigade Association was formed and began laying its own plans for the dedication of monuments to two of the brigade's regiments, the 69th and 71st Pennsylvania, in July. When the Union men heard that Pickett's veterans planned to be present in Gettysburg at the same time, they eagerly proposed a joint reunion of the two commands.

The Southerners' plans, however, encountered difficulties almost immediately. The GBMA vetoed the placement of any Confederate monument within the Union lines, citing its long-standing policy that all unit monuments be sited on their original lines of deployment rather than at any forward position they subsequently occupied during the engagement. John Bachelder of the GBMA said he had received "bushels of letters" opposing the idea of a Rebel monument on Cemetery Ridge, including one from the national commander-in-chief of the GAR, while the governor of Ohio threatened to use his state's national guard "to prevent such a 'sacrilege.'" Not even a visit to Gettysburg by three prominent veterans of Pickett's Division to plead their case in person could sway the leaders of the memorial association. As a result, in early May, the Pickett's Division Association resolved not to hold a reunion at Gettysburg that summer after all.[8]

When the Northern veterans caught wind of these developments, they immediately swung into action to try to salvage the situation. John W. Frazier, secretary of the Philadelphia Brigade Association, wrote to Charles T. Loehr, his

7 Ibid., 62-63.

8 Ibid., 94-95.

counterpart with the Pickett's Division Association, to inform him "of our deep regret at the possibility of the contemplated reunion between your Division and our Brigade Associations, not taking place in July next at Gettysburg. We regret this all the more because we had intended to extend such a welcome as your unsurpassed bravery merited, and I was instructed to earnestly request you not to forego your desire to hold your first reunion at Gettysburg, July 3d, but to meet there as the guests of the Philadelphia Brigade." In a subsequent letter, he told Loehr, "if not all your Association, we still hope a strong committee—not less than one hundred—will be appointed at your meeting on June 1st, to represent your Association, at Gettysburg, as the honored guests of the Philadelphia Brigade. If your Association could understand how very anxious we are to meet and welcome you, I am sure you would not fail in coming."[9]

To the Northerners' delight, Pickett's veterans agreed and on the evening of July 2, more than 300 of them joined an equal or larger number of Philadelphia Brigade men and, amid shouting and cheers as fireworks burst overhead, "the re-united forces—Yankee and Johnny Reb—marched to a medley of airs from the railroad station to the Diamond" in the center of Gettysburg and thence to the courthouse for a joint "campfire" and reunion. The next day, they assembled at the foot of Seminary Ridge and marched "arm-in-arm, the Blue and the Gray" across the fields to the stone wall at the Angle where, the historian of the Philadelphia Brigade Association reported in the same measured tones that would characterize the speech-making in 1913, "the Blue and Gray clasped hands in Fraternity, Charity and Loyalty, with men and angels as approving witnesses of a scene such as was never before witnessed upon any Battle-field in the history of battles since the beginning of time."[10]

Newspapers on both sides of the Mason-Dixon line were enthralled. "NOW AND FOREVER! Reunited on the Battleground of Gettysburg" trumpeted the *Philadelphia Inquirer*, while the *Atlanta Constitution* declared it a "remarkable" occasion that would serve to strengthen the "ties of a common country, a common lineage, a common tongue." Sallie Pickett, the general's widow, called it "a display of chivalry and heartfelt rivalry, wherein the men of Pennsylvania vied with our own cherished sons in doing honor to us." She felt certain that "the brave and loyal hearts of both North and South are firmly cemented under the old Stars and Stripes, the emblem of our fathers."[11]

9 John W. Frazier, *The Reunion of the Blue and Gray: Philadelphia Brigade and Pickett's Division* (Philadelphia, 1906), 78, 82.

10 Ibid., 86, 113.

11 Reardon, *Pickett's Charge*, 99, 103.

The 1887 reunion of Pickett's and Webb's men not only helped further solidify the image of Pickett's Charge as the fulcrum upon which the fate of the Confederacy had turned; it also gave to the survivors a second, parallel role in the popular imagination as exemplars of national reconciliation and healing. "It is exceedingly appropriate," said John Frazier of the Philadelphia Brigade Association to the crowd gathered at the courthouse on July 2, "that this first Re-union of old-time foes, now friends forever, should be held here at the High Water Mark of the Rebellion, and that this Re-union should be a meeting of the two Commands that must forever stand out in the pages of American history, as the Commands that created that distinction."[12]

The two groups met again the following year in Richmond, and once more in 1906 at Gettysburg, where the Yanks presented to their old adversaries a sword that Michael Specht of the 72nd Pennsylvania claimed was Armistead's; he had picked it up when the general fell mortally wounded and kept it in his possession ever since. According to Carol Reardon, "The bonds between the Philadelphians and the Virginians remained strong for years."[13]

Veterans from Tennessee, Alabama, and especially those from North Carolina, spent decades attempting to paint a fuller picture of the third day's assault for a public increasingly enamored with the tragic epic they had come to know as "Pickett's Charge." In addition to the 37th North Carolina, the 11th North Carolina claimed that some of its men also had penetrated the Union line. The 18th North Carolina pointed to the westward jog in the wall behind which the Union defenders waited, as well as its greater height along their front, and declared that their dead and wounded could be found "at the stone fence, the height of a man's chin, eighty yards further in their front than the stone fence about 2 1/2 feet high, in front of Pickett's line." But outside of their own states, their efforts were largely for naught. Twenty-five years after the battle, the editors of *St. Nicholas*, the most popular children's magazine of the day, could still write that "those on the left faltered and fled. The right behaved gloriously. Each body acted according to its nature, for they were made of different stuff. The one of common earth, the other of finest clay. Pettigrew's men were North Carolinians. Pickett's were superb Virginians."[14]

Still, as the veterans of the Old North State returned to Gettysburg in 1913, they had high hopes of finally setting the record straight. "North Carolina is going to be conspicuous in the Gettysburg reunion," Julian Carr told the *Charlotte*

12 Frazier, *The Reunion of the Blue and Gray*, 90.

13 Ibid., 10; Reardon, *Pickett's Charge*, 103.

14 Reardon, *Pickett's Charge*, 140, 150.

Observer. "The story of North Carolina's part at Gettysburg has never been told by North Carolinians; always by soldiers of other States. We purpose to let the world know what North Carolina soldiers did in the memorable battle . . . Our men went farther up the hill than did Pickett's men at Gettysburg. General Pickett had three brigadiers, two of whom were killed; but the average number of soldiers killed among the North Carolina troops was 47 1/2 to 15 1/2 in Pickett's command."[15]

*   *   *

Unfortunately for Carr and his comrades, it was not to be. From the moment Pickett's veterans reached Gettysburg, they were the center of attention, easily identifiable by their white silk badges, which were six inches long by two and a half inches wide, with a gilt strip and star at the top and the legend "Pickett's Men, 1863–1913. Sic Semper Tyrannis, July 3rd, Gettysburg." They were eagerly sought out by reporters, who described them as "gray-clad survivors of the forlorn hope which stormed Cemetery Ridge in vain on July 3" and "the worst sufferers of the memorable action at Gettysburg." These were the men, the *Philadelphia Inquirer* declared, "whose memories hold more of the tragedy of the battle than any other soldiers."[16]

"The confederates most sought after in the camp were Pickett's men," noted D. S. Miller, a II Corps veteran from Watertown, New York. "Everybody wanted to shake hands with the men who had survived that tempest of lead and iron that they faced in the most magnificent charge recorded in history. When one was found, he was soon surrounded by eager listeners."[17]

"When we got over the wall there," said one veteran of Lane's brigade gesturing toward the Emmitsburg Road, "we marched as if on parade; but I said to my comrades, 'Boys, we aren't going to take it. It's too far across.' Most of the boys didn't think that way, though." Winfield S. Bird of Alabama thought "there might have been a different story to tell of the charge" if only Wilcox's Brigade had come up sooner, but F. W. Nelson of the 56th Virginia took a bleaker view. "The charge was hopeless from the start," he declared. "Lee believed his army invincible. Stonewall Jackson was gone and there was no one to counsel." J. N. Small, a veteran of the 2nd Virginia in Jackson's old brigade, also thought there would have been "a different tale to tell" if his old commander had been present. "I remember

---

15 "At Gettysburg," *Charlotte Observer*, June 26, 1913.

16 Blake, *Hand Grips*, 44; "Survivors of Pickett's Charge Revisit Scenes," *Philadelphia Inquirer*, July 1, 1913; "'Rebel Yell' Awarded Governor Tener at Veterans' Exercises," *Philadelphia Inquirer*, July 2, 1913.

17 "Reminiscences of Gettysburg," *Watertown Daily Times*, July 9, 1913.

how the men of the brigade, lying near Gettysburg, smarted under their inaction the night before the second day's fight," he told a reporter from the *Baltimore Sun*. "It seemed that we were wasting time that was precious. . . . Jackson would have kept us going all night, until he reached the position he would have picked out for the attack in the morning."[18]

Miller, the II Corps veteran, found that most of the Southerners he spoke to "blamed Gen. Longstreet for their failure. 'He seemed to have a grouch,' one said, 'and did not accord Lee the hearty support that should have been given him. He sulked and argued with Lee, trying to have him change his plans, and when Pickett made the charge with his division, he saw them slaughtered without sending him any aid, though he had two fresh divisions lying there as a reserve."[19]

It was hard to get a word in for the Union defenders, never mind the North Carolinians, but Union veteran Robert Drummond tried. "[You] find yourself looking out in sadness and yet in admiration over that <u>mile of almost level ground,</u> over which the best and bravest of the South marched through shot and shell and musketry and grape and canister from every side," he wrote to a friend in North Carolina, "and find yourself asking the question, why did all this bravery and courage fail, and you are simply told, because the Second Army Corps—equally brave and courageous—lay behind and upon that Stone Wall, made up of the best and bravest of the North, determined that the <u>ground should not be taken</u>."[20] [Emphasis in original.]

*   *   *

The reunion's organizers had designated 2:00 p.m. on July 3 as the moment when Pickett's Charge would be reenacted. In deference to the veterans' age and the blistering heat that had once more enveloped the battlefield, the Virginians, fewer than 100 in number, would form up on the Emmitsburg Road rather than cover the whole distance over which they had advanced 50 years earlier. They would be met at the wall by almost 200 survivors of the Philadelphia Brigade, each of whom would have two small souvenir badges, courtesy of Wanamaker's department store in Philadelphia: one to keep and one to pin on an old adversary after clasping hands across the wall at the Angle. The bronze badges were attached to red, white, and blue ribbons and bore the words "Philadelphia Brigade" and

---

18 "Pickett Day' for South," *Baltimore Sun*, July 4, 1913; "Gettysburg Fifty Years Afterward," *Outlook*, July 19, 1913; "Survivors of Pickett's Charge Revisit Scenes"; "Jackson His Reliance," *Baltimore Sun*, July 3, 1913.

19 "Reminiscences of Gettysburg," *Watertown Daily Times*, July 9, 1913.

20 Drummond to Mangum.

"Pickett's Division" along with the II Corps flag and the dates "1863-1913."
"Presented by John Wanamaker through the Philadelphia Brigade as a token of
peace" was inscribed on the reverse side.

"There was not a man there who had not belonged either to the divisions of
Pickett or Pettigrew or to Webb's Division [sic] of Hancock's Corps," the *New York
Times* told its readers before sharply narrowing the focus, where it would remain for
the balance of the historic day. "Of the 5,000 who charged [i.e., Pickett's division],
only about 2,000 returned to the Confederate position. The Philadelphia Brigade
numbered about 1,200 men, and lost 453 in killed and wounded."[21]

Around 2:30 p.m., the Virginians emerged from the shade of their tents along
Confederate Avenue and began to make their way toward the Emmitsburg Road,
where William Weldon Bentley of the 24th Virginia, president of the Pickett's
Division Association, marshalled them into a rough column of fours behind a shot-
riddled Confederate battle flag and Kesnech's Municipal Band from Richmond.
Thousands of spectators, veteran and non-veteran alike, were already crowding the
Angle, along with every reporter and photographer fortunate enough to not be
covering Governors' Day in the big tent.

As the band played "Dixie" and "a cruel, broiling sun beat down," the old men
stepped off, some walking with the aid of canes, others shading themselves with
umbrellas, through fields of knee-high wheat and timothy grass. They advanced
slowly toward the Union line, "for the timothy in the field was high and its plowed
surface was not easy for world-weary feet" responding to the commands of Bentley
and his adjutant for the day, Thomas C. Holland of the 28th Virginia, "a soldier
of the old school . . . a man with the courtesy of the South." Holland had enlisted
in the first days of the war and fought with the 28th from First Manassas through
the Peninsula campaign, where he was shot through both legs while leading a
charge at Gaines' Mill. Promoted to captain and given command of Company
G, he returned to the regiment at the end of October 1862. On the third day at
Gettysburg, he was one of the men who breached the center of the Union line with
Armistead, before being felled by a Minie ball that broke his jaw and barely missed
his spine before exiting the back of his neck. Captured where he fell, Holland spent
almost two years as a prisoner of war on Johnson's Island in Sandusky, Ohio. After
the war, he moved to Missouri, where he married, raised three children, taught
school, and ran a store in Reform.[22]

21 "Veterans Will Reproduce Pickett's Famous Charge," *Philadelphia Inquirer*, July 3, 1913; "Pickett's
Charge Fifty Years After," *New York Times*, July 4, 1913.

22 "Pickett's Charge Fifty Years After"; "Gray Men Totter to Bloody Angle," *Washington Post*, July
4, 1913; "Charge Made in Peace," *Los Angeles Times*, July 4, 1913; "Blunders Spoil the Rehearsal of
Pickett's Charge," *Philadelphia Inquirer*, July 4, 1913; T. C. Holland, "With Armistead at Gettysburg,"

"It is a steep ascent just before you get to the stone fence," a *New York Times* reporter wrote, "and some of us younger men found it hard climbing through that brush; but the old men didn't seem to regard it as a difficult thing at all." Edmund Berkeley of the 8th Virginia, at 90 the oldest survivor of Pickett's Division, decided not to personally reenact the charge in which he and his three brothers, all officers in the regiment, had been wounded and all but he captured. He was driven out to the Angle in an automobile, as were Dan Sickles and Mrs. Longstreet.[23]

At last Pickett's men reached the wall only to discover that "[n]o blue uniforms shone over the wall. Nothing but a rink of curious spectators confronted them." The Philadelphia Brigade veterans were still struggling through the crowd. The Virginians looked around uncertainly. "Well," one drawled, "where are the Yanks?" drawing a laugh from his comrades. Holland sized up the situation and briskly commanded, "Column right, forward march." The Confederates moved off parallel to the wall until they reached some shade and sat down to await developments.

When the Union men finally succeeded in elbowing their way through the crowd, "one of the many directors of the scene ran down to the Confederates resting beneath the trees and ordered them to move up at once." Unfortunately, he led them back up the wrong side of the wall, and "they found themselves wedged between automobiles and visitors and behind the Union line." Observing the scene from one of those automobiles, Berkeley remarked to his companion, "We didn't have that much confusion fifty years ago, did we?"

Finally, Holland "led the gray veterans through a narrow lane which he forced, until they reached the stone wall and could again cross into their rightful position fronting the Union line." The two lines were finally facing each other, but the crowd continued to jostle the veterans, as they jockeyed for the best view of the climactic moment, and "showed absolutely no respect for the men who had waited patiently for fifty years to take part in the great event."[24]

Congressman J. Hampton Moore of Philadelphia now mounted the wall to deliver the occasion's formal remarks. "He spoke at some length," the *New-York Tribune* noted, "of the valor of both sides and the sublimity of the reunion, while the merciless sun fairly roasted his audience and caused one old man to be borne away on a stretcher." As Moore concluded his address, one of Pickett's men brought forward their battle flag, while from the other side of the wall a

---

Confederate Veteran, Vol. 29, No. 2 (Feb. 1921), 62; Isham C. Holland, untitled article by Holland's grandson in *Gates Camp Gazette*, newsletter of Elijah Gates Camp No. 570, Typescript, Sons of Confederate Veterans.

23 "Pickett's Charge Fifty Years After"; "Blue and Gray Act Pickett's Charge," *New-York Tribune*, July 4, 1913.

24 "Blunders Spoil the Rehearsal of Pickett's Charge"; "Blue and Gray Act Pickett's Charge."

When the time came to reenact Pickett's charge, the old men found they had to elbow their way through a scrum of spectators, reporters, and photographers just to reach one another at the wall. *Library of Congress*

Philadelphia Brigade veteran advanced with the flag of the II Corps. The two ensigns were crossed over the wall, and between them was unfurled an American flag, which the 71st Pennsylvania presented to the Virginians. R. W. Dowthat of the 11th Virginia, a retired professor from West Virginia University, accepted it on behalf of his comrades, saying that they loved that flag and would remain faithful to it unto death, at which a Rebel yell burst from the gray line.[25]

The speeches over, the two lines surged forward. Mark D. L. Boone of the 57th Virginia, a 78-year-old farmer from Franklin County, was the first to reach across the wall and shake hands with J. L. Rockwell of the 106th Pennsylvania, a mere youth of 72. With that, "the engagement immediately became general all along the line" as the Union veterans helped their old foes over the wall and embraced them. The reporters, meanwhile, zeroed in on any Confederate who had made it over that wall a half-century before. C. P. Deering of the 28th Virginia told of being hit and falling beside his mortally wounded colonel, who turned to him and asked, "Wheah is the colors?" before expiring. Pointing to Holland, he said that his old company commander had made it "fully fifty feet beyond the spot

25 "Blunders Spoil the Rehearsal of Pickett's Charge"; "Blue and Gray Act Pickett's Charge."

When at last Pickett's men and the Philadelphia Brigade veterans reached the wall there were handshakes and embraces all around but the surging crowd made it impossible for the photographers to frame a "money shot" for the newspapers, so this one had to be staged. *Library of Congress*

where Armistead fell" before being wounded and later, side-by-side with Armistead in a field hospital, had witnessed the gallant brigade commander's death. "The tall Southerner probably bears more poignant memories of the charge than any other of the eighty-five survivors," the *Philadelphia Inquirer* opined. As he stood on the spot where he had fallen 50 years before, Holland heard a Union veteran describing to his companion how he had killed a Confederate officer on that same spot. Holland turned to the man and said, "I am the man you killed, but I'm a pretty lively corpse. Here is where the ball entered my left cheek, and here is where it came out the back of my head."[26]

D. B. Easley of the 14th Virginia also told of breaching the Yankee line, only to find himself surrounded. "I dropped my gun and they just let me pass behind them. Then I saw Armistead come along and put his hand on that cannon and

---

26 "Pickett's Charge Fifty Years After"; "Blunders Spoil the Rehearsal of Pickett's Charge"; Holland, "With Armistead at Gettysburg," 62.

fall. . . . [H]e was an old man, past sixty. Think of that," he said as tears filled his eyes. "But when I saw he was dead, I grabbed up a gun, though I had surrendered, and reached for some ammunition, but just then I saw three bayonets pointed at my breast and I put it down." The sight that riveted all eyes, however, noted by reporters from every major newspaper on the scene, was a pair of 74-year-olds: Isaac E. Tibben of the 71st Pennsylvania and William H. Turpin of the 53rd Virginia, "dressed in the uniforms they wore on the day of the fight." Tibben "had on his old blue coat and trousers, his blue forage cap with its white clover leaf above the visor and a knapsack and a roll bearing his initials and the number of his regiment," while Turpin "wore the oldest, most faded gray coat in the world, tied together with soiled cotton strips in lieu of buttons. A tattered campaign hat crowned his gray-brown head, and his feet were bandaged in old burlap, in strips of cotton and in parts of old socks. His outfit gave one a sudden and vivid realization of the destitution as well as the desperation attending Confederate campaigns." When the two embraced at the wall to the applause of the crowd, the *New-York Tribune* declared it "the climax of the reunion."[27]

"If the gentle and strong spirit of Lincoln could today revisit the field of Gettysburg," intoned the *Atlanta Constitution*'s editors, "he would see there a fulfillment of all his visions. . . . The men who died at Gettysburg, whether in blue or gray, did not indeed 'die in vain.' The harvest of their sacrifice is a country that no longer nurses sectionalism to make it bitter . . . [a] republic purged of hate and unworthiness, seared clean of dross by the most fiery ordeal in any nation's history." At Gettysburg, echoed the *Philadelphia Evening Bulletin*, "is being written an answer to the inspired and lofty thought of Lincoln such as even he, with all his profound love and intuitive understanding of this country, could hardly have foreseen. . . . To the everlasting honor of these veterans may it always be gratefully remembered that they who had the most cause not to forgive have ever been the most magnanimous in forgiving."[28]

The most insightful comment on the day, however, may have come from Union veteran Thaddeus Kenderine. In a lengthy article published in his hometown paper after the reunion, he observed, "The talk about Pickett's charge was interesting, as there were eighty-five of the men who were in it present in camp. . . . But much that has been told is from hearsay, till each narrator believes he heard and saw what he got from others, each of whom was an innocent Ananias himself."[29]

27 "Pickett's Charge Fifty Years After"; "Blue and Gray Act Pickett's Charge."

28 "Gettysburg," *Atlanta Constitution*, July 2, 1913; "The Men of Gettysburg," *Philadelphia Evening Bulletin*, June 30, 1913, reproduced in *Pennsylvania Commission Report*, 195.

29 Kenderine, "After Fifty Years," Part 1, *Newtown Enterprise*, July 12, 1913.

*   *   *

Following the conclusion of the ceremony at the Angle, Dan Sickles was driven back to the big tent, where he made a dramatic entrance, carried in by three state policemen in the midst of the Governors' Day speeches. Vice President Marshall had opened the proceedings with a paean to "the glory [of] the common soldier, North and South," which he undoubtedly wished more of them were present to hear instead of being gathered on Cemetery Ridge for the Pickett reenactment. It was, he declared, "vain to speak of right or wrong upon this occasion. Rather let us remember that this could happen only in America; that no where else upon the habitable globe could men, who fifty years ago had engaged in stormy conflict, meet and clasp hands as brethren under the same flag." Reinforcing yet again the moral equivalence at the center of the Lost Cause narrative, he assured the veterans of both sides, "I would not have you yield one jot or tittle of that faith and devotion in the cause for which you fought, but I would have you believe that this day we are a re-united people."[30]

Nine of the 11 governors who spoke represented states that had remained loyal to the Union, but most were too young to have served in the war. The other two—William Hodges Mann of Virginia and James B. McCreary of Kentucky—were Confederate veterans, and they made sure no one had missed the vice president's point. McCreary, who fought with the 11th Kentucky Cavalry, reminded the audience how eagerly former Confederate soldiers and their sons had rallied to the flag "when the tocsin of war was sounded a few years ago, at the beginning of the Spanish-American War" and asserted, "There are no more patriotic people at the present time than Confederate veterans." He pointed with pride to the fact that the chief justice of the Supreme Court, Edward J. White, was a Confederate veteran, as was Horace H. Lurton, an associate justice, and averred that "the great and crowning act" of his own life had been "to help place the statue of Robert E. Lee, the great general of the Civil War, in Statuary Hall in the Capitol Building at Washington, with the statues of the most distinguished sons of the Republic, and by the side of the statue of George Washington, our first President."[31]

McCreary was followed by Dan Sickles's erstwhile upstairs tenant, Gov. William Sulzer of New York, who kept his remarks brief, perhaps in deference to the fact that the day before, a front-page story in the *New-York Tribune* had announced

---

30 Vice President Marshall's remarks, reprinted in *Pennsylvania Commission Report*, 136.

31 McCreary's remarks, as reprinted in the *Pennsylvania Commission Report*, 140-141.

that the married governor was the subject of a breach-of-promise suit filed by "an attractive woman, about thirty-five years old, who formerly lived in Brooklyn."[32]

Governor Mann of Virginia then stepped forward to bring the focus back where it belonged. "We are not here to discuss the Genesis of the war," he said, and as for the men who fought, "We should admire their courage, rejoice in their ability and be proud of their achievements without regard to the States from which they came or the uniform they wore." As with Bennett Young of the UCV and other speakers throughout the week, it was understood that the men being referred to were white. Belief in white racial superiority was simply a given in America in 1913; a pervasive, unquestioned assumption on both sides of the Mason-Dixon line. And so Mann could declare with evident satisfaction and no hint of cognitive dissonance, "We believe that we are setting an example for the whole world, and that the principle upon which this government is based is the true principle, and will sooner or later be followed by every civilized nation. We are rejoicing that our Government has established for itself high ideals of truth, justice, and rights; that in this year of grace nineteen hundred and thirteen, men of every class have their rights respected and no man, however great, is entitled to special privileges."[33]

*   *   *

Almost as soon as the big tent had been cleared at the conclusion of the Governors' Day ceremony, it began to refill for a special program for the veterans of New York State. One of the featured speakers was Andrew Cowan, Kentucky's representative on the Pennsylvania Commission. Born in Ayrshire, Scotland, at age seven he had emigrated to America with his parents, settling in Cayuga County, New York. In July 1863, he was a 21-year-old captain in command of the 1st New York Independent Battery, which was hurriedly ordered into position just south of the copse of trees at the Angle to plug a gap left by the withdrawal of another battery that had been badly damaged in the opening cannonade. As Pickett's men advanced, Cowan's six 3-inch ordnance rifles opened fire, and did not cease until the Confederates were on top of them and they were down to their last round, which was, as the inscription on their monument succinctly puts it, "Double canister at 10 yards."

After the war, Cowan settled in Louisville, Kentucky, where he and two partners opened a leather business. The enterprise prospered and Cowan became one of Louisville's leading citizens, crossing paths often with Confederate veteran Bennett Young; they both were on the organizing committee for the Southern Exposition,

---

32 "Governor Sulzer Sued by a Woman," *New-York Tribune*, July 2, 1913.

33 Mann's remarks were reprinted in the *Pennsylvania Commission Report*, 144-145.

were patrons of the Polytechnic Art Gallery, and helped lead the successful effort to create the city's park system. Now he prefaced his remarks on the battle by raising a piece of unfinished business: the peace memorial. Noting the many monuments that already dotted the battlefield, he declared that they "possess an educational value too great to be measured by their cost." He continued:

> Comrades, should not a Peace Monument be erected on this battlefield of Gettysburg, in commemoration of this wonderful reunion of more than 50,000 soldiers in blue and gray who fought bravely and on so many other battlefields of the Civil War, for the principles in which both sincerely believed? The survivors of that terrible war, through which it was forever established that this nation, under God, should not perish, returned to the paths of peace, and wherever they went they strove to heal the nation's wounds and make the waste places fruitful again. They and their sons and daughters have made the richest and freest land on earth; and through them, without regard to sectional lines, the spirit of peace and good will between us has been growing sweeter and stronger. Shall we not highly resolve to do all in our power to influence Congress and the States to erect a Peace Monument which shall be grander than any now here, or which may be erected hereafter on this great battlefield.[34]

Cowan's call to action was well-received, and he and a number of other veterans, including former UCV commander-in-chief Irvine Walker, began strategizing how best to proceed.

*   *   *

As evening drew on, many of the governors—whose own accommodations were not under canvas but in dormitory rooms on the Pennsylvania College campus, overseen by a professional hotelier hired for the occasion—visited with their states' veterans in the big camp. Governor Ralston of Indiana "feasted on rice fritters, potatoes, pork and beans, roast beef, apple pie, bread and butter and coffee" alongside the Hoosiers, and his wife gamely declared it "the best meal we have had since we came here." Governor Cox of Ohio, the former newspaper publisher who had saved the day when the Buckeye veterans arrived to find their tents taken on Tuesday morning, opted for supper in the press camp, but afterward joined the Ohioans. "Boys," he told them, "I am in receipt of an invitation to visit the Confederate Camp this evening, and as you boys met them fifty years ago, I would like to have you go with me, and show me how to do it." So John Morris

---

34 "Address of Colonel Andrew Cowan," *New York State Commission Report*, 53.

and his fellow veterans "fell in line with our Governor leading, and marched over to the Gray Camp, and were very cordially received."[35]

Once there, they settled in for the night's big event: a fireworks display that reportedly cost the Pennsylvania Commission $10,000. The Pain Fireworks Display Company, whose pyrotechnic spectaculars had been a favorite of Coney Island crowds for 30 years, needed 10 rail cars to transport everything required for the show, including "nearly 100,000 square feet of lance and frame work used for set pieces, 4,000 shells ranging from 3 inches to 30 inches in diameter . . . one complete carload of rockets and two tons of red, white and blue fire." By nightfall, every road and thoroughfare south of town all the way to Little Round Top was jammed with cars—at least 2,500 by most estimates—carrying thousands of non-veteran visitors, some from as far away as Baltimore and Philadelphia.

At 8:45 p.m., a signal gun was fired from behind Little Round Top to begin "a great salvo of dynamite guns and belching mortars, in turn followed with hundreds of bursting bombs and rockets, interspersed with . . . gigantic set pieces, the latter covering the entire face and crest of Little Round Top." For nearly two hours, the show went on, "hurling long sizzling serpents into the air and sending colored shooters far out over the battlefield and the tents of the veterans encamped there." Some shells burst high in the air to form individual corps badges, or the emblems of various states represented in camp, at which "men from that portion of the Union rose to their feet with Yankee cheers or rebel yells." The largest set piece created a waving American flag, 80 feet tall and 200 feet long, visible for miles around, while the finale portrayed a soldier of the Army of the Potomac shaking hands with a soldier from the Army of Northern Virginia, beneath which a fiery inscription read, "There is no North or South now."[36]

As the non-veteran spectators in their cars inched along the roads surrounding the camp after the last rocket had fizzled out, the veterans settled down outside their tents, Yanks and Rebs mingled together everywhere. The air had finally cooled down and according to the *Detroit Free Press*'s man in camp, "No one wanted to go to bed. There was a good deal of laughing and hilarity among the North Carolinians." Sometime around 4 a.m. a band started up and began marching through the Virginia camp:

35 "Ralstons Eat from Pan on Field, Best Meal Since Leaving Indiana," *Indianapolis Star*, July 4, 1913; Morris, "Notes of the Trip to Gettysburg 1913," SUVCW.

36 *Pennsylvania Commission Report*, 171; "The Great Handshake," *Gettysburg Compiler*, June 25, 1913; "Making Preparations for President Wilson," *Philadelphia Inquirer*, July 3, 1913; "Fireworks for the Veterans," *Philadelphia Inquirer*, July 4, 1913; "Many See Fireworks," *Adams County News*, July 5, 1913.

With a shout of joy the Virginians catching hold of the visiting federals, trailed after the band and as the parade passed camp after camp, the old men fell into line.

A strong voice took up "Marching Through Georgia.". . . Led by the band, they sang it clear into the midst of the northern camps and then the union soldiers joining the parade with their own band insisted on "Dixie" until the bandsmen were breathless.

Round and round the camp they went until finally the merry din roused from sleep Brigadier General Liggett, U.S.A., commanding the reunion camp. The general appeared in his pajamas, cheered lustily and laughed with a chorus of 5,000. In the bright sunlight the veterans went to bed to get a little rest. . . . The story of that night will be told many times in small towns and villages all over the United States.[37]

*   *   *

If General Liggett returned to his cot following the Virginians' serenade, it was only a brief respite, for at 5:00 a.m., the 5th U.S. Infantry band struck up an Independence Day medley of "America," "Yankee Doodle," "Marching Through Georgia," "Dixie," and other popular tunes. Through the streets on the east side of the great camp the bandsmen marched, rousing the veterans, who responded with cheers. "The effect was electrical," said Iron Brigade veteran Jerome A. Watrous.[38]

For veterans of the Irish Brigade, the day began on a more solemn note at St. Francis Xavier Church in town, where a requiem high mass was celebrated for the repose of the souls of their deceased comrades. The men of the United States Signal Corps Association had held their own reunion in the big tent on Thursday, but this morning a group led by Charles DeWitt Marcy climbed to the summit of Little Round Top and wig-wagged a message to another group, including George Carr Round, on Seminary Ridge: "Peace on earth, good will to men." Round responded with "Glory to God in the highest," to which Marcy replied, "Let us have peace-Grant." Those on Seminary Ridge offered the final word: "Duty, the sublimest word in our language-Lee."[39]

In its original conception, the Pennsylvania Commission had envisioned July 4 as a truly spectacular culmination of the great reunion. With the chief justice of the Supreme Court presiding and hundreds of dignitaries looking on, the president would lay the cornerstone of the peace memorial to the hosannas of a 5,000-voice choir. But Congress had scuttled the memorial, and when the commission's eleventh-hour invitations finally reached them, both President Woodrow Wilson

37 "Parade, Big Feature at Gettysburg," *Detroit Free Press*, July 5, 1913.

38 "Veterans Cheer Patriotic Airs," *Los Angeles Times*, July 5, 1913.

39 "Peace Messages Wigwagged," *Baltimore Sun*, July 5, 1913.

and Chief Justice Edward J. White pleaded previous engagements. So "the commission decided that the Fourth of July should have no set program, but that the veterans should indulge the final hours of the encampment in farewells and a tightening of the bond of sympathy and understanding between the North and South." Wilson's decision was not well-received, especially among residents of the Keystone State who had poured so much time and treasure into organizing the reunion. "If that was a Confederate celebration at Gettysburg next week Wilson would be there," fumed the *Chambersburg Repository*, "likely all week. Watch Woodrow get the Union veterans' vote in 1916, nit."

Then on Saturday, June 28, just as the camp was about to open, Wilson telegraphed Governor Tener to say that he had reconsidered and would be able to make a brief speech to the veterans after all. According to the *Philadelphia Inquirer*, the reversal came at the behest of Rep. A. Mitchell Palmer of Pennsylvania. The *Gettysburg Star and Sentinel* thought it "seemed to savor of a forced decision due to newspaper criticism," and the official statement from Joseph Patrick Tumulty, Wilson's private secretary, did nothing to dispel that notion, conveying more petulance than enthusiasm: "The President has felt constrained to forego his chance for a few days of much needed rest in New Hampshire next week because he feels it his duty to attend the celebration at Gettysburg on Friday, the Fourth of July."[40]

"I had declined the invitation to Gettysburg along with all others and very much as a matter of course," Wilson wrote to his wife, who was already in New Hampshire, the day after his belated acceptance,

. . . and it had practically gone out of my mind, as I think you know. But yesterday Mitchell Palmer called me up and sought an interview with me about it, saying that at first he had looked upon the matter with a good deal of indifference, as something I could afford to put upon the same footing with other invitations, but that, as the event drew nearer and he listened to the talk about it, among our friends in the two houses and out of them, he came to see that it was something we had to take very seriously indeed. It is no ordinary celebration. It is the half-century anniversary of the turning battle of the war. Both blue and gray are to be there. It is to celebrate the end of all feeling as well as the end of all strife between the sections . . . If the President should refuse to go this time and should, instead, merely take a vacation for his own refreshment and pleasure, it would be hotly resented by a very large part of the public. It would be suggested that he is a Southerner and out of sympathy with the occasion. In short, it would be more than a passing mistake;

40 Editorial from Chambersburg Repository, quoted in *Adams County News*, June 28, 1913; "Wilson Going to Gettysburg July 4," *Philadelphia Inquirer*, June 29, 1913; "50th Anniversary Is Here," *Gettysburg Compiler*, July 2, 1913; "Making Preparations for President Wilson"; "President Woodrow Wilson Visits Veterans' Camp," *Gettysburg Star & Sentinel*, July 9, 1913.

it would amount to a serious blunder. And so I surrendered—the more readily because all this would have been a serious misapprehension of my own real attitude. Nothing, while I am President must be suffered to make an impression which will subtract by an iota from the force I need to do the work assigned to me.[41]

Impelled by that political calculus, Wilson and Palmer travelled by special train from Washington. They arrived at 11:00 a.m. at the Western Maryland station in town, where Governor Tener was waiting with an automobile and a detachment of mounted state troopers to serve as an escort. They drove down streets lined with cheering townspeople, veterans, and non-veteran visitors as a battery of the 3rd U.S. Artillery fired a 21-gun salute from the college grounds. Outside the big tent, a squadron of the 15th U.S. Cavalry was drawn up, their sabres flashing in the sunlight in salute. Wilson paused for a moment before entering the tent to allow the newspaper photographers to snap pictures of him standing between two veterans, one Yank, one Reb. He entered the tent to the strains of "Hail to the Chief" and the cheers of the 10,000 gathered within and made his way to the stage.

"Friends and fellow citizens, I need not tell you what the battle of Gettysburg meant," Wilson began. "These gallant men in Blue and Gray sit all about us here. . . . In their presence it were an impertinence to discourse upon how the battle went, how it ended, what it signified! But fifty years have gone by since then, and I crave the privilege of speaking to you for a few minutes of what those fifty years have meant": "peace and union and vigor, and the maturity and might of a great nation." Wilson, pivoting to his real theme, added that the work of building that nation was by no means complete. "The days of sacrifice and cleansing are not closed."

The military metaphor of a nation in arms, united for a cause behind a strong, wise, dispassionate leader, unconstrained by that antediluvian construct, the Constitution, appealed deeply to Wilson, and he pressed it upon the veterans and the scores of reporters in the great tent. "I have been chosen the leader of the Nation," he said. "Whom do I command? The ghostly hosts who fought upon these battlefields long ago and are gone? These gallant gentlemen stricken in years whose fighting days are over, their glory won?" No, the host Wilson had in mind was "the people themselves . . . undivided in their interest, if we have but the vision to guide and direct them and order their lives aright in what we do. Our

---

41 Arthur S. Link, ed., *The Papers of Woodrow Wilson*, 69 vols. (Princeton, NJ, 1978), 28:11-12. A year later, Wilson blundered again when he declined the invitation of the GAR to speak at Union Memorial Day ceremonies in Arlington National Cemetery but accepted one from the UDC to speak at the dedication of the new Confederate monument at Arlington less than a week later. Faced with a growing outcry led by GAR posts around the country, Wilson suddenly found room in his schedule to accommodate both events.

Before entering the big tent to deliver his brief remarks, President Woodrow Wilson paused for a photo op with Confederate and Union veterans. *Pennsylvania State Archives*

constitutions are their articles of enlistment. The orders of the day are the laws upon our statute books. . . .The recruits are the little children crowding in. The quartermaster's stores are in the mines and forests and fields, in the shops and factories. Every day something must be done to push the campaign forward, and it must be done by plan and with an eye to some great destiny."[42]

The president spoke slowly, "but the breeze that played under the side of the tent and the restless feet of those who hastened in made it difficult for the old men in the rear seats to hear and understand," the *New York Times* reported. The staunchly Democratic *Gettysburg Compiler* thought Wilson's speech was "superb" and said it was met with "enthusiastic applause," but the *Times* observed that it "was interrupted only once or twice with cheering that seemed perfunctory."[43]

And then he was done. Fifteen minutes after arriving at the big tent, Wilson was walking back to his private rail car, which had been backed onto the spur that ran through the encampment. He mounted the observation platform at the rear of the car, shaking hands with the veterans that crowded around below. As the train slowly began to move, some of the old men trotted along behind until the Secret

42 Wilson's remarks were reprinted in the *Pennsylvania Commission Report*, 174-176.

43 "Gettysburg Cold to Wilson's Speech," *New York Times*, July 5, 1913; "The Celebration Message," *Gettysburg Compiler*, July 9, 1913.

President Wilson was in Gettysburg less than an hour and his remarks to the throng in the great tent were brief and not especially well received. Jacob Cress, a veteran of the 138th Pennsylvania, judged the speech "a very poor thing." *Library of Congress*

Service men, fearing an accident, forced them back. The president had been in Gettysburg for precisely 46 minutes.

According to the *Times*, "The comments on the speech afterward were not complimentary. Some who spoke unfavorably of it referred to Lincoln's address at the same place on Nov. 19, 1863, but most confined their comments to an expression of opinion that the President had not been in camp long enough to catch the sentiment that prevailed. Their view was 'It's a good speech and ought to have been made at some other place, but not at Gettysburg.'"[44]

"In all his speech he never once mentioned the name of Lincoln," one old Confederate complained. "Too bad," said a Union man, "that he could not have remained as long as Mr. Lincoln did almost fifty years ago, and that he might have said something as great and long lived as President Lincoln's Gettysburg address." Jacob Cress, who had grown up in Gettysburg and served in the 138th Pennsylvania, judged the speech "a very poor thing for a president of this great republic to 20,000 [sic] old soldiers, who saved this great nation in its time of distress from the hands of its enemies."[45]

44 "Gettysburg Cold to Wilson's Speech."

45 "Bay State Veterans Charge Grand Central," *New-York Tribune*, July 6, 1913; "Veterans Cheer Patriotic Airs"; Jacob W. Cress, Diary, Typescript, Vertical Files, 11-61-B: Participant Accounts, GNMP Library.

The veterans received Wilson cordially enough, wrote a reporter for the *Indianapolis Star*, but "it is no secret in camp here that the soldiers were disappointed in President Wilson because he first decided not to attend this celebration, which will become a part of the nation's history, and later with some reluctance consented to make a brief stop here." Perhaps unsurprisingly, Mrs. Longstreet's view was rosier. "A Virginia President," she told her readers, "on the natal day of American liberty stood on the tilt yard of American chivalry, and, joining two great epochs in American history, issued a challenge to patriotism and a bugle call to battle for the Republic which Washington founded and Lincoln saved."[46]

* * *

At precisely noon, as the president's train steamed north in the 93-degree heat toward Harrisburg, a bugle call rang out and every soldier in the reunion camp came to attention. The huge American flag was lowered to half-staff and a 48-gun salute began to boom out. Veterans stopped what they were doing, uncovered their heads, and for five minutes, the whole camp fell silent in a final tribute to the dead. Many wept.

"Into each heart had come memories almost unbearable," the *Philadelphia Inquirer* noted. "Not one of them but had lost comrades in the battle and since. Many are alone in the world. To them for months this reunion had meant more than power and glory to the crowned heads of Europe. Behind it they did not reckon. But in their tribute to the dead came the realization that second Gettysburg was over, that the world would go on just the same, and that life would take on the same channel for them as it had before the anniversary."

After lunch, many veterans began preparing to leave. They lined up before the commissary tents to turn in their blankets, then went back to their tents to pack and say their final goodbyes before heading for the train stations. "They bravely chaffed about attending the centenary of the Gettysburg fight, but they knew only too well that they had attended their last and greatest reunion," observed a reporter from the *Indianapolis Star*. The veterans of Richmond's R. E. Lee Camp of the UCV, gracious to the end, held one last reception, at which they served punch to the ladies and "sang songs, told war stories, and made speeches" before they too prepared to board trains for home. The old Rebels had been "the object of the greatest welcome during the week [and] were given rousing send-offs when on the

46 "Indiana Veterans Homeward Bound," *Indianapolis Star*, July 5, 1913; "Wilson's 'Bugle Call,'" *New York Times*, July 5, 1913.

way to their trains and cheer after cheer followed their every appearance as they started homeward."[47]

In mid-afternoon, a rumor swept the camp that Dan Sickles had died, and veterans rushed to the press section, where they were relieved to find it was not so. He had himself driven over to the Southern camp later in the afternoon, which snuffed out the last of the rumor.

Chester Durfee and his comrades assembled and marched out of camp to the Western Maryland station to await the special train that would return them to Minnesota. "At 4:10 p.m., July 4th, 1913, our train moves slowly away amid cheers upon cheers for the Old 1st Minnesota, the waving of flags and cheering as we kept passing the mass of people was something long to be remembered by us. With the thousands of Good Bye, Come again Comrades, which was answered by Yes we will meet again fifty years from today God bless you . . . we passed out of sight of the Great Battlefield, and City of Gettysburg, Pa, no doubt for the last time."[48]

The North Carolinians departed believing that they had made some progress in setting the record straight on their role in Pickett's Charge. Bennett Young, the UCV commander, had visited their section of the camp "and in the course of his speech said he was convinced from what he had heard here this week that the North Carolina motto, 'First at Bethel, furtherest at Gettysburg and last at Appomattox,' was true." Three veterans from Raleigh, judges all, "who have been here during the week looking after the work given them in securing data as to where the North Carolina troops fought, believe they have ample proof that the Tar Heel troops went furthest in Pickett's famous charge, and when they get back home they intend to make public the information secured."[49]

Before he headed for the train station, one 70-year-old veteran of the 79th Pennsylvania, whose wife had passed away in January, stopped by the offices of the *Gettysburg Times* to place an ad. It read: "An old soldier wishes to correspond with widow or maiden lady in view of matrimony. Good home, house furnished, health, no encumbrance. Address James A. Nimlow, Mount Nebo, Lancaster Co., Penna."[50]

By evening, the army officers estimated that between 10,000 and 15,000 veterans remained in camp. "[T]he shades of night are beginning to fall over the

---

47 "Wilson's Speech Wins Veterans," *New-York Tribune*, July 5, 1913; "Richmond Would Celebrate," *Baltimore Sun*, July 5, 1913; "Pathetic Scenes Mark Departure of Blue and Gray," *Philadelphia Inquirer*, July 5, 1913; "Few Veterans Remain Here," *Gettysburg Times*, July 5, 1913.

48 Durfee, "Our Trip to Gettysburg."

49 "Maj. W. A. Guthrie of Durham Stricken at the Big Reunion," *Greensboro Daily News*, July 4, 1913; "National Pensions for Confederates in Near Future," *Greensboro Daily News*, July 6, 1913.

50 Advertisement, *Gettysburg Times*, July 7, 1913.

field of Gettysburg," noted Robert Drummond, "and the monuments and statues stand out like spectres in the distance. The electric lights are sparkling throughout the tented City for the last time, for by tomorrow night it will be almost a deserted City. While standing here . . . the silvery notes of a bugle float out over the great camp and send a thrill to everyone who hears them."[51]

*   *   *

Saturday morning the exodus continued as temperatures climbed back into the 90s once more. Thousands of veterans lined up along the railroad tracks to await their trains, where "they fell like sheep under the sun's rays" and "Red Cross wagons and ambulances were clanging loudly through the streets on their way to and from the hospitals." Thankfully most of the heat prostrations were relatively minor, but not all. H. H. Hodges was telling those waiting with him at the Western Maryland station how he had gone out to the Angle just after daybreak and filled a suitcase with soil that he planned to spread in his front yard in Union Hill, North Carolina. "I will plant flowers there, so I can always remember when we of the South met the men of the North the second time at Gettysburg." His listeners thought he was looking weak, and urged him to retreat to the shade of the waiting room. "I am feeling sickly," he admitted, "for that suitcase was heavy. I had to tote it from the Bloody Angle here. . . . [but] I would willingly carry it all the way to my old home." At that, he suddenly clutched his chest and fell to the platform. He was the ninth, and final, veteran to die at the reunion. Western Maryland officials promised to send the soil south so that it could be placed in his grave.[52]

Before they departed, a group of prominent veterans on both sides, including former commanders-in-chief of the GAR and UCV, passed a resolution "to bear testimony to the complete success of the reunion and to the rich blessings that have come to us as individuals and will surely flow in refreshing streams to every portion of our reunited country" and to recommend "the formation of an organization of the Blue and the Gray, to meet in national convention at least once each year." The *New York Times* even reported that a movement was afoot, endorsed by Governor Mann of Virginia and Bennett Young of the UCV, "to have a reunion of the armies of the North and South at Richmond in April, 1915, on the fiftieth anniversary of the evacuation of the capital of the Confederacy."[53]

---

51 Drummond to Mangum, July 4, 1913.

52 "Blue and Gray Quit Gettysburg for All Time," *Philadelphia Inquirer*, July 6, 1913; "Dies at Railway Station," *Gettysburg Star & Sentinel*, July 9, 1913.

53 *Pennsylvania Commission Report*, 219; "Gettysburg Cold to Wilson's Speech."

On Saturday night, with fewer than 300 veterans remaining in camp under their care, the army officers were able to relax. "[A]fter a week of the hardest sort of work, [they] made merry tonight at a dinner in the big mess tent which they have used jointly with the newspaper correspondents. Gen. Liggett presided, and all the officers present were felicitated over the wonderful success of what has been described as an army camp that will stand as a model for all the countries of the world for years to come." The medical officers had particular reason to feel proud, and relieved. They had treated almost 10,000 cases, 744 of whom were admitted to one of the camp hospitals, and yet by the end of the week the death toll was just a fraction of what they had feared might occur, and lower even than what the actuarial tables predicted for a population of more than 50,000 men in their seventies and eighties over the course of a week. The dinner was followed by a reception and dance at Little Round Top, hosted by the officers of the 5th Infantry and the 15th Cavalry, to which prominent Gettysburg citizens as well as the Union and Confederate officers still in camp were invited.[54]

The reporters and photographers who had sweated and scrambled for stories all week also celebrated. They organized the Gettysburg Memorial Press Association, with Union veteran William D. Mann, editor of *Town Topics*, as president, "to hold its first meeting on the battle ground on July 2, 1963, during the celebration of the centennial of the battle." According to the *Baltimore Sun*, "All promised to be present."[55]

"Night came down upon the deserted camp," wrote Walter Blake. "The numberless brown tents were without their old soldier boys. The laugh and the jest had ceased. No camp fires glimmered in the gloom; no smoke from the kitchen fires drifted past the camp streets. Gone! Gone, most probably never to see again each other. The old Boys in Blue and Grey have gone their ways, taking with them the recollections of one of the happiest weeks in all their lives."[56]

*   *   *

H. H. Hodges may have been the last veteran to die in Gettysburg during the reunion, but he was not the final casualty of the great event, as newspaper accounts in the days after the camp closed make clear. Two Union veterans who had been transported to the hospital in Harrisburg, one for heat prostration, the other for a broken hip, both succumbed the week after the reunion. John Hermance, an

---

54 "Gettysburg Camp All But Deserted," *New York Times*, July 6, 1913; "Dance on Little Round Top," *Baltimore Sun*, July 6, 1913.

55 "Newspaper Men Organize," *Baltimore Sun*, July 3, 1913.

56 Blake, *Hand Grips*, 198.

81-year-old veteran of the 67th New York, was found dead in the bed of a small stream near the railroad tracks in Canton, Pennsylvania, having apparently fallen from the train that was carrying him home. Joseph Husted of the 82nd New York died at his home on Sunday "as a result of over exertion in the trip to Gettysburg," as did 85-year-old John E. Young at his niece's home in York, Pennsylvania. The same fate befell Confederate veteran Washington Hands of New Orleans, who died at the home of his brother-in-law and sister on Thursday, July 10 "following a stroke of paralysis . . . brought on, it is thought, by the excessive heat during the reunion." William Nicholas, a retired Newark policeman and GAR member who likewise had been wearied by the journey and the heat, dropped dead as he stepped into a saloon in West Orange, New Jersey, where he was visiting his daughter on the way home from the reunion. A 76-year-old Indiana veteran got off his homebound train in Cincinnati and after it departed without him, he "was found in the station in a fit of temporary insanity, induced by the extreme heat." He was brought to the hospital, where he died.[57]

W. H. Rugg, the 12th Massachusetts veteran from Washington State who had a premonition that the journey across the continent would do him in, died just as his homebound train crossed the Idaho-Washington border. "The Great Northern Railway's physician accompanying the party did everything possible, but the aged veteran was beyond medical aid."[58]

*   *   *

When Governor Mann of Virginia got wind of the press reports claiming that he and Bennett Young favored a reunion of the Blue and Gray in Richmond in 1915, he was quick to respond. "There was absolutely no foundation for such a report," he told the *Richmond Times-Dispatch*:

I have not said anything of the sort to any one, and am not in favor of any such celebration. The Gettysburg reunion was an entirely different affair. The spirit of Gettysburg was of friendship and kindly relations. It was not a celebration of victory or of defeat. It was an effort to bring the old soldiers together to cement kindly relations, and to further the idea that all are American citizens. There were no questions asked and no comment made as to the past, but all were on a common footing. . . .

57 "Veteran Killed by Fall from Train," *New York Times*, July 3, 1913; "Gettysburg Veteran Dead," *New-York Tribune*, July 6, 1913; "One More Death," *Gettysburg Times*, July 7, 1913; "Dies as a Result of Injuries Here," *Adams County News*, July 12, 1913; "Three Veterans Die," *Adams County News*, July 12, 1913; "Veteran Dies on Way Home," *Baltimore Sun*, July 12, 1913; "Old Soldier Dies from Heat Affects," *Brazil Daily Times*, July 12, 1913.

58 "Orting Veteran Dies on His Journey Home," *Seattle Times*, July 10, 1913.

Such a friendly gathering of American citizens who were soldiers in both armies on the field of Gettysburg was a very different thing from the proposed celebration of the passing and fall of a government. I participated with pleasure and pride at the celebration just closed at Gettysburg, but any reunion which celebrated the fall and burning of Richmond would be woefully inappropriate.[59]

---

59 "Does Not Favor Reunion in 1915," *Richmond Times-Dispatch*, July 6, 1913.

Chapter 8

There Will Never Be Any Such Gathering of Men Again

Aafter five years of planning and preparation, setbacks and controversies, and a total expenditure of $1,175,000—equivalent to more than $30 million today—the great reunion was over. "The people of the United States have every reason to congratulate themselves upon the success of the celebration just concluded upon the battlefield of Gettysburg," wrote the editors of the *Charleston News and Courier*. "The genuineness of the celebration, the absence of any untoward incident, the spirit of brotherhood there manifested show how completely this country has purged itself in the short space of fifty years of every vestige of sectional bitterness. That the metamorphosis has been so complete is an amazing thing."[1]

Editorial writers across the country agreed. "As a moral spectacle, the analogue of the event cannot be cited from ancient, medieval or modern history," declared the *Christian Science Monitor*. "This event must compel the attention of the world, especially at a time when so many nations beyond seas are tense with internal and external problems that indicate no such dominating unity of patriotism." Many drew comparisons with the bloodier passages of European history. "Can we imagine within so short a time as fifty years the surviving English Cavaliers and Puritans holding a joint celebration on some field which decided the destiny of the nation and impartially and sincerely doing honor to Cromwell on the one side and Charles I on the other?" asked the *Baltimore Sun*. "The third generation after the War of the Roses in England continued to transmit to its posterity the

1 "The Wounds Healed," *Charleston News and Courier*, July 5, 1913.

bitterness of the strife," the *Indianapolis News* averred. "Long after all who had a personal part in the French Revolution were dead, its influence was felt in the politics of the country. With us after fifty years, and while here are survivors by the thousands of the greatest Civil War of history, are found brave men ready to clasp hands and fight the old battles over in comparisons of memory sweetened by honest admiration for bravery on both sides."[2]

The editors of the *Richmond Times-Dispatch*, however, struck a slightly more somber chord:

> As a token of the future, this anniversary reunion holds a deep and fruitful lesson for the people. We rejoice that the South can send its old soldiers to join in the spectacle by right of past valor and present patriotism: we are glad that no spirit of regret or bitterness has entered into this anniversary time. Yet he must be very ignorant of the deep hearts of our Southern people who thinks that any showy reunion can blot out the memory of the real Gettysburg. Not in a brief half-century can we forget the somber and gigantic emotions that five years of war wrought into the spiritual fabric of our life. No oratory, however sincere; no mingled flags, however beautiful and prophetic; no friendly meetings of former foes, however sweet and kindly and human, can touch into sunlit song our cemetery regions, still and holy and dedicated with tears to an ideal, priceless because in its defense we paid so much. The South gave to this nation at its birth, and the South loves and serves this nation now, but the South cannot forget her grief. It is too soon.
>
> This cannot be misunderstood by those who know the solemn facts of sacrifice and death. There is no backward path of joy after eternity had laid its shadow on the soul. There may be serenity, faith, even fresh hope, for the ever-building future. These great things we bring to the field where our chivalry broke against an iron fate. We keep forever our pride and our memories.[3]

*   *   *

The citizens of Gettysburg breathed a heartfelt sigh of relief. In addition to entertaining the veterans themselves, they had successfully accommodated more than 50,000 non-veteran visitors over the course of the week. The state police had made just 23 arrests, including two horse thieves, one unlicensed peddler, and 17 "suspicious characters" who were given the bum's rush out of town. "Gettysburg has done itself proud," the *Gettysburg Times* declared. "[N]o town or city ever had

---

2 "On to Gettysburg as Friends," *Christian Science Monitor*, June 28, 1913, quoted in *Pennsylvania Commission Report*, 191; "Gettysburg Past and Present," *Baltimore Sun*, June 30, 1913; "The Gettysburg Reunion," *Indianapolis News*, March 29, 1913, quoted in *Pennsylvania Commission Report*, 188.

3 "The Memory of Gettysburg," *Richmond Times-Dispatch*, July 2, 1913.

a celebration of such magnitude and passed through it with such little difficulty and such absolute satisfaction to all concerned." The editors went on to claim, with pride but perhaps something less than complete accuracy, that "not one word of complaint was heard at any time over ill treatment by Gettysburg people, but on the contrary there was always some one ready to praise the town and its people."[4]

Some veterans exhibited a similar tendency when it came to refuting reports of drinking during the reunion. Massachusetts veteran Ansel Ward thought that "although the saloons seemed to do fairly well, there was hardly to be seen anywhere a man who was really intoxicated or unable to manage himself." A GAR member from Michigan declared that the old Rebels, in particular, "were on their good behavior. I heard it remarked time and again that only one confederate had taken a drop or two too much." Judge Ogden Hiles of Salt Lake City thought the Southerners' officers "had impressed upon them that they must not drink too much, with the result that their bearing all through the week was marked by a manly courtesy, beautiful to see." J. A. Watrous went further, writing in the *Los Angeles Times* that "in the whole week I did not see one soldier of either side under the influence of liquor. It was the best behaved vast body of old gentlemen that the sun ever smiled upon." Robert McCulloch, a Confederate veteran and clearly not a man to content himself with half measures, offered this assessment in a speech to the City Club of St. Louis: "In all the camp there were no sick men, there were no drunken men, there were no complaining men, there were no ill-natured men; all were hearty and jolly and happy." Union veteran John C. Delaney offered a dissenting view but placed the blame for the veterans' drinking during the reunion not on the old soldiers themselves but on "the greedy sellers of that which destroys man's reason," the proprietors of Gettysburg's drinking establishments. "Never did a town the size of Gettysburg make such perfect arrangements to debauch human nature," he thundered. "The hotel and saloon keepers seemed to tax their genius to provide wholesale means to trap my comrades. . . . Their one paramount thought, hope and ambition was to swell their bank account at the expense of the boys in blue and the boys in gray."[5]

Delaney's minority report notwithstanding, the veteran leaders who had worked so hard to make the event a success basked in the afterglow of a job well

---

4 "Arrests During Camp," *Harrisburg Telegraph*, July 12, 1913; "Gettysburg May Well Be Proud," *Gettysburg Times*, July 5, 1913.

5 "Vets in Reunion Have Royal Time," *Springfield Union*, July 5, 1913; "Muskegon Veteran Searches Gettysburg Camp Two Days to Find Brother—He Does," *Muskegon* [MI] *Chronicle*, July 11, 1913; "Back from Gettysburg," *Salt Lake Telegram*, July 17, 1913; "Veterans Break Camp on Field of Gettysburg," *Los Angeles Times*, July 6, 1913; Robert McCulloch, "The 'High Tide at Gettysburg,'" *Confederate Veteran*, Vol. 21, No. 10 (October 1913), 475; "Impressions of the Gettysburg Reunion," *Harrisburg Telegraph*, July 12, 1913.

done. "It will go down in history as an event fraught with more power for good than any gathering since the signing of the Declaration of Independence," said former GAR commander-in-chief Albert Beers. "It will forever cement the differences of the states which brought on the Civil War." Confederate veteran Andrew J. West, Georgia's representative to the Pennsylvania Commission, wrote to field secretary Lewis Beitler, "Taking it all in all the World's history has failed to furnish anything equal to the success of the Gettysburg reunion. Everybody came away happy. It has been the talk of all who attended from this section." Union veteran Ell Torrance wrote, "Ever since I was Commander-in-Chief [of the GAR] I have been doing all within my power to bring about a good understanding between the North and the South and especially to establish a close fraternal relationship between the soldiers of the two armies, and I can assure you that it has given me a world of satisfaction to know that the 'Nation's wounds' have been healed within my lifetime."[6]

"Such was its magnitude, such was the impress of its spirit and such was its pleasure," B. H. Teague, commander of the South Carolina division of the UCV, wrote to the editors of *The State* in Columbia, "that in the language of a veteran one will cease dating every happening as occurring 'since the war,' but as 'since the Gettysburg reunion.'"[7]

For the men on both sides, the reunion had been an event unlike anything they had ever experienced, and its impact was profound. "We needed this reunion to bring the country closer together than ever," noted F. H. Litchfield of the 7th Massachusetts, "and there is no doubt in my mind but what it has accomplished its purpose." "There never has been nor there never will be any such gathering of men again. The good effects were simply inestimable," wrote North Carolina veteran A. H. Boyden to his new friend Robert Drummond in New York. "It has cemented and absolutely blotted out whatever little hatred might have remained in the hearts of the men who wore the Gray." W. H. Sanders, the 11th Alabama veteran who had reunited with Union sharpshooter Frank Cobb at Gettysburg, travelled back to Hudson, Michigan as Cobb's "highly honored guest" and 200 townspeople turned out for a reception in his honor "on the water works lawn" that featured speeches by the mayor and others, including Sanders himself, and musical entertainment by a quartet of singers.[8]

6 "Bay State Veterans Charge Grand Central," *New-York Tribune*, July 6, 1913; Letter, Andrew J. West to Lewis Beitler, July 22, 1913, Commission Correspondence, RG 25.24, Box 5; Letter, Ell Torrance to Lewis Beitler, August 28, 1913, Commission Correspondence, RG 25.24, Box 23.

7 B. H. Teague, letter to the editor, *The State*, July 7, 1913.

8 "Bay State Veterans Charge Grand Central"; Letter, Archibald Henderson Boyden to Robert Drummond, August 4, 1913, Drummond Reminiscences, CU; "Hudson Citizens Welcome Veterans," *Adrian* [MI] *Daily Telegram*, July 14, 1913.

Union veteran Frank Cobb [left] and Confederate veteran W. H. Sanders first met on the banks of the Rappahannock River in 1863. They reunited at Gettysburg in 1913. *Hudson Museum*

Colonel Thomas S. Hopkins, the District of Columbia's representative to the Pennsylvania Commission, believed the reunion would have far-reaching results, "for every man who was there and felt the spirit of that reunion, whether he be from the North or the South, will go home and preach good will for the rest of his life." Union veteran Walter Blake agreed: "When all the Yanks get through telling all their children and their grandchildren and their neighbors of the wonderful conclave . . . and when all the Johnnys get through telling all their friends and relations the same things, a new state of feelings will have come into existence. All the old sores of by-gone days will be healed." The Carr's Brigade Gettysburg Committee voted unanimously to send a message of thanks to the seven Confederate veterans who had shared their campsite at the Rogers house, saying that their brigade reunion "would have failed of the great success we had hoped for, had it not been for the enthusiastic, cordial and patriotic co-operation from you and your associates; words fail to express the influence a week's sojurn with you has had in strengthening our belief that the future will see a prosperous and united country." S. A. Cunningham, editor of *Confederate Veteran*, thought the best explanation for the good feeling at the reunion was to be found in the fact that "the men invited were those who engaged in the battle. They were men who fought at the front. . . . Such men never entertain personal animosity. When a battle was over they always did what they could to relieve the suffering of the wounded enemy in their hands whom they genuinely respected."[9]

The departing Confederates could indeed reflect with satisfaction on the reception they had received. "Many old Union vets, when they saw us, would run up to us and throw their arms around us fellows in grey and hug us," recalled 15th Alabama veteran Michael J. McGuire. "I verily believe the Rebs enjoyed the reunion more than the Yanks," said Virginian Louis D. Hilliard. "We were the guests of our former enemies who were trying to provide a good time for us and we had it." The old Rebels "could not buy refreshments if a union man was in hearing," declared the *Detroit Free Press*. "Down in Gettysburg town it was the commonest thing in the world to hear 'put that money up, comrade. You can't spend anything here. It's confederate money anyhow.'" "All was peace and joy," according to North Carolina veteran John T. B. Hoover. "The Federals were exceedingly kind. The glad hand was extended by them [and] embraced with delight. I delivered an address in the Michigan tent and explained many things I thought had never been heard before by my audience. They gave me an ovation and the many who shook my hand after the speech proved their sincerity and appreciation."[10]

"The Yankees told the Johnnies that their repulse at Gettysburg was no discredit to them, as they were on an enemy's ground, and were fewer in numbers," said Thaddeus Kenderdine, "that the Civil War was simply fighting out a little matter unattended to by the framers of the Constitution, as to whether the State or the confederation of the States was the custodian of the people's rights and destinies; that we were now all a united people, ready to build more mutual dreadnaughts; to place a chip on the mutual shoulder and defy the world."

Kenderdine thought some of the cordiality between Union and Confederate veterans "may have been on the surface, and if there was a reservation in the actions of the Southerner, and a semblance of subserviency in him from the North, we must remember that the first felt the sting of the anguish of defeat, and the latter the sense of owing the apology of a victor to a fallen foe who had striven valiantly for what he thought was right." Throughout the reunion, he had been impressed with "the commanding appearance" of the Southerners. "In their new gray uniforms, corded hats, white mustaches and imperials, such as many wore, they won the

9 "Veterans Rush Home," *Washington Post*, July 6, 1913; Blake, *Hand Grips*, 25-26; copy of Carr's Brigade letter in Commission Correspondence, RG 25.24, Box 6; S. A. Cunningham, "Gettysburg, Gettysburg," *Confederate Veteran*, Vol. 21, No. 8 (August 1913), 377.

10 "M. J. McGuire Tells of His Trip to Gettysburg," *Montgomery Advertiser*, July 7, 1913; Louis Daniel Hilliard, "1863—Reunion at Gettysburg—1913," Louis Daniel Hilliard Papers, Library of Virginia (LV), Richmond; "Parade, Big Feature at Gettysburg"; John T. B. Hoover, "The Reunion of the 'Blue and Gray' Held at Gettysburg, Pa., July 1st to 5th, 1913," Typescript, Vertical Files: 11-61 B: Participant Accounts, GNMP Library.

impression. Many of them were lawyers and politicians and they looked like born leaders of the masses." But there were limits to his admiration. "Some of their talk was objectionable, but generally applauded by over-effusive Northern soldiers or camp visitors. The 'nameless crime' (when committed by blacks), justifying any lawlessness from hanging to burning at the stake was put forth, and undertaken to be offset by an account of a white man being lynched for killing his mother-in-law. . . . I thought if the 'era of good feeling' had to be bought at such a price the dickering had better stop."[11]

William P. Strickland, a New York veteran living in Minnesota, was one of the many Union men who came away from the reunion with a new opinion of their former foes. "I never realized that the Confederates were such jolly good fellows," he said. "They are some of the best men I have ever had the pleasure of meeting." Howard B. Arrison, a veteran of the 1st Pennsylvania Light Artillery, wrote to Irvine Walker of the UCV "to tender you my sincere thanks for all you did to make it possible for me to meet so many men from the old Confederate army. . . . It has permanently altered my point of view and forever changed my thinking. I tell all my friends that you men are 'first-class Americans,' and that is enough for anybody." Massachusetts veteran Frank H. Bell agreed. "The finest sight I ever saw in my life was the reception we got from the Johnnies Wednesday night. Two thousand strong, the Massachusetts delegation, headed by the Norwich band, marched over into the Confederate camp. You ought to have heard those yells. You ought to have seen the way we were received. They couldn't do enough for us.'"[12]

Indeed, the old Rebels had particular reason to look back on the week with satisfaction. "I feel, with the other Confederate veterans that were there, that the South was given full honor for its heroic record," Georgian W. P. Whitaker wrote to *Confederate Veteran*. "And as we came away," another told a gathering back home after the reunion, "there was this reflection and sweet memory: There had been no apology, no explanation, no expression of regret, no humiliation, no retraction, no recanting." If the Southerners had been expected to acknowledge "that the South was foolish and therefore wrong in withdrawing from a Union in which her dearest rights were violated, then I am sure that not a corporal's guard of Confederates would have attended," declared the Reverend James H. McNeilly of Nashville. "We still believe that our cause was right, that we were justified in defending it to

---

11 Kenderdine, "After Fifty Years," Parts 1, 2, and 3.

12 "'Yank' Says 'Rebels' Jolly Good Fellows," *Duluth News-Tribune*, July 8, 1913; Letter, Howard B. Arrison to C. Irvine Walker, reprinted in *Charleston News and Courier*, July 26, 1913; "Bay State Veterans Charge Grand Central."

the last extremity, and that the victory of the Federal government was the triumph of might over right."[13]

The secret to the great reunion's success, Irvine Walker felt, boiled down to this: "Every one simply ignored the differences which led to the war between the States. . . . The peace prevailing during that week at Gettysburg was made possible by entombing on the field all the disputes and clamors which led to the clash of arms on that spot fifty years ago. This was what the old gray-haired veterans who met at Gettysburg did—they simply ignored the dissensions of the past. Each recognized that the other did his duty as he saw it. It was useless to discuss further an 'unsettleable' question. They settled it on the only practicable basis, by burying it beyond resurrection."[14]

That interment had been in progress for years. Major elements of the Lost Cause narrative, from the unparalleled strategic genius of Lee and Jackson to the cruel and capricious impact of Reconstruction on white Southerners, had long since gained widespread acceptance throughout the North. Even Union veteran Thaddeus Kenderdine, whose clear-eyed observations about the reunion stand in sharp contrast to so much of the contemporary news coverage, could write that, "Considering that the South had so much to lose, and lost it, I give them all consideration for the graceful way they bowed to the inevitable, and if they kicked against carpet-bag and negro domination, we would, in their places, certainly have resented them also." Union veterans remained proud of their role in ending the evil of slavery, but they were also, like most Northerners, sympathetic to white Southerners' desire to maintain effective social and political control over the black population. As Caroline Janney argued in *Remembering the Civil War*, "most white Unionists had believed in 1861, as they did in 1865 and into the postwar years, that they were socially, culturally, physically, and mentally superior to African Americans." Even within the integrated ranks of the GAR, where black veterans successfully ran for leadership positions within the state department organizations, only rarely did they rise to one of the top three positions in the chain of command. "White veterans obviously believed that black veterans deserved a seat at the table," Barbara Gannon observed, "but usually not at the head." Moreover, men who had fought one another on a hundred battlefields knew first-hand the courage and valor of their wartime foes, and that shared experience of combat served at once to distance Union and Confederate veterans from their non-veteran fellow

---

13 "A Georgia Veteran at Gettysburg," *Confederate Veteran*, Vol. 21, No. 10 (October 1913), 539; McCulloch, "The 'High Tide at Gettysburg,'" 476; "Comment of Rev. James H. McNeilly, D. D., of Nashville," *Confederate Veteran*, Vol. 21, No. 10 (October 1913), 556.

14 Letter, C. Irvine Walker to J. M. Schoonmaker, August 15, 1913, quoted in *Pennsylvania Commission Report*, 223.

citizens, and to draw them closer to one another. For the veterans of both sides, said Dixon Wecter, "the huge retrospective shape of the war remained, on the horizon of their minds, forever. For most, it was their one soul-shaking experience. The majority of Civil War soldiers . . . had actually been in battle, met fire, and seen the visage of death. To show their scars to family, and the cracker-box circle at the village store was an act of diffident pride; other things, not visible, eluded even the power of words."[15]

With each passing year, the distance between the veterans and the civilian world only seemed to grow greater, the bonds between Blue and Gray stronger. The Gilded Era fortunes amassed by men like John D. Rockefeller and Andrew Carnegie—both of whom had hired substitutes to serve in their place during the war—made them the new models of American success at the same time that many veterans, as Gerald Linderman notes in *Embattled Courage*, "realized that they had not achieved the goals they had set for themselves two decades earlier. The 'pursuits of peaceful industry' had not always proved as remunerative as they had anticipated, and they sought explanations. One took the form that while nonparticipation had given the magnates a head start, participation had continued to hobble soldiers even after they were able to join the race."[16]

The Reverend Emory J. Haynes, a minister for many years in Brooklyn and New York City, also was a regular contributor to the editorial columns of the *New York World*, the *Evening Mail*, and other papers. He was a student at Wesleyan University and had just turned 18 when the Civil War ended, but his 33 years as a pastor of churches in New York, Brooklyn, and Boston brought him into contact with many veterans of the war. In an essay published a few weeks after the reunion, he reflected on the conflict's cost:

> War breaks up a man's life. It is an unnatural trade in which the young man engages just at the time he should be starting his career as a blacksmith, a lawyer or a farmer. That is the unspoken cruelty of countries which demand certain early years in the army. It is not easy to get back into the factory or bank after the routine of daily drills. The bugle call differs from the factory whistle.
>
> Our own great war killed thousands who never yet have died. They never could, however, come back. Even if a merchant kept the boy's place, yet the mustered out boy often was utterly unfitted for the place. War twists the mind; it distorts the faculties. . . .

15 Kenderdine, "After Fifty Years," Part 2; Janney, *Remembering the Civil War*, 200; Gannon, *The Won Cause*, 25; Wecter, *When Johnny Comes Marching Home*, 154.

16 Gerald F. Linderman, *Embattled Courage: The Experience of Combat in the American Civil War* (New York, 1987), 285.

Such of that great army as did, with most violent effort, wrench the mind back so that they succeeded in civil life did a wonderful feat. And they were the minority. The hurt and harm of war in bodily wounds are the least of the ills it inflicts.

All over this country today are soldiers' homes, as well managed as could be asked. But they are pathetic spots of sorrow, the ruins of war. There are, everywhere, homes where men once soldiers live under their own roof. But they are shot through by shells that only the dwellers there can count. It is not the same home, nor the same career behind it, that would have been except for the war. The deflection of purpose and fortune no other man knows. But the brave man himself. A thousand times he whispers it to himself. "If I had not gone to the war! But do I regret it? Not I."[17]

The reunion had been a chance for these men to gather in unprecedented numbers with fellow veterans who understood it all, perhaps for the last time. In many ways, 1913 felt like the hinge upon which the door to a new age was swinging open. In February, an exhibit of some 1,100 paintings, drawings, and sculptures "purporting to illustrate the 'advance' from Ingres and Courbet through Cezanne, Manet, Gaugin, and Van Gogh to Matisse and the Post-Impressionists, and finally to the Cubist 'incoherencies' of Picasso, Picabia, and Marcel Duchamp" had opened at the 69th Regiment Armory in New York City, home of one of the most storied regiments of the Irish Brigade. In four weeks, the Armory Show drew 56,000 visitors and upended the art world. That same month, the final ratification of the 16th Amendment cleared the way for the imposition of a new federal income tax before Christmas. In March, thousands demonstrated in Washington for women's suffrage two days before the inauguration of President Wilson, whose own vision for the country's future had scant room for tradition or the celebration of past glories. That same month saw the deaths of Harriet Tubman in Auburn, New York, and J. P. Morgan—who, like Rockefeller and Carnegie, had avoided service in the Civil War by paying $300 for a substitute—in Rome. In April, President Wilson pressed a button in the White House, and 200 miles away in New York City, the Woolworth Building, at 792 feet the tallest building in the world, was illuminated in a blaze of electric light. Six weeks later, "The Battle of Gettysburg," a five-reel silent movie that critics called "one of the most striking pictures of war ever visualized" and the producers modestly described as "the most stupendous effort ever put forth in motion pictures," had its New York premiere.[18]

17 "The Soldiers' Home," *Lexington* [TX] *Leader*, July 27, 1913.

18 Paul M. Angle, *Crossroads: 1913* (New York, 1963), 54-55; Advertisement, *Duluth News-Tribune*, July 20, 1913; advertisement, *Seattle Times*, July 3, 1913. "The Battle of Gettysburg," directed by Thomas H. Ince, cost $75,000 to produce and employed as many as 3,000 extras in the big battle scenes. No copy is known to survive. For more on the larger social, economic, and political context in

Hand in hand. The picture may have been posed but the sentiment it captured was real. For the men on both sides, the reunion had been an event unlike anything they had ever experienced and its impact was profound. *Pennsylvania State Archives*

*   *   *

If the door to a new era was opening, veterans on both sides knew only too well that the one to theirs was closing, and they hoped that before it did, the good feelings and positive press generated by the reunion could help them revive their dream of a peace memorial on the field of Gettysburg. Back home in Louisville on July 19, Andrew Cowan wrote to Irvine Walker, "I think we ought to carefully select at least 40 Charter Members, one from each State, if possible," for a new organization to press their case. He continued:

If you will write me that you have started out to get the consent of one prominent Confederate for each [Southern] state, to be named as one of the charter members, I will then write to Judge Torrance asking for his cooperation, and requesting him to name an influential man for each Northern State. . . . Now we must <u>hustle</u> for it is of the highest importance to get the Southern names first and foremost. . . . Don't think of me for the head of the Association, as you suggest. I have never in my whole life sought for

which the reunion occurred, see Charles Emerson, *1913: In Search of the World Before the Great War* (New York, 2013).

prominence and it is the last thing I desire in this project. We must elect a big, broad-minded, Southern gentleman as President of the Association, with as many Vice Presidents as we have material for. I shall gladly pay all the expenses incurred up to the organization of the Association you have planned.[19]

The Gettysburg Peace Memorial Association was formally launched, and articles of association adopted, on September 17, 1913, in Chattanooga, Tennessee, with Confederate veteran and former secretary of the navy Hilary A. Herbert as president, Walker as secretary, John H. Leathers of the UCV as treasurer, and Union veteran Thomas S. Hopkins as chairman of the executive committee. Joshua Chamberlain and Evander Law were named honorary presidents. The directors and state vice presidents included *Confederate Veteran* editor S. A. Cunningham and several others who had served as representatives to the Pennsylvania Commission, along with Union veteran and former U.S. pension commissioner James Tanner. Among the 120 founding members were Governor Mann of Virginia and several former commanders-in-chief of the GAR and UCV. In short order, U.S. Rep. Swagar Sherley of Kentucky introduced a bill "to create the Gettysburg peace memorial commission and authorizing that commission to locate the place and erect a memorial on the Gettysburg battle field to commemorate the peace celebration on the fiftieth anniversary of that battle" and appropriating "the sum of $500,000, or so much thereof as may be necessary."[20]

For that sum, the veterans envisioned a memorial along the lines they had first proposed almost two years before: "an imposing gateway, or entrance, to the Gettysburg National Military Park . . . signifying National Unity and Peace, the structure to be pierced by a spacious arch, or gateway, and to be surmounted by a heroic statue of Abraham Lincoln reading his Gettysburg address, and in the act of making the immortal declaration 'That the government of the people, by the people, for the people, shall not perish from the earth.' It is our judgment that such a work . . . standing as a Benedictus above this great bivouac of our patriot dead . . . would be, for all time, an eloquent object lesson in American unity, valor, and good-will."[21]

Cowan appealed to Speaker of the House Clark, who had seen at least a small portion of the great reunion firsthand, for support, framing the issue as one of some

19 Letter, Andrew Cowan to C. Irvine Walker, July 19, 1913, Vertical Files 17-5: Peace Memorial Efforts, GNMP Library.

20 Gettysburg Peace Memorial Association, Brochure, Vertical Files: Eternal Peace Light Memorial, Adams County Historical Society; "Form Gettysburg Peace Memorial Association," *Louisville Courier-Journal*, November 19, 1913.

21 Commission Minutes, 27-28.

urgency. "Before we pass over to rest in 'that bivouac of the dead,'" Cowan wrote, "we would see erected on the battlefield of Gettysburg, by our reunited country a memorial of the fraternal peace and good will manifested there only fifty years after that great central battle of the War was fought. It is for that patriotic purpose we shall appeal to Congress for an adequate appropriation, and the appointment of a Commission, to accomplish. Other appeals for public monuments can wait, but for us who are nearing the end of the last march, the present Session of Congress probably presents the last opportunity to make our appeal."[22]

Clark replied that he would be "very glad indeed to do what I can to help" but went no further. Sherley's bill was referred to the House Committee on the Library, and Cowan hastened to write to Rep. James L. Slayden of Texas, the committee's chairman, stressing that "Texans came to the Fiftieth Anniversary Celebration in numbers, and went back home prouder of their deeds on that great battle field, and with a new feeling of respect and good will for their old time enemies in blue. . . . I pray that Congress may realize the fitness of erecting a great Peace Monument, in commemoration of an epoch in the history of our people, and I beg you to remember that the Texas U.C.V. were first to adopt Resolutions in its favor." Slayden was active in the American Peace Society and one of the original trustees of the Carnegie Endowment for International Peace, but he was unmoved by Cowan's appeal. "I have no idea what view the Committee will take of the proposal to spend half a million dollars for a monument for Gettysburg," he wrote to a colleague. "Personally I have thought that battlefield had all the monuments any possible sentiment or condition could demand, but it appears that I was mistaken. No doubt committee hearings will be granted and the opinion of the Committee subsequently developed."[23]

When those hearings were held, Cowan put the case simply and poignantly. "Why should we commemorate the [reunion] with a monument? Because, gentlemen, nothing like that fraternal meeting has ever been seen in the history of the world. I believe that without such a permanent memorial the significance of the event may be lost for future generations."[24]

22 Letter, Andrew Cowan to Champ Clark, December 15, 1913, Vertical Files 17-5: Peace Memorial Efforts, GNMP Library.

23 Letter, Champ Clark to Andrew Cowan, December 17, 1913; Letter, Andrew Cowan to James Slayden, January 10, 1914; Letter, James Slayden to Admiral Watson, January 10, 1914, Vertical Files 17-5: Peace Memorial Efforts, GNMP Library.

24 House Committee on the Library, *Hearings on H.R. 11112: A Bill to Erect a Memorial on the Gettysburg Battle Field to Commemorate the Fiftieth Anniversary of That Battle, February 18, 1914* (Washington, D.C., 1914), 10.

It soon became clear that securing an appropriation from Congress was not the only hurdle to overcome. Perhaps emboldened by their warm reception at Gettysburg, the Louisiana division of the UCV passed a resolution declaring that "any act of Congress approving such a Peace Monument, or making appropriations therefor, shall specifically state that such act or appropriation is in the name of Abraham Lincoln and Jefferson Davis, the great and loyal Presidents of the United States and the Confederate States during the strife of 1861 to 1865, giving to each as the loyal and devoted executive head of their respective people equal honor for their devotion. Any peace monument which can not be made in the spirit of this amendment would be a mockery, a delusion, and a snare, because President Davis was as much a representative of his people as President Lincoln was of his, and those who followed the one are just as loyal to our present United States as are the followers of the other."

At its national convention that November, the UDC quoted the Louisiana resolution in full and "most heartily endorse[d] the action of the Louisiana Division," while the UCV, in its national meeting, was unable to pass a resolution in support of the peace memorial after the Louisiana delegates moved an amendment stating "that all moneys appropriated by Congress shall be with the declaration that it is intended to give equal honor to President Jefferson Davis, as the leader of the South, with Abraham Lincoln, as the leader of the North."[25]

Undaunted, the members of the association soldiered on and, according to Hilary Herbert, "The first day of August we were confident that the House Committee on the Library would recommend the passage of a bill appropriating $100,000 for the memorial. But, like a thunderbolt from a clear sky, came the fearful outbreak of war among the nations of Europe. The financial systems of the world collapsed, and it became evident that our own Government would face a Treasury deficit at the close of the present fiscal year." As a result, Representative Slayden informed them, "The exigencies of the present situation make it absolutely necessary that Congress limit appropriations to the actual necessities of the Government."[26]

Herbert, the association's president, and Hopkins, the chairman of the executive committee, sent a circular letter to the members breaking the bad news. "We comfort ourselves," they wrote, "with the knowledge that the Hon. Swagar Sherley, M.C., author of the bill and its indefatigable supporter, the Hon. Champ

25 *Minutes of the Twentieth Annual Convention, United Daughters of the Confederacy* (Raleigh, 1914), 104-105; *Minutes of the Twenty-fourth Annual Meeting and Reunion of the United Confederate Veterans* (New Orleans, 1914), 122-124.

26 "Gettysburg Memorial Given Setback by War and Deficit," *Louisville Courier-Journal*, October 29, 1914.

Clark, Speaker of the House of Representatives, and the Hon. Oscar Underwood, Majority Leader, warmly approved the bill. . . . We also had good reason to believe that a majority of the members of the Committee on the Library were in favor of it. But too long deliberation, the illness of members and the European war, defeated our hopes." After briefly reviewing the association's finances, the two old veterans sounded "Taps" for the peace memorial effort. "Colonel Andrew Cowan has been seriously ill since July 24th but is now convalescent. General Joshua L. Chamberlain, U.S.V., one of the two honorary Presidents, and Colonel S. A. Cunningham, U.C.V., of the Board of Directors, have answered the summons of the Great Commander." Dan Sickles, who had first championed the idea of a peace memorial four years earlier was also gone, dead of a cerebral hemorrhage at 94. "After paying all bills, including the expense of this statement, a balance of about two hundred and seventy-five dollars will remain in the hands of Treasurer Leathers. With the approval of the Executive Committee, President Herbert will send [a] check for the amount to the American Red Cross Society, Washington, D.C."[27]

It would take another quarter-century for the peace monument to be built. None of the organizers of the Gettysburg Peace Memorial Association would live to see it dedicated.

*   *   *

If some veterans feared that without a permanent memorial the passage of time would efface the public's memory of the great reunion, for many attendees it seemed destined to be long remembered as an occurrence of historic significance. "To the youth of this nation the inspirational value of this day on Gettysburg's field will outweigh the sordid accumulations of all the Rockefellers the world will ever produce," Mrs. Longstreet told her readers. "It has been one of the most beneficial events in our history whose value will last for generations," the *Philadelphia Inquirer* declared in a July 6 editorial. "It is a great thing for a man to have said that he fought at Gettysburg. It is even greater to say that he was there last week at the Reunion, and the third and fourth generations will be proud of ancestors who participated in either or both." Elsie Tibbetts, back home in Maine with her veteran father, agreed. "All that the great Reunion of the Blue and the Gray means to the American people is yet to be realized. It will be realized more and more with the flight of years—it will be talked about and written about as long as the American people boast of the dauntless courage of Gettysburg."[28]

27 Letter, Thomas S. Hopkins and Hilary Herbert to the members of the Gettysburg Peace Memorial Association, October 29, 1914, Vertical Files 17-5: Peace Memorial Efforts, GNMP Library.

28 "Mrs. Longstreet with Blue and Gray"; "A Glorious Victory," *Philadelphia Inquirer*, July 6, 1913, quoted in *Pennsylvania Commission Report*, 208; Tibbetts, *From Maine to Gettysburg*, 204.

But it was not to be. As the old soldiers themselves faded away, so too did the public's memory of the 1913 reunion. Newspaper clippings yellowed and were filed away. Of the thousands of letters and postcards the veterans wrote from the reunion camp, some found their way into archives and libraries, while others fell victim to a century's worth of spring cleanings. It is to be hoped that some are yet preserved among family papers in attics across America, for surely that is what the veterans themselves would have wished. Because for all the hyperbole in newspaper editorials and politicians' speeches, the fact that more than 53,000 veterans from both sides of a bloody, bitter civil war were sufficiently reconciled to come together in fellowship less than 50 years after the last gun had fallen silent was truly remarkable, and the role they had played in reuniting and healing the nation— imperfectly, incompletely, at a terrible cost to their black fellow countrymen, but nonetheless in the end, lastingly— is deserving of remembrance.

Daniel Snyder of Berryville, Virginia, a veteran of the 11th Virginia Cavalry, certainly believed that. As the year drew to a close, he sat down to compose a letter:

> My dear daughter, Mrs. Daisy Brittingham,
>
> I turn over to you on this Christmas Day of 1913, these badges worn by me at the Reunion held at Gettysburg on the 1st, 2nd, 3rd, and 4th days of July, 1913, of both armies after 50 years had elapsed.
>
> Fifty-five thousand old veterans who wore the Blue and wore the Gray from every state of the Union meeting in the spirit of fraternity. Historians will record as the grandest event in the history of this or any other country on the globe.
>
> Preserve these badges and hand them down to one of your children as relics of the greatest Civil War in the history of nations.
>
> Your fond, affectionate father,
>
> Daniel C. Snyder[29]

---

29 Letter, Daniel C. Snyder to Daisy Brittingham, December 25, 1913, Daniel C. Snyder Collection: Correspondence, 1896-1922, Clarke County Historical Association, Berryville, VA.

Appendix

State Breakdown of Veterans Attending the Reunion

	Union Veterans	Confederate Veterans	Total
Alabama	0	200	200
Arizona	7	3	10
Arkansas	50	25	75
California	90	10	100
Colorado	11	1	12
Connecticut	350	0	350
Delaware	303	13	316
Florida	0	150	150
Georgia	35	250	285
Idaho	45	0	45
Illinois	450	15	465
Indiana	540	25	565
Iowa	360	4	364
Kansas	125	5	130
Kentucky	75	25	100
Louisiana	0	125	125
Maine	540	3	543
Maryland	800	280	1,080
Massachusetts	1,600	100	1,700
Michigan	830	14	844
Minnesota	400	22	422
Mississippi	0	120	120
Missouri	250	172	422
Montana	14	8	22
Nebraska	230	8	238
Nevada	0	0	0

	Union Veterans	Confederate Veterans	Total
New Hampshire	740	10	750
New Jersey	2,800	109	2,909
New Mexico	1	0	1
New York	8,440	60	8,500
North Carolina	0	1,265	1,265
North Dakota	162	3	165
Ohio	900	100	1,000
Oklahoma	87	48	135
Oregon	75	7	82
Pennsylvania	21,800	303	22,103
Rhode Island	370	7	377
South Carolina	68	301	369
South Dakota	121	4	125
Tennessee	0	300	300
Texas	0	130	130
Utah	67	9	76
Vermont	665	4	669
Virginia	50	3,228	3,278
Washington	152	15	167
West Virginia	562	563	1,125
Wisconsin	625	25	650
Wyoming	0	0	0
District of Columbia	380	105	485
Veteran Signal Corps	63	0	63
Total	**45,233**	**8,174**	**53,407**

Source: *Report of the Pennsylvania Commission for the Fiftieth Anniversary of the Battle of Gettysburg,* revised edition (Harrisburg, PA, April 1915), 36-37.

Bibliography

Official Publications

The War of the Rebellion: A Compilation of the Official Records of the Union and Confederate Armies, 128 vols. Washington, D.C.: Government Printing Office, 1880-1901

Manuscript Collections

Adams County Historical Society, Gettysburg, PA
    Vertical Files: Eternal Peace Light Memorial

Clarke County Historical Association, Berryville, VA
    Daniel C. Snyder Collection: Correspondence, 1896-1922

Cornell University, Division of Rare and Manuscript Collections, Ithaca, NY
    Robert L. Drummond Reminiscences

Gettysburg National Military Park Library, Gettysburg, PA
    Vertical Files 11-61-B: 50th Anniversary, Grand Reunion 1913: Participant Accounts
    Vertical Files 11-61: 50th Anniversary Grand Reunion: General Information
    Vertical Files 17-5: Peace Memorial Efforts

Library of Congress, Manuscripts Division, Washington, D.C.
    Daniel Edward Sickles Papers

Library of Virginia, Richmond, VA
    Louis Daniel Hilliard Papers

National Archives and Records Administration, Washington, D.C.
    Record Group 15: Civil War Veteran Pension Files
    Record Group 94: Civil War Military Service Records

New-York Historical Society, New York, NY

American Historical Manuscript Collection

Pennsylvania State Archives, Harrisburg, PA

  Record Group 25: Fiftieth Anniversary of the Battle of Gettysburg Commission

Rhode Island Historical Society, Providence, RI

  George N. Bliss Papers

Southern Historical Collection, University of North Carolina, Chapel Hill, NC

  Julian Shakespeare Carr Papers

South Caroliniana Library, University of South Carolina, Columbia, SC

  William Fuller Jewson Papers

U.S. Army Military History Institute, Carlisle, PA

  Wendell W. Lang, Jr. Collection

Virginia Historical Society

  Lomax Family Papers

Washington State Library, Olympia, WA

  Manuscript Collection

Newspapers

Adams County [PA] *News*, 1910-13

Adrian [MI] *Daily Telegram*, 1913

Atlanta Constitution, 1913

Auburn [NY] *Daily Advertiser*, 1913

Auburn [NY] *Democrat Argus*, 1913

Baltimore Sun, 1913

Boston Globe, 1913

Boston Herald, 1913

Brazil [IN] *Times*, 1913

Buffalo Evening News, 1913

Charlotte [NC] *Observer*, 1913

Charleston [SC] *Evening Post*, 1913

Charleston [SC] *News-Courier*, 1913

Chatham [NJ] *Record*, 1913

Cincinnati Enquirer, 1913

Cleveland Plain Dealer, 1913

Daily Progress [Charlottesville, VA], 1913

Dallas Morning News, 1913

Detroit Free Press, 1913

Duluth [MN] *News-Tribune*, 1913

Flint [MI] *Daily Journal*, 1913

Fort Worth Star-Telegram, 1913

Gettysburg Compiler, 1910-13

Gettysburg Star-Sentinel, 1910-13

Gettysburg Times, 1910-13

Grand Rapids [MI] *Press*, 1913

Greensboro [NC] *Daily News*, 1913

Harrisburg [PA] *Patriot*, 1913

Harrisburg [PA] *Telegraph*, 1913

Hartford [CT] *Courant*, 1913

Houston Post, 1913

Indianapolis Star, 1913

Jackson [MI] *Citizen Patriot*, 1913

Jersey Journal, 1913

Kalamazoo [MI] *Gazette*, 1913

Kansas City Star, 1913

Lexington [KY] *Leader*, 1913

Los Angeles Times, 1913

Louisville [KY] *Courier-Journal*, 1913

Lowell [MA] *Sun*, 1913

Montgomery [AL] *Advertiser*, 1913

Muskegon [MI] *Chronicle*, 1913

New York Times, 1913

New-York Tribune, 1913.

Newtown [PA] *Enterprise*, 1913

Oregon Daily Journal, 1913

Olympia [WA] *Recorder*, 1913

Pawtucket [RI] *Times*, 1913

Philadelphia Evening Bulletin, 1913

Philadelphia Inquirer, 1913

Pittsburgh Press, 1913

Pittsburgh Post-Gazette, 1913

Racine [WI] *Journal*, 1913

Richmond Times-Dispatch, 1913

Salt Lake Herald, 1913

Salt Lake Telegram, 1913

Salt Lake Tribune, 1913

Saulte Ste. Marie [MI] *Evening News*, 1913

Seattle Times, 1913

Springfield [MA] *Daily News*, 1913

Springfield [MA] *Union*, 1913

Syracuse Journal, 1913

The State [Columbia, SC], 1913

The Tennessean [Nashville, TN], 1913

Trenton [NJ] *Times*, 1913

Washington Post, 1913

Watertown [NY] *Daily Times*, 1913

Wilkes-Barre [PA] *Times-Leader*, 1913

Winston-Salem [NC] *Journal*, 1913

Periodicals

Boys' Life (1913)

Confederate Veteran (1910-13)

The Harvard Graduates' Magazine (1919)

The North American Review (April 1892)

Webster's Weekly (July 1913)

Primary Sources

Published

Blake, Walter H. *Handgrips: The Story of the Great Gettysburg Reunion*. Vineland, NJ: G. E. Smith, 1913.

Blumenson, Martin, ed. *The Patton Papers, 1885-1940*. Boston: Houghton Mifflin Co., 1972.

Fiftieth Anniversary of the Battle of Gettysburg 1913: Report of the New York State Commission. Albany, NY: J. B. Lyon Co., 1916.

Frazier, John W. *The Reunion of the Blue and Gray: Philadelphia Brigade and Pickett's Division*. Philadelphia: Ware Bros., 1906.

Haskell, Frank A. *The Battle of Gettysburg*. Sandwich, MA: Chapman Billies, 1993.

Jaquette, Henrietta Stratton, ed. *Letters of a Civil War Nurse: Cornelia Hancock, 1863-1865*. Lincoln, NE: University of Nebraska Press, 1998.

Kenderdine, Thaddeus Stevens. *Personal Recollections and Travels at Home and Abroad*. 4 Vols. Newtown, PA: n.p., 1917.

_____. "After Fifty Years, or Scenes and Incidents Connected with the Gettysburg Semi-Centennial," *Newtown Enterprise*, Part 1 (July 12, 1913), Part 2 (July 19, 1913), Part 3 (July 26, 1913).

Kenfield, Frank. "Fiftieth Anniversary of the Battle of Gettysburg," *Vermont at Gettysburg, July 1863 and Fifty Years Later*. Rutland, VT: Marble City Press, 1914.

Link, Arthur S., ed. *The Papers of Woodrow Wilson*, 69 Vols. Princeton, NJ: Princeton University Press, 1978.

Longstreet, Helen D. *Lee and Longstreet at High Tide*. Philadelphia: J. B. Lippincott, 1904.

Longstreet, James. "Lee in Pennsylvania," in Alexander K. McClure, ed., *The Annals of the War Written by Leading Participants North and South*. Philadelphia: Times Publishing Co., 1879.

Minutes of the Twentieth Annual Convention, United Daughters of the Confederacy. Raleigh, NC: Edwards & Broughton, 1914.

Minutes of the Seventeenth Annual Convention, United Daughters of the Confederacy, North Carolina Division. New Bern, NC: Owen G. Dunn, Printer, 1913.

Minutes of the Twenty-fourth Annual Meeting and Reunion of the United Confederate Veterans. New Orleans: Hauser Printing, 1914.

Proceedings of the 48th Annual Encampment of the Dept. of Pennsylvania, G.A.R. Harrisburg, PA: Wm. Stanley Ray, State Printer, 1914.

Proceedings of the 53rd Annual Encampment of the Dept. of Ohio G.A.R. Columbus, OH: F. J. Heer Printing, 1919.

Rauch, William H. *Fiftieth Anniversary of the Battle of Gettysburg and Twenty-sixth Annual Reunion of the "Old Bucktails" or First Rifle Regiment, P.R.V.C.* Philadelphia, 1913.

Report of the Pennsylvania Commission for the Fiftieth Anniversary of the Battle of Gettysburg, revised edition. Harrisburg, PA: Wm. Stanley Ray, State Printer, April 1915.

Rodgers, Sarah Sites, ed., *The Ties of the Past: The Gettysburg Diaries of Salome Myers Stewart, 1854-1922.* Gettysburg, PA: Thomas Publications, 1996.

Tibbetts, Elsie Dorothea. *From Maine to Gettysburg 1863-1913.* Bangor, ME: Bangor Co-Operative Printing Co., 1913.

U.S. Congress, House Committee on the Library. *Hearings on H.R. 11112: A Bill to Erect a Memorial on the Gettysburg Battle Field to Commemorate the Fiftieth Anniversary of That Battle, 18 February 1914.* Washington, D.C.: Government Printing Office, 1914.

Vermont at Gettysburg, July 1863 and Fifty Years Later. Rutland, VT: Marble City Press, 1914.

Secondary Sources

Adams, Michael C. C. *Living Hell: The Dark Side of the Civil War.* Baltimore: Johns Hopkins University Press, 2014.

Angle, Paul M. *Crossroads: 1913.* New York: Rand McNally, 1963.

Blight, David W. *Race and Reunion: The Civil War in American Memory.* Cambridge, MA: Belknap Press/Harvard University Press, 2001.

Buck, Paul H. *The Road to Reunion, 1865-1900.* Boston: Little Brown & Co., 1937.

Buckley, William. *Buckley's History of the Great Reunion of the North and the South.* Staunton, VA: self-published, 1923.

Coco, Gregory A. *A Strange and Blighted Land: Gettysburg: The Aftermath of a Battle.* El Dorado Hills, CA: Savas Beatie, 2017.

Connelly, Thomas L. & Bellows, Barbara L. *God and General Longstreet: The Lost Cause and the Southern Mind,* Baton Rouge, LA: Louisiana State University Press, 1982.

Corrington, John William. "Reunion. Gettysburg: 1913," in *The Lonesome Traveler and Other Stories.* New York: G. P. Putnam's Sons, 1968.

Coski, John M. *The Confederate Battle Flag: America's Most Embattled Emblem.* Cambridge, MA: Belknap Press, 2005.

Cox, Karen L. *Dixie's Daughters: The United Daughters of the Confederacy and the Preservation of Confederate Culture.* Gainesville, FL: University Press of Florida, 2003.

Creighton, Margaret S. *The Colors of Courage: Gettysburg's Forgotten History.* New York: Basic Books, 2005.

Davis, William C. *The Cause Lost: Myths and Realities of the Confederacy*. Lawrence, KS: University Press of Kansas, 1996.

_____. "Felix Huston Robertson," in *The Confederate General*, edited by William C. Davis and Julie Hoffman. 6 Vols. Harrisburg, PA: National Historical Society, 1991.

Dearing, Mary R. *Veterans in Politics: The Story of the G.A.R.* Baton Rouge, LA: Louisiana State University Press, 1952.

Desjardin, Thomas A. *These Honored Dead: How the Story of Gettysburg Shaped American Memory*. Cambridge, MA: Da Capo Press, 2003.

Dew, Charles B. *Apostles of Disunion: Southern Secession Commissioners and the Causes of the Civil War*. Charlottesville, VA: University of Virginia Press, 2001.

Eeman, Carl. *Encampment: A Novel of Race and Reconciliation*. Round Lake, NY: Melange Press, 2009.

Emmerson, Charles. *1913: In Search of the World Before the Great War*. New York: Public Affairs, 2013.

Flagel, Thomas R. *War, Memory, and the 1913 Gettysburg Reunion*. Kent, OH: Kent State University Press, 2019.

Fleche, Andre M. "'Shoulder to Shoulder as Comrades Tried': Black and White Union Veterans and Civil War Memory," *Civil War History* (June 2005), Vol. 51, No. 2, 175-201.

Foster, Gaines M. *Ghosts of the Confederacy: Defeat, the Lost Cause, and the Emergence of the New South*. New York: Oxford University Press, 1987.

Gallagher, Gary W. & Nolan, Alan T. eds., *The Myth of the Lost Cause and Civil War History*. Bloomington, IN: Indiana University Press, 2000.

Gannon, Barbara A. *The Won Cause: Black and White Comradeship in the Grand Army of the Republic*. Chapel Hill, NC: University of North Carolina Press, 2011.

Goulka, Jeremiah E., ed. *The Grand Old Man of Maine: Selected Letters of Joshua Lawrence Chamberlain, 1865-1914*. Chapel Hill, NC: University of North Carolina Press, 2004.

Guelzo, Allen C. *Gettysburg: The Last Invasion*. New York: Alfred A. Knopf, 2013.

_____. "Mad Dan," *The Civil War Monitor* (Summer 2013), Vol. 3, No. 2, 48-55.

Heseltine, William B. *Confederate Leaders in the New South*. Baton Rouge, LA: Louisiana State University Press, 1950.

Hessler, James A. *Sickles at Gettysburg: The Controversial Civil War General Who Committed Murder, Abandoned Little Round Top, and Declared Himself the Hero of Gettysburg*. El Dorado Hills, CA: Savas Beatie, 2009.

Holland, Isham C. Undated article from *Gates Camp Gazette*, newsletter of Elijah Gates Camp No. 570, Sons of Confederate Veterans.

Janney, Caroline E. *Remembering the Civil War: Reunion and the Limits of Reconciliation*. Chapel Hill, NC: University of North Carolina Press, 2013.

Jordan, Brian Matthew. *Marching Home: Union Veterans and Their Unending Civil War*. New York: Liveright Publishing, 2014.

Keneally, Thomas. *American Scoundrel: The Life of the Notorious Civil War General Dan Sickles*. New York: Anchor Books, 2002.

Kinchen, Oscar A. *General Bennett H. Young: Confederate Raider and a Man of Many Adventures*. West Hanover, MA: Christopher Publishing, 1981.

LaFantasie, Glenn W. *Twilight at Little Round Top: July 2, 1863—The Tide Turns at Gettysburg*, Hoboken, NJ: John Wiley & Sons, 2005.

Linderman, Gerald F. *Embattled Courage: The Experience of Combat in the American Civil War*. New York, Free Press, 1987.

Marten, James. *Sing Not War: The Lives of Union and Confederate Veterans in Gilded Age America*. Chapel Hill, NC: University of North Carolina Press, 2011.

Martin, David G. *Gettysburg July 1*. Cambridge, MA: Da Capo Press, 1995.

McConnell, Stuart. *Glorious Contentment: The Grand Army of the Republic, 1865-1900*. Chapel Hill, NC: University of North Carolina Press, 1992.

McPherson, James M. *Ordeal by Fire: The Civil War and Reconstruction*. New York: Alfred A. Knopf, 1982.

Moe, Richard. *The Last Full Measure: The Life and Death of the First Minnesota Volunteers*. St. Paul, MN: Minnesota Historical Society Press, 1993.

Noyalas, Jonathan A. *Civil War Legacy in the Shenandoah: Remembrance, Reunion & Reconciliation*. Charleston, SC: The History Press, 2015.

Page, Thomas Nelson. "A Southerner on the Negro Question," *The North American Review* (April 1892), Vol. 154, No. 425, 401-413.

Pfanz, Harry W. *Gettysburg: The Second Day*. Chapel Hill, NC: University of North Carolina Press, 1987.

Piston, William Garrett. *Lee's Tarnished Lieutenant: James Longstreet and His Place in Southern History*. Athens, GA: University of Georgia Press, 1987.

Pollard, Edward A. *The Lost Cause: A New Southern History of the War of the Confederates*. New York: E. B. Treat, 1866.

Prince, Cathryn J. *Burn the Town and Sack the Banks: Confederates Attack Vermont*. New York: Carroll & Graf, 2006.

Reagan, Charles Wilson. *Baptized in Blood: The Religion of the Lost Cause*. Athens, GA: University of Georgia Press, 1980.

Reardon, Carol. *Pickett's Charge in History and Memory*. Chapel Hill, NC: University of North Carolina Press, 1997.

Rosenburg, R. B. *Living Monuments: Confederate Soldiers' Homes in the New South*. Chapel Hill, NC: University of North Carolina Press, 1995.

Shaffer, Donald R. *After the Glory: The Struggles of Black Civil War Veterans*. Lawrence, KS: University of Kansas Press, 2004.

Silber, Nina. *The Romance of Reunion: Northerners and the South, 1865-1900*. Chapel Hill, NC: University of North Carolina Press, 1993.

Simpson, John A. *S. A. Cunningham and the Confederate Heritage*. Athens, GA: University of Georgia Press, 1994.

Smith, Diane Monroe. *Fanny and Joshua: The Enigmatic Lives of Frances Caroline Adams and Joshua Lawrence Chamberlain*. Hanover, NH: University Press of New England, 2013.

Stewart, George R. *Pickett's Charge: A Microhistory of the Final Attack at Gettysburg*. Boston: Houghton Mifflin, 1959.

Swanberg, W. A. *Sickles the Incredible*. New York: Charles A. Scribner's Sons, 1956.

Tyler, Lyon Gardiner. *Men of Mark in Virginia*. 5 Vols. Washington, D.C.: Men of Mark Publishing Co., 1907.

Wecter, Dixon. *When Johnny Comes Marching Home*. Westport, CT: Greenwood Press, 1944.

Weeks, Jim. *Gettysburg: Memory, Market, and an American Shrine*. Princeton, NJ: Princeton University Press, 2003.

_____. "A Different View of Gettysburg: Play, Memory, and Race at the Civil War's Greatest Shrine," *Civil War History* (June 2004), Vol. 50, No. 2, 175-191.

Wert, Jeffrey D. *General James Longstreet: The Confederacy's Most Controversial Soldier*. New York: Simon & Schuster, 1993.

White, William Lee & Runion, Charles Denny, eds. *Great Things Are Expected of Us: The Letters of Colonel C. Irvine Walker, 10th South Carolina Infantry, C.S.A.* Knoxville, TN: University of Tennessee Press, 2009.

Williams, Rusty. *My Old Confederate Home*. Lexington, KY: University of Kentucky Press, 2010.

Index

About the Author

John L. Hopkins is a communication and public relations professional with more than three decades of experience in strategic communication planning, issues management, media relations, crisis communication, news and feature writing, and team building in higher education, nonprofit, and agency settings. He was born and raised in New York City, earned a bachelor's degree in political science from Williams College, and was transplanted to the Midwest in the mid-90s. John and his wife, Apple, have three grown daughters and one sweet, goofy golden retriever. This is his first book.